The F[illegible]
His Dancers

Also by Rob Elliott

Don't Blame Me I'm Only The Triangle Player
The Food Maze
How To Eat

The Fool And His Dancers

Tales Of Dark Morris From The Wild Welsh Border

Rob Elliott

Silurian A-Z

Anarchically black, cheekily disdainful, each face grimaces haughtily, inciting jealous knavery. Lasciviously mauling nubile onlookers, prurient quirkily raffish Silurian teasers unsettle virgins with X-rated yuletide zest.

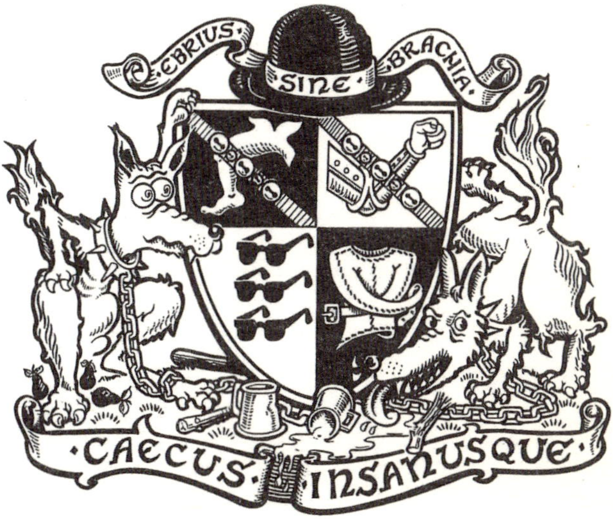

First published in Great Britain in 2017 by Rob Elliott

A Cataloguing in Publication record for this book is available from the British Library

Printed by Orphans Press, Leominster

ISBN: 978-0-9558425-2-8

To my two sons and best friends,
George and Edward

Contents

Caution

• • • • •

This is essentially a book about friendship, fun and the bonds that unite people in a common cause. It is about comradeship, trust and mutual respect – with a healthy disrespect for the entrenched thinking of the status quo. And it just happens to be set against a backdrop of morris dancing.

I believe the Morris dance is a vital part of England's cultural heritage, and I welcome this opportunity to look at it in some detail. As much as this is a tale of a band of brothers, strong personalities with a common goal, it is also a story of a paradigm shift in the concept of Morris. The characters in this narrative were the pioneering revivalists of Welsh Border Morris. Their experiences and my subsequent reflections have resulted in some imaginative thinking on my part as to the possible primal origins of this eccentric yet visibly esoteric custom. Much has changed since those iconic dancers and their charismatic Fool thrilled the crowds around three decades ago, but their legacy lives on in the myriad Border sides that dance today. I have written neither a history book nor an academic tome, although I do examine some of the references to Morris down the ages, but I suggest that any examination of this kind has limited potential.

It is my belief that an academic or scientific approach to the human condition is valuable, but that it is only part of our toolkit. Enhance this formalised approach with imagination, vision and creativity and the resulting ideas might bring us a little closer to the holistic truth. Let us not forget that in the long and fascinating story of humankind, every 'great leap forward' has been prompted by visionaries. Thus I believe we need vision in our present age more than ever, and that includes trying to map the route Morris has travelled over many centuries, to ascertain its relevance and discuss where it might take us from here. We cannot visualise the bigger picture by staring intently at a few pieces of the jigsaw. Neither can we challenge anything unless we understand it. So please read my story with an open mind and set aside any preconceptions about Morris and its origins. See it for what it is – a story and some thoughts about how music, ritual and celebration might have sustained all ancient cultures. Read it without prejudice and then let the discussions begin.

Silurian dramatis personae

In the 48 years since the inception of this enigmatic morris side, many have joined, danced and played, and many have moved on, to be replaced by others. I salute them all for their time on stage, but listed below are the characters in this particular drama.

DAVE JONES – 'JONESY'
Founding father and ardent researcher

The Triad of Rhythm

DION COCHRANE
drummer from another world

COLIN ROBINSON – 'BURCO'
brass-playing UED (Unpredictable Explosive Device)

JOHN WILLIAMS – 'WILLY'
The Music, and the dancers' Fool

Band Support

STEVE GLENNIE-SMITH – 'SUPER STEVE'
inscrutably eccentric accordion player

MIKE MASSEY
bones player, possibly unique in a morris side

DAVE PARKIN
cornet-playing biker (and roadie for Wrathchild)

TONY PRICE
cool side drummer (nice shades)

MICK QUINN
bass drummer and hug therapist

MARTIN RUSSELL
tenor sax player with a PhD

JOHN SMITH
fiddler on the hoof

Hardcore Dancers

CARL 'PRETTY BOY' BROUGHTON
dashing babe-magnet with a rose between his teeth

KEITH CLOSE
the avatar of level-headedness; with flashing feet

VAS DESHMUKH
precision dancer with PhD in something very clever

KEITH FRANCIS – 'WILF'
one-time Bagman of the Ring and Mayor of Ledbury

ANDY GRIFFIN
moves like lightning; sleeps with his eyes open

JETHRO HILL
a Northumbrian accent and a PhD

GORDON LILLEY
an original Silurian

NEIL MALVERN
from Malvern, obviously

CHRIS MULVEY
dancer, singer, ceilidh caller, plasterer

ROGER PAGE
tall, but short feathers in his hat

MIKE RUST
a Silurian asset – but defected to the Ironmen

BERNIE SMART
quiet, but like a cluster bomb when needs must

DAVE SMITH – 'SMUDGE'
stings like a butterfly, floats like a bee

DAI THOMAS
Welsh, great dancer and wrestler

STUART WATTS
pipe and tabor player and surreal ventriloquist

And also . . .

ROB ELLIOTT
dancer, band support, observer and narrator

Part One

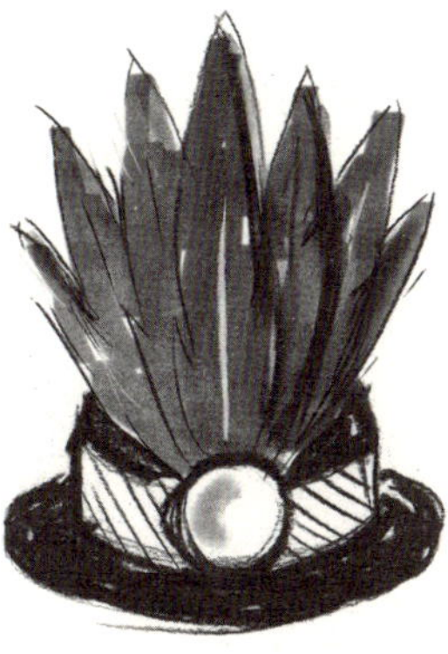

Before I Start...

• • • • •

It is 2016, and the time of the ancient celebration of Beltane, which most people today recognise only as May Day. Merriment fills the air and the pubs around Upton-upon-Severn in Worcestershire. A grey-haired man, with matching goatee beard and a silver earring in his left ear, stands unnoticed in the crowd outside The King's Head. Hands in pockets, he wears an ageing Royal Navy greatcoat, collar turned up against the unseasonable cold. In the swirling human sea of onlookers, drinkers and passers-by, he observes the blackened faces and ragtag costumes of the many Welsh Border Morris sides present for the town's annual folk festival. A space clears in front of the pub as one of these sides limbers up to dance. It's all rag strips and ribbons, personalised paraphernalia, bristling pheasant feathers, bells and sticks. At the heart of the band is a solid core of melodeon, fiddle and drum. The grey-haired man is caught in the flow of the music, rocking gently in its rhythm. It's a good band, but the man senses something missing, and he thinks to himself, "What they need in there is a decent triangle player."

I am that man, and I did play the triangle. Not any old triangle though. This was a triangle that had been made for me out of a length of 10mm reinforcing steel bar, tuned to be compatible with the keys of D and G, and which I played with two six-inch nails to create what that Afro-Caribbean group, Osibisa, once described in their own music as 'criss-cross rhythms that explode with happiness'. Why did I have two nails? Well, one for the tune and the other for the beat. Simple.

My presence that day outside The King's Head was the first time this century that I had ventured into Upton for their folk festival, but in the past this had been familiar territory for me. A long time ago, in a galaxy far, far away . . . I became a part of that entity called Silurian, erstwhile magical morris dancers from another dimension. I travelled with them, from the hesitancy of their Cotswold persona, performing the dances from that specific part of England, through their coming out as an unabashed black-faced Border side, up and over the bell curve of their inspirational talent and growing fame, to gently sliding down the other side. My growing despondency with the prospect of decline came to a head at the Thaxted Ring Meeting in 1998 and I left before the old century was out.

The Silurian Morrismen of Ledbury, to give them their original full and somewhat cumbersome title, first drew breath in 1969. The only other event of any note in that year, with an equally lengthy title, was the Woodstock Music and Art Fair. For reasons which should require no explanation, both these weighty names were quickly stripped down to one word labels. Woodstock became an overnight legend and Silurian did not. Its time was yet to come. To the credit of Dave Jones the founder, however, he did at least keep the word 'Border' in his head, eventually adding it to that unwieldly original moniker. From its inception, the side did promote the dances of the Welsh Border even in the face of ridicule from the really serious Cotswold devotees, whose commitment stemmed from the fact that the Cotswold dances were 'collected' by a dedicated folklorist, Cecil Sharp. Which is why, for a long time, the Silurian boys kept the black-faced Border dances to themselves, trotting them out to a supportive local audience each Boxing Day in Ledbury, whilst the rest of the time they mostly performed Cotswold dances.

It took ten years to get around to adding the word 'Border' to the name, but within the space-time continuum that cloaks the more ethereal outlands of the Welsh borders, this was a mere blip. And, as any lepidopterist will tell you, time is irrelevant inside a cocoon. Once the true Border Butterfly had emerged from the cocoon, however, the Cotswold Caterpillar was but an old memory. This brightly coloured winged creature took to the air and dazzled, enchanted and hypnotised those who saw it. Silurian truly was greater than the sum of its parts, squeezing out of the cocoon as a single entity, not a hotch-potch of motley individuals. Quickly gathering strength as it fed off its own energy, it recharged itself with every public appearance. The idea of a 'dance display' was dismissed as redundantly old-fashioned. Performance, pure theatre and *meaning* replaced it. Dance spots became a dizzying energy exchange as Silurian grabbed the onlookers, gave them a good shake and woke them up. The spectators had no choice but to be involved, and dancers and audience together became part of a bigger idea. On occasions, the energy was so palpable that the heys, rounds and crossovers of the dance were seemingly creating a powerful gyre, a spiralling vortex that sucked people in.

I am sure that anyone reading this has experienced moments when life seems a little unreal, a kind of parallel universe – those magical times when someone can hit a high without really being able to explain why or how. A perfect example of this would be the American athlete, Bob Beamon, who exceeded the world long jump record by nearly 22inches (55cms, if you must) at the 1968 Mexico Olympics. His record stood for 23 years.

Over an all too brief period of about five years, Silurian was right in that zone, able to create those energy exchanges almost at will. That does not mean that we were all in a permanent state of euphoria during those years. There were many off days, days when we couldn't muster a strong side to do a gig, many dreadful venues, and other days when everything went wrong or when some internal dissention disrupted the bond that held us in union. But when the venue was right and there was an audience full of expectation, we could easily weave the spell and have them in our thrall. We involved them – their energy willed us to dance. We gave as good as we got. When everything was right, we were transported – the audience too. For the brief span of a dance, we could rise to another level, become something else. There were occasions when the ground we covered in a rounds or a figure-of-eight was so expansive that we would wake from the dance bemused. "What happened there?" one of us would ask, or, "How did we manage that?"

Nothing lasts forever of course, although some would argue that everything lasts forever, but this may not be the place to get into the semantics of Zen and quantum physics. Let's just say that life and the environment within which it exists is seemingly chaotic but fractal by nature. Thus one small variation in what may look like an unpredictable pattern can create an unexpected but perfectly logical configuration in a new direction. In the case of Silurian, its life took the shape of a seven-year transition from Cotswold to Border, a rapid rise to a five year peak and then an inevitable slide down the gentle slope to mediocrity, precipitated by fractal changes in the line-up of band and dancers. Yet the legend lives on. Silurian in name is still alive and physical parts of it are seemingly well. Change is an infinite process, never motionless. And, against all odds, Silurian still appears to be part of that process.

From my point of view, having spent nearly a quarter of a century as a dancer, band member (graduating from triangle to snare drum to oboe) and one-time squire of this enigmatic clutch of eccentrics, I have undying affection and loyalty for them as the one-time innovators of change. I like to visualise them in a tribal context, going through youth into initiation as warriors before the onset of familial responsibility and finally reaching the status of elders, imparting wisdom and knowledge to the next generation of would-be warriors . . . and I can hear you saying, "You're having a laugh, aren't you?" Perhaps I am being a little fanciful, but the original mystique of Silurian has morphed into Myth, so much so that many of the bad memories have faded, because every trough falls between two peaks, and therefore the good times outnumber the bad.

The last peak I personally enjoyed was around twelve months before I left the side, when Silurian was invited to the Killorglin Puck Fair in the south-west of Ireland. Most of the Irish audience had no idea what hit them that weekend, so surprise was on our side, but once again we were blessed with a warm reception and the energy exchange was enough to light up half the town. In any case, it would be a sad day indeed to arrive in any Irish town in celebratory mood and not be buoyed up by the *craic* (which was 'fierce' in Killorglin that weekend) and the pure delirious Irishness of it all. A little of the flavour of that weekend can be tasted in Appendix 2.

By contrast with the positive vibe of the Killorglin Puck Fair, our presence at the Thaxted Ring Meeting in 1998 ended on a sour note as we delivered on the last afternoon what was the nadir of Silurian performances. I won't describe that episode in detail, but I will say that, for me, it seemed that another brittle lump of credibility had fallen from what had once been the towering edifice of Silurian. I felt we lost the cachet that had once been bestowed upon the side by the vicar of Thaxted, who had pronounced Silurian to be 'anarchic but genteel'. He had welcomed our presence in his town, remarking also that our closest imitators at that time were 'vulgar by comparison'. I knew, on that day in 1998, we had let him and ourselves down, and that it was us who had become vulgar.

So, that did it for me. I wanted no more of this downward slide. I didn't leave in a huff, but I didn't stay much longer. When I did leave, my disenchantment was complete and Morris was no longer an important part of my life. Since that Thaxted weekend, the best part of two decades has passed, but a spontaneous decision to visit Chepstow for the 2016 wassail blew oxygen onto embers that I did not realise were still faintly glowing. To see so many Border sides in one place woke me up double quick. Suddenly I am interested again. I am intrigued with how Border Morris has developed, and even more intrigued to hear the name Silurian uttered by some in respectful tones. I once tried to tell the story of Silurian in the lengthily titled *Don't Blame Me, I'm Only The Triangle Player*. It was written whilst I was deeply embedded in the side, and all I was doing was making an attempt to record the details while I could still remember them. Now older, and hopefully wiser, I find myself updating the original narrative from what is now a more detached perspective, and this book is the result.

Much has changed since *The Triangle Player* was written. Border Morris has moved on, and some of the mystique that must have once been innate in this kind of dancing, and that Silurian stirred into life, is finding its way back. This is exciting. At the same time, however, I am disappointed to see that, when it comes to blacking up, there are still so many people who *just don't get it*. At the time of writing, the Shrewsbury Folk Festival organisers have bowed to the threat of legal action and proclaimed that, from the 2017 Festival onwards, they will not be booking morris sides who black their faces. It is a disturbing reflection on modern-day thinking to see that even the heritage of an ancient dance culture can fall victim to erroneous received wisdom, misinformation, rumour and misguided Political Correctness.

Theories, opinions and academic postulations abound in a discussion that has been going on in earnest for at least fifty years. It seems that the earliest reference to morris dancers with black faces cites some kind of courtly entertainment in the reign of Henry VII, and black faces tend to feature in many references to morris dancing since that time. The erudite or academic approach to such references can all too easily miss the point, however – or indeed 'points', plural.

For instance, some who cite the reference to a 15th Century courtly entertainment would have us believe that morris dancing began here, subsequently devolving to the 'common people' thereafter. I would suggest this is the wrong way round. It is more likely that the dance existed at village community level and was brought into court (and probably glammed up a bit) by order of the monarch. Let's face it, the elite ruling classes have a long history of relying on the commoners to provide them with all they need, from food to cannon fodder to cathedrals. I can imagine Good King Henry saying to his flunkies, “Those guys I saw dancing in the village last week – get them in here!” Why are there no earlier references? Probably because it was of no interest to royalty until Henry VII decided he wanted ‘something different’ for his party piece. Now, I may be subject to accusations of presenting an ‘argument from silence’ here, so let me make myself clear. I am only guessing. Or, more accurately, I am employing intelligent guesswork based on thorough research.

Another problem we face, and another point that is easily missed, is that all known references to morris dancers, black-faced or otherwise, were written by the ‘literary classes’. Until the 19th Century, only a small percentage of the populace could read and write. Much of what was written came from what we might call the ruling authority, whether regal or administrative. As such, writing could say what the writer wanted it to say, and would often carry bias. A report on rowdy morris dancers would cast them in a bad light, because it was probably written by the Magistrate's Court clerk. The more contemporary references to morris dancers simply being unemployed itinerant labourers, blacking their faces to avoid recognition whilst putting on a short display to justify begging for money is, I believe, an example of biased reporting. Or simply too much reliance on anecdotal stories. That's not to say this never happened – I just think it does not constitute fully rounded research unless a few caveats and questions are introduced.

Without those caveats and questions, we can all too easily sink into the mire of fake news (you know, the stuff that used to be called ‘propaganda’). The worst example of this is to suggest the black-faced morris dancers are connected with minstrel shows – a suggestion that is so absurd as to be asinine in the extreme. Morris dancers with black faces are mentioned four hundred years before anyone ever dreamed up the idea of a minstrel show, the first of which is noted as having been performed in 1843. It was an American form of ‘entertainment’ and was clearly racist in its lampooning of 'African-Americans' (slaves, actually, back then) as dim-witted lazy buffoons. The fact that it should migrate to the UK in the 20th Century in the form of *The Black and White Minstrel Show* is, I am sure, a deep and uncomfortable embarrassment to all clear-thinking people today. But it has nothing to do with morris dancing. And, in its turn, I suspect that morris has nothing to do with imitating the Moors. It is said that there was a 16th Century French dance called the *Morisque*, supposedly a derivation from the Spanish *morisco* (Moor). Thus it has been mooted that morris is probably of Moorish origin, and the blacked-up face has been put forward as proof of this theory. Such a proposition seems to invert the order of facts. That tireless researcher, Tracy Boyd www.sacredthreads.net, tells us through her very detailed investigations that "the faces were not blackened because the dancers represented Moors, but rather the dancers were thought to represent Moors *because their faces were blackened* [my italics]."

Having done my own comprehensive research, I find myself agreeing with Tracy Boyd. I would add that those from the PC lobby who pontificate on the origins of morris with the supposed voice of authority would benefit from delving a little deeper. Further research will reveal to them that what is now called morris dancing has a very long history that takes us right back to a time many millennia before the invention of monotheistic religions. We are looking at mystical spiritualism in a time of organised hunting and the earliest days of agriculture. From this we can see that the morris, in whatever form it first existed, is too involved with hunting, agrarian customs and rites of ancient Britons to be any kind of import from abroad. As for trying to agree on a true etymological grounding for the word 'morris', it is in my opinion a waste of effort, as nothing can be proved conclusively. Yet all the arguments continue to rage, and the PC lobby, still without any concrete historical foundation, is getting ever more belligerent.

Back in 1994, there was a conference at Cecil Sharp House

on the theme of *Morris – the Good, the Bad and the Ugly*, at which Vas Deshmukh (another stalwart Silurian man) and I gave a presentation on behalf of Silurian. The situation I see today suggests that the Good in Morris is probably better, whilst the Bad and the Ugly are probably worse, and thus I cannot revisit the original *Triangle Player* without addressing these issues in a little more detail, as you will come to see.

Chapter 1
Sharp Notes

• • • • •

*"Step gently down, you've nought to fear
With Jockey to the fair..."*

I asked a question twenty-five years ago, and I ask it again now: what is it that makes anyone want to be a morris dancer anyway? Who would willingly, without bribery or coercion, actually want to dress up with flowers around their hat and bells on their shins, just to skip around with all that flouncy hanky waving and such? All that hopping about like hallucinating rabbits, leaving yourself open to ridicule and public scorn.

Though most people are able to call up this caricature of a morris dancer, most dancers do not project such an image. Yet, even today, I have seen some dance displays that are shamefully bad. At the time when I first became aware of morris dancing it had always suffered from a bad press. It was often met with sniggers or self-conscious shuffling of feet when brought up in conversation. It was sent up on TV, or shrugged off by visitors to this country as being yet another example of British eccentricity. For the full effect of this negativity, try talking about it with a bunch of labourers on a building site. Watching the kind of morris dancing that can so often still be seen out there, it is easy to understand all those negative reactions, but has it always been like that? Does anyone care anyway, and does it make any difference whether they do or not?

It's time for a little history, so I can put my story into context.

This quirky pastime is all supposed to have started a very long time ago, but nobody knows exactly when. Hundreds of years ago certainly – possibly even thousands. It was well known by Shakespeare's time, and the earliest written reference seems to be during the reign of Henry VII. And morris dancers have been mentioned from time to time in various documents down the years since then. I could, at this stage, quote a long list of all known references to morris since the birth of the universe, but luckily for you this will not be necessary, as it has been done so often elsewhere. This is not an academic dissertation, but it is an opportunity for me to set before you some salient facts, connections and intelligent guesses. More importantly, we need to examine some erroneous beliefs, the pitfalls of tradition and the difference between myths and Myth. Just to be clear on this last point, let's introduce a capital letter. Let's say that myths are simply ideas or stories that are believed by many but are not true, whereas Myth is an important cultural concept from a time before written language. Myth concerns legendary stories, usually centred on heroes, fabled beings or events, with or without a basis in fact, that help to 'explain' the origins of a cultural practice or natural phenomena. Many myths abound when it comes to morris dancing, whereas the story of Silurian has become Myth in itself.

Certain self-proclaimed cognoscenti say that morris dancing started as a pagan fertility ritual. Well, maybe. 'Pagan' suggests pre-Christian, so there we have two thousand years straightaway. Twenty-first Century Man indulging in fertility rituals from two millennia ago? Hard to believe, considering the nature of change. Today 'indulging in fertility rituals' sounds like something you could be arrested for. Certainly not an excuse anyone is likely to get away with when confronted by an inquisitive Officer of the

Law, shining a torch onto the back seats of parked cars. In any case, I suggest that your average Cotswold-style morris dance doesn't cut it as a fertility ritual, though they do contain very visible traces of ancient rites. Much of this kind of ostensibly arcane chatter entered popular culture about fifty years ago with folk revivalists and Robin Hardy, the director responsible for *The Wicker Man*. This film quickly reached cult status, allegedly because it dealt with the subject of fertility rites but more likely because it featured the physical attributes of certain female members of the cast. If it was fertility rites their antics were describing, then much has been lost in translation into morris, or at least the type of morris that dominated the twentieth century. Since the dawn of the new millennium, however, some interesting new diversions have taken place, which we will consider in due course.

So, going back to the idea of tradition . . .

"It's traditional!" you will hear morris dancers assert. Some go as far as to describe morris as 'traditional men's ritual dances'. It's a difficult word, 'tradition'. One thing is certain – the word tends to feature in the justification of folk culture of any sort, not just dancing. But it has a touch of the weasel about it, often frolicking through the lexis with the equally dubious word, 'authority'. As with all discussions of this nature, we need to get back to basics to understand what we are looking at, so let's start with a dictionary definition. The dictionary says *tradition* is:

1. a custom, opinion or belief handed down to posterity, esp. orally or by practice.
2. artistic, literary, etc., principles based on experience, practice and continuous development of any one of these.

Taking the first of these definitions, we notice the word 'orally'. A custom, opinion or belief handed down by word-of-mouth . . .

hmmm. Can you hear those alarm bells? That's the warning that word-of-mouth transmission is about as accurate as the weather forecast – it starts well but soon fragments into speculation and guesswork.

Back in the last century, there was a briefly popular party game called Chinese Whispers, involving passing a message from one person to another until it comes back to the originator. It's a silly game, usually played by a bunch of people encumbered by an excess of alcohol and a dearth of creative ideas. However, anyone who has participated in it will realise how much a story can change in five minutes. So, what about five hundred years? Rumours, stories, recipes . . . anything passed on by word-of-mouth, changes slightly from person to person. Small details are altered, forgotten, misheard or misconstrued; others are deliberately left out as being insignificant, whilst little embellishments are added to the bits each individual likes best. So, for all we know, what we now call morris dancing may have started off as an egg-and-spoon race, or Hunt the Thimble.

"Not so!" I hear the purists cry, "what about Cecil Sharp?" Others say, "Oh, never mind about Cecil Sharp. We all know this stuff is pagan!"

Both these points are valid and will be explored but, before that and for the sake of thoroughness, let's look at the second definition of 'tradition'.

This describes it as 'principles based on experience, practice and continuous development of a body of, say, art'. Or, if you prefer, it is an artistic or literary principle based on accumulated or continuous usage, as in: 'the tradition of the Dutch school of painting'. It depends on which dictionary you consult. So, an academic tradition relies on being passed on from generation to generation but, like its oral sibling, it is tinkered with and grows as time goes on. Any new variations, interpretations or embellishments, are added to the body of knowledge, provided that they are in keeping with its basic principles.

Therefore, to recap, we have this so-called pagan fertility ritual, the principles of which have been handed down orally over the centuries from father to son (*traditionally* of course, it is argued that the dancers were always men), added to, subtracted from and generally modified and refined to produce what we now call morris dancing.

Not quite true.

What we now call morris dancing is akin to something which awoke a weary traveller, one Cecil Sharp, visiting friends in Headington, Oxfordshire in 1899. It was Boxing Day morning of that year, and C. Sharp (quite likely known to his mates as D Flat) was reputedly asleep at the local inn, doubtless still totally trashed after the full Christmas blow-out the night before. He was woken by the sound of small tinkling bells and a tuneful concertina outside his hostelry. Looking out of his window, chamber-pot presumably at the ready to douse this disturbance, he was amazed to see a group of lunatics (you could say that in 1899, before the 21st Century Thought Police turned it into an indictable offence) colourfully dressed and cavorting about with sticks and handkerchiefs. He enquired politely as to, "Who are these idiots, what are they doing and *why are they doing it outside my window at this time of the morning*!?" The answer he was given was, "Morris dancing."

It must have been some kind of a Damascus moment for our hero because, having found out that Morris was potentially on the red list of cultural extinctions, he resolved to write down the tunes and dance steps before they were lost, thus preserving them for posterity, and of course creating in the process a tradition. After exhaustive and painstaking research, he had finally logged all the different morris dances he could find, filling five volumes – not bad for something that was looked upon as endangered. Being the academic he was, and having picked up the ubiquitous Victorian mania for collecting and cataloguing, he soon had all the dances classified in a kind of musical taxonomy of 'traditions' – there's that word again. Thus he had them listed under the Adderbury tradition, the Bledington tradition, etc. He even found some dances were common to more than one local variation – same tune, different steps, as in, for example, Jockey To The Fair, *Adderbury*, or Jockey To The Fair, *Brackley*, Jockey To The Fair, *Sherborne*, Jockey To The Fair, *Bledington*, Jockey To The Fair . . . etc.

Another noteworthy morris celeb, Lionel Bacon (born in 1910) used Cecil Sharp's manuscripts and tomes as the main source material for his own personal aide-memoire, which was eventually published in 1974 as *A Handbook of Morris Dances*, containing hundreds of different dances and variations. The Black Book, as it is popularly known, became the definitive bible for all would-be morris men, but it was available only to those approved by the exclusively male Morris Ring. More on that later. To be fair, the Black Book and Sharp's original volumes contain an extraordinary amount of material which may otherwise have been lost, but as collections they are much like a museum collection of butterflies, all neatly arranged to show the differences between species and derivatives. Colourful but lifeless, preserved for posterity. And that's a problem. Preservation of this sort for what should be a living, ever-changing expression of culture is a kind of death, an embalming. These are the dances 'as collected'. All growth stops here. Boxing Day 1899 may have actually been a sad day for morris. What Cecil Sharp inadvertently created was a kind of archive, but also an ever-growing enthusiasm for this particular custom as it existed *at the time*. Eager disciples spread the word devotedly, embracing Sharp's teachings and doing their best to perform the dances as collected, keen to demonstrate the differences between the 'traditions'.

Like kids with new toys, they had all the dances laid out in front of them to gaze upon and linger over. Play with one, put it down, play with another. Certainly a sense of wonder, perhaps tinged with childlike innocence, must have inspired these followers of Sharp. Continuity was also established at this time, reinforcing the custom of dancing the morris especially at certain times of the year, such as May Day. In a number of places of course, the dances had been performed 'since nobody can't remember when'. But also nobody can't remember *why* either. The Headington men, for example, had been dancing for years before that famous appearance in 1899, but I doubt if anyone, even at the end of the nineteenth century, could hint at why Boxing Day might have been significant, and no one would have been able to join the dots between dancing at the time of the winter solstice and dancing on May Day.

Cecil Sharp died in 1924, but the enthusiasm with which he had fired his supporters lived on, and three years later some of the leading lights amongst them were laying the ground rules for an 'Association of Morris Dancers'. This culminated in the formation in 1934 of the Morris Ring of England, a loose federation of morris sides designed to preserve and publicise the morris. Annual gatherings have taken place since then, and they now run at four or five per year, with the Essex town of Thaxted becoming Morris Mecca, having hosted a Ring meeting every year since 1934.

For those of you beginning to lose the will to live at this point, bear with me. My observations are all about creating context for this story, and thereby must include a brief dissertation on the wider folk revival which coloured the last quarter of the 20th century. I am a real eye witness from that period, and I am passing this valuable information on to you regardless of expense and/or possible reprisal from other morris dancers or from those whose memory simply differs from my own.

Back to it, then. The Morris Ring grew and grew, with a steep rise in its popularity in the mid- to late-sixties, when the hippie culture from our transatlantic chums sparked the renaissance of all things Folky that had been smouldering away for years in this country. Without warning it seemed, everyone was weaving their own clothes and singing down their noses. Those who didn't want the bother of weaving got away with it by wearing cream-coloured Arran sweaters or Cornish fishermen's smocks, and those who couldn't sing did so anyway. Nothing happens in isolation of course. Hippies and the Woodstock festival were as much a part of the whole as the sudden compulsive urge in this country to get back to our musical roots, and all of it part of something much bigger. The 1970s were what might be called interesting times, but not in the sense of that oft-quoted Chinese curse (that's a myth, for the record).

Popular at the time was the concept of the dawning of the age of Aquarius, and it was evident that many people felt so strongly that change was in the air that the media, always keen to ridicule anyone questioning the status quo, soon dubbed them New Agers. As with so much of the nonsense that appears in the media, reports on the behaviour of these perceived provocateurs missed the point. Because the term 'New Age' was applied to everything that challenged the status quo, anyone asking awkward questions was splashed by the wildly wielded tar brush, and the prevalent mood was misunderstood and erroneously analysed. Yet the zeitgeist couldn't be denied, and through the 1970s these free thinkers began to search for something long lost, something to give life some meaning. Books on Zen and other arcane Oriental philosophies became popular, and the age of the How-To book was upon us. How to find yourself, how to change your life, how to touch your own soul, how to grow your own vegetables, weave your own clothes . . .

Those in the vanguard of this search never considered themselves to be New Agers. At 'street level', that epithet was reserved for certain individuals out there on the borders of idiocy. The questioners were mostly middle-class thinkers, people with enough comfort and security and time on their hands to be able to philosophise with their mates over a pint or two down the pub. They were looking for something to believe in, carrying the latest album by The Albion Band under one arm and a copy of *Zen and the Art of Motorcycle Maintenance* under the other. I know, because I was there and I was one of them.

In another reality in another part of society, a different kind of rebellion was going on, that gave birth to a hitherto unseen manifestation of folk culture a million miles away from the cosiness of morris dancers on the village green. The kind of folk songs being sung here came straight out of a world of economic and social hardships, much like the 18th and 19th century ballads being sung in the folk clubs. Equally poignant and hard-hitting, these new songs came from marginalised and exploited individuals, but their music was hijacked by the media and entrepreneurs like Malcolm McLaren and given the label of 'punk'. Don't worry, I am not going to expand this into a thesis on the folk roots of punk music. It is just interesting to note how change at that time manifested itself in different strata of an increasingly divided and unequal society.

Going back to our middle-class devotees of the folk revival, the last quarter of the 20th century saw an upsurge in folk festivals. No folk festival was complete without a few morris sides, and pretty soon they seemed to be everywhere – fetes, steam engine rallies, carnivals and indeed their very own Ring Meetings. Many born-again countrymen and would-be rustics also appeared at these events, kitted out in the kind of waistcoats Grandads used to wear, red-spotted neckerchiefs, moleskin trousers and collarless shirts. The women swelled the profits of burgeoning businesses like Laura Ashley that quickly latched onto the demand for floaty cotton print dresses, whose wearers drifted around the folk festivals with their long frocks dragging in the dust or mud. The sentimental, campfire-side American folk songs that had surreptitiously sneaked into our midst were quickly discarded in the search for the real thing. English folk tradition, having survived this post-war American takeover, finally came home to a rapturous welcome. 20th Century *Homo sapiens* was high on the nostalgia drug and obsessed with 19th Century *Homo rusticana.*

The folk clubs and festivals thrived as the '70s and '80s rolled out. There was brisk trade in the antique shops and market stalls, which became oases in the shopping desert, besieged by hordes of folkies desperate for old garments, pewter tankards and other essential accoutrements. Clothed in these symbols of a forgotten time and armed with their must-have accessories, they then felt the part, joining in with the rousing choruses of yesteryear. Before long, everybody was Rounding the Horn or Hunting the Bonny Black Hare-O, the latter being found in the most alarming places, such as on the girlfriend's legs and under her arms, a clear demonstration of the new tendency to be more natural. Once again the media stepped in, got it wrong as usual and proclaimed that this was the onset of the new hard edge of Feminism – a threat to the established patriarchy. It was nothing of the sort of course. It's just that the natural look was in, helped in no small way by the visibly hirsute East European female athletes that dominated the Olympic Games during the last quarter of last century. Heike Drechsler, Marita Koch, Silke Gladisch, Katrin Krabbe . . . where are you now?

This revivalist interest in folk history, especially in the musical side of it, helped the cause of morris dancing enormously. Morris was Folk and Folk was Okay. The interest was such that the Morris Ring soon had sides (a team of morris dancers is called a 'side') from all over the country trying to join. Unlike the early days, the 'officers' of the Ring had a huge choice and were able to elect only those sides which could demonstrate dancing of an acceptable standard. A sharp rise in the popularity of morris dancing obviously put pressure on the Ring officials to supervise and regulate the growth. Clearly, standards had to be set, and those sides that failed to reach the required standard were not invited to join the elite.

Here we have a great example of the Our Gang Syndrome, whose symptoms were seen in some of the rules that had been introduced. For instance, sides wishing to join the Ring had to 'dance in', performing a demonstration show dance in front of Ring members, usually at a Ring meeting. Then it was marks out of ten, maybe a pat on the head and a little sticky gold star to press onto your hat. Usually entry into the Ring by this means was a foregone conclusion, because no budding member side would attempt to 'dance in' unless they were fairly confident of success. Failure was too horrible to contemplate, conjuring up visions reminiscent of Caligula's gladiatorial arenas – public humiliation with the thumbs-down signal of death, right foot amputated, 'REJECT' branded on foreheads with red-hot irons and the victims cast into the dungeons, where there was weeping and wailing and groaning of non-Ring sides. By contrast, those who were given the thumbs-up got in with a demonstration of their eligibility to dance the morris as collected by Sharp, and as interpreted by his early disciples.

All right and proper, you might say. It is ostensibly a good thing to preserve one's culture and social customs, and the reasons behind the formation of the Morris Ring were admirable. Unfortunately, the Ring gradually became a victim of its own popularity. Its ever-increasing size necessitated more administration and gave it a bureaucratic character, not helped by the little rituals that permeated ring meeting weekends, particularly during the Saturday night feast, with its speeches and toasts to Cecil Sharp and the reigning monarch. A little too much of the Old School Tie for my personal taste.

Dropping to the next tier below the Ring meetings, morris men were busy organising their own Ales, Feasts, Days of Dance and the like. Some of the sides involved in these events (ring meetings in miniature) also had a tendency to be elitist and were much concerned with the fancy footwork and different traditions. Consequently, some of those gatherings of morris men were just a bit too introspective. The dances were for the *dancers* – those watching as well as those performing. Sometimes it was all a bit too narcissistic. All self-congratulation and mutual admiration –

a very long way from pagan ritual. But not a million miles away from Round Table with bells.

Returning for a moment to our Victorian dance hunter, Cecil Sharp, this might be a good time to point out that it was not only dances from the Cotswold villages that he picked up. During his travels he discovered a wealth of folk culture in the Welsh Border counties of Herefordshire, Shropshire and Worcestershire, but little more than scattered traces of any morris tradition. Because the information available was so scant, the whole idea of morris in these counties was dismissed as a corrupted form of the dance and therefore of little significance.

Thus the dances of the Cotswold villages became the definitive demonstrations of the Morris. Anything that was not Cotswold was viewed with suspicion and deemed degenerate, or passed off as carnival dancing, particularly as morris dancers on the Welsh Border had blackened faces. Predictably, a touch of 'us and them' appeared. Anything not done as per the Black Book (Black Book: good; black face: bad) was frowned upon and variously labelled as 'rubbish', 'made up' or 'untraditional'. There were many Cotswold sides that came and went in this period whose approach to the tradition was original, sympathetic and fresh. Some of these so-called non-Ring sides were acting on a 'We'll show them' impulse; others were genuinely and purposefully demonstrating novel and valid interpretations of what they thought morris should be. Whilst allowing that there was room for innovation and interpretation, the Ring condemned these inventive and avant-garde dancers as frivolous. Despite this anally retentive attitude, the Ring – no pun intended – continued to grow in strength and popularity.

Publicity material that was handed out to the curious (who both read it avidly) at Ring meetings and other morris events generally included a potted history of morris dancing. As the feminist movement gathered momentum in its demands for equality, the Ring was unmoved. It continued to emphasise the fact that these were traditional *men's* dances, not in any way 'social' like all those folky barn dance things, but ritualistic in nature and therefore Very Important. And, being very important, were therefore, by definition, Male. This attitude went down really well with the women, needless to say – about as well as a porterhouse steak at the Vegan Annual Dinner. Unable to equate Very Important ritual dances with Very Boring old duffers adorned with ostentatiously decorated hats, they decided they could do better.

By the early '70s, there seemed to be morris men around every corner. They had become commonplace and familiar to the public. Familiarity, as we all know, breeds contempt, and so it was that morris drifted into a bad patch. At times it seemed that everyone was doing it but no one wanted to watch it. Thus the women found morris one of the easier male fortresses to storm. With the men caught off their guard, the all-female Morris Federation was formed in 1975 and it was not long before there seemed to be morris *women* around every corner. Some of these were all aggression and pint pots, showing the men how they thought it ought to be done; others were more feminine and coyly sexual, doing dances that looked like morris but weren't. All this scared the socks off quite a lot of men, whose dancing improved enormously. But it was too little too late. The women were here to stay.

A further assault on the bastion of androcentric traditional dancing took the form of yet another version of the Ring – this one called Open Morris. Yes, you've guessed it: open to all, and the natural magnet for those sides that featured male and female dancers together. All very well, but by the early 1980s there were three formal organisations around the simple idea of ancient ritual dancing. Personally (and I emphasise that it is my personal opinion), I couldn't be doing with all the bureaucratic stuff, AGMs and bookkeeping that goes with any organisation, and I still can't. Back in those distant days, I felt that there was something very wrong with the whole idea, but I struggled to define my objections, so I just kept quiet.

Between what had become the two extreme views of morris dancing – all-male or all-female – many were drawn to the simple compromise of 'mixed morris', as it was known then. In those early days, this was a weird little hybrid that generally looked like a country dance with bells, though many of its supporters defended it as being 'a valid interpretation of morris dancing which fits in exactly with the new non-sexist equality-conscious Nineties and is the way morris will be done in the future'. Fast forward to the 21st Century and we see that political correctness can indeed have an uncanny ability to predict its own future. Sadly, in handing out behavioural guidelines about misunderstood social issues, it so often misses the point. Not so much up the creek without a paddle, but deliberately throwing the paddles overboard because they are made in China.

Meanwhile, unnoticed by the sparring factions of organised morris, a different revolution was quietly beginning to gather pace. A Welsh-born Herefordshire man, with the commonplace name of David Jones, was becoming increasingly annoyed with the fact that the so-called remnants of morris dances found in the Welsh Border counties were still being dismissed as a redundant form of Cotswold Morris. A committed folk revivalist, he knew from his knowledge and experience that the Morris once thrived in the Borders. More importantly, he believed that, rather than being a degeneration of the Cotswold style, the Border tradition was a much older form of the dance. He invested much time and effort into researching his subject thoroughly in order to lay the evidence before a jury of his peers and reverse the judgement. He was determined to put Border Morris on the map, and his labours began in earnest at the end of the sixties, when he left the Hereford Morrismen to set up a side in his home town, calling it The Silurian Morrismen of Ledbury. The concept and understanding of morris was about to be changed dramatically.

Chapter 2
The Long and Winding Road

• • • • •

"Hal an tow, jolly rumbalow,
We were up long before the day-oh,
To welcome in the summer,
To welcome in the May-oh.
The summer is a-coming in
And winter's gone away-oh..."

In a way, Dave Jones fell into the same trap that snared Cecil Sharp – the belief that collating extant references to morris dancing was enough to animate the tradition and clothe it with vitality and relevance. But the result of such activity is merely to retrieve no more than a single frame from a very long film. The Morris Ring had already waded out of its depth to float its boat of 'men's ritual dances', and was all too soon floundering in the quicksand of misandrist confrontation. Unable to elaborate on their stock phrase, they had no effective answer when the women asked, "Why does it have to be *men*'s dances?"

Dave Jones was running the same risk, but he had one thing on his side. He maintained vociferously that Welsh Border Morris represented a much older lineage than its Cotswold counterpart, thus playing the 'ancient rite' card. Unable to present a comprehensive detail-perfect notated collection to rival the work of Cecil Sharp and Lionel Bacon, he was thinking on his feet. By claiming that Border dances were so much older than Cotswold, he was venturing into uncharted territory. In his more reflective moments, he imagined that these older dances, by then almost certainly lost in their original form, may well have had a pre-Christian genesis. The word 'ritual' took root in his thinking and steadily grew into the grander concept of 'pagan ritual male fertility dances'. He was right on track with this, but inadvertently lost a bit of focus. His research in trying to find enough past evidence to support his thinking revealed that there were many references to morris dancing itself as far back as the 16th Century. Satisfied that a four-hundred-year legacy was enough to prove his point, he set about publicising what he had discovered, but with the clear ulterior motive of amassing enough detail to create his own Border side.

The four key words, 'pagan', 'ritual', 'male' and 'fertility', were left hanging in the air like smoke on a becalmed winter morning.

Once a genie is out of the bottle, it's best to give it something to do. Your wish is its command and, without a wish to fulfil, there is a risk that the now disgruntled genie will wander off and get up to all sorts of mischief. This seems to be what happened to the phrase 'pagan fertility ritual' with specific reference to morris dancing, to the extent that it has lost its essence, though not the cachet of the word 'pagan'. Although there are many people who comprehend the true significance of the word, and some very clear indications that this awareness is being displayed in thoughtful and creative ways, there are many others who bandy it about like some glittering trophy of trendy tokenism, knowing next to nothing about the word's meaning, history or significance.

Looking at the etymology, we see that the word comes from the Latin, *paganum*, which simply means 'villager'. When Christianity was taken up as the state religion of the old Roman Empire, it thrived in the cities and towns. Out in the sticks, the villagers were still happy with their old gods and were soon spoken of derisively by the newly Christianised urbanites, in the same way that modern city dwellers might call their country cousins yokels or bumpkins. Before long, the villagers of ancient Rome became *paganus* (or 'pagan'), 'people who don't believe in God', and were ostracised and demonised by the Church. At a basic level, therefore, pagans are simply those people whose belief system pre-dated and was condemned by Christianity. Examining their culture, as it existed in those heady days before the tightening grip of Canon Law squeezed the fun out of life, might give us more clues about the people that the word described.

When a word acquires an *-ism*, it's a sure sign that it has become the subject of a takeover bid to turn it from a communal Myth-based belief into something 'organised'. Sad to say, such is the fate of paganism. Organisation brings with it the opinions and prejudices of those who love to organise, resulting in erroneous theories, such as the conviction that 'pagan' is synonymous with 'Celtic', another word that has also been hijacked – an inherent problem of labelling. Pagan is a generic word; Celtic describes a group of linguistically linked tribal peoples that occupied an extensive part of the European mainland and the British Isles by 275BCE. For the purposes of this investigation, I will restrict my references to those Celts who lived in the western areas of Britain at the time of the Iron Age, say around 500BCE.

Evidence suggests the Celts came to Britain from central Europe via the Basque region of Iberia through Brittany into Cornwall, although this theory has its critics. They say there is also evidence to suggest the Celts spread eastwards from the western shores of Europe (i.e. the Iberian peninsula, Britain and Ireland), eventually reaching as far as modern-day Turkey. Much has been written about this fascinating culture, but there is still room to explore the idea of pagan ritual fertility dances. All culture is of course part of a flow. Everything is connected. Celtic culture, as seen in Britain in the Iron Age, contained elements also seen in ancient Rome and Greece. Setting aside for the moment the debate around whether or not the culture arrived in Cornwall via Spain, let's just say that at least part of the Celtic culture in Britain was in full working order in 500BCE. It is reasonably certain that, in seeking traces of what we now call morris, we find the closest parallels in the Basque country, but it is the linguistic clues that are more intriguing. The old Cornish language is closely related to Basque, a Pre-Indo-European language descended from the original Neolithic root language of a culture that centred on the Great (Earth) Mother. This connected the early settlements of Anatolia (Turkey, more or less) through the centres of Crete and Greece to the Berbers of North Africa and into Iberia.

Hold that thought, because I am going to come back to the Great Mother.

Before that, we need to look at some other fundamental aspects of culture that are relevant to this inquiry. A central idea was that a sense of 'place' had sacred significance and the boundaries around a community's 'place' must be protected and regularly renewed and sanctified. The understanding that everything is connected, and at the same time is in a state of constant flow, prompts me to suggest that this sense of place has a history. Humans were at one time hunter-gatherers. Where animal herds were in abundance, hunting became organised as humans became increasingly reliant on this important source of food.

Soon enough, ritual would have grown up around the hunt, led by a shaman or priest. Its purpose would be the re-enactment of the hunt as a way of influencing the outcome by attempting to find a way into the spirit of the animals. Such a re-enactment would no doubt involve dance in some form, to the beat of drums and other percussion instruments. Hunters and dancers would clothe themselves in animal skins and masks (of which painted faces might be the simplest form), initially perhaps as camouflage, but more importantly to put themselves 'inside' the animal – to become its spirit.

Without the herds, the community would face starvation, so this food source was vital. Any encroachment on the hunting grounds would be a serious threat, dealt with by chasing off or even killing any intruders, and the ritualised dance is likely to have doubled as a means of psyching up the warriors in preparation for conflict. Eventually, the whole idea of protecting hunting grounds would have become more formal and, as the hunters perhaps began to settle into at least semi-permanent communities, the now formalised ritual would have become an integral part of the protection of 'place' and its boundaries.

The importance of boundaries is primal, tribal and ubiquitous. Boundaries were always marked in some way, most usually with stones, which may be named or decorated with carvings. Those recovered from the Babylonian culture depict carvings of goddesses and womb symbols – we can see that the idea of the Great Mother has a very long history. So fundamental is the importance of boundaries that, to this day, the ceremony of 'beating the bounds' still takes place in certain parishes in England and Wales, but now conducted by the local vicar. Yet another ancient rite usurped by the Church.

In the Celtic world of well-established farming and pastoral communities the turning of the earth cycle determined the need to renew the boundaries. At each of the eight cardinal points in the cycle, the veil that separates the physical world from the ethereal world is at its thinnest and can be briefly opened. These were liminal times, when those involved in the appropriate rituals 'stand at the threshold' between how they perceived themselves in the pre-ritual world and what they would become once the rite had been completed. Even today, we can be subject to liminal times, for example, that period of transition between passing your degree exams and the subsequent receiving of the beribboned certificate at the awards ceremony. At the more spiritual level of re-affirming the boundaries, things are 'neither this nor that', the veil is there but not there and a mystical atmosphere permeates proceedings.

I cannot imagine that such proceedings were enacted without a sense of excitement, joy and eager anticipation, particularly in the innately egalitarian partnership-based Goddess-worshiping agrarian societies. We know virtually nothing of these times, but it is not difficult to envision, with the help of the many clues we have, that a real sense of ritual marked these occasions, and that music and ceremony were core facets of society. Tracing the boundary had a dual purpose, as it still does today. The rite was designed to draw out evil and banish it from the perimeter, whilst at the same time protecting those within the sacred space. As described above, the idea of having dancers present goes all the way back to a time when the hunting of animals was essential to human survival, and their presence was not simply cosmetic. It was vital in creating the link between the human world and the cosmic, harmonising the activities of mortals with the patterns of the spirit world. Rituals are of necessity constructed in fine detail, and it is the adherence to this detail that makes them work. It ensured the continuity of those fragile boundaries whilst bringing together macrocosmic and microcosmic worlds. In a ritualistic context, dance steps are not there just to make the dance visually appealing. Certain patterns – for example, the circle and the figure-of-eight – have a magical quality, as they create and hold cosmic energy, and the dance is woven with the intent of making this happen.

By the time we reach Celtic times, hunting and gathering had morphed into an agrarian way of life. Celebrations around the earth cycle of birth, growth, death and rebirth were centred on 'mother earth', once again revered by modern neo-pagans, and certainly a concept that speaks of affection and empathy and sounds like common sense. An agrarian society becomes more inventive in its ceremonies and other distractions. For example, ritual dance patterns mimicked the gyres implicit in labyrinths and indeed in the game of Nine-Men's-Morris, both of which were originally cut into the turf as part of the festivities. The design of the Nine-Men's-Morris 'board' is a square within a square within a square, the underlying symbolism of which is about the delineation of boundaries not to be crossed, that thin line that separates the sacred from the profane. It is a design that goes back to at least 1400BCE, carved by stonemasons in Egypt, but may well be considerably older.

This may not be the place to discuss the full implications of the mysticism of the number nine, but if you think you are a cat with nine lives and you want to go the whole nine yards, dressed to the nines, knowing that a stitch in time saves nine and possession is nine points of the law, you may well end up on cloud nine, doing your 9 x 9 Sudoku puzzles or attempting to get nine squares of the same colour on each face of your Rubic's cube. You may be into numerology and understand the implications of the nine-year cycle of change, or you may be an advocate of the Mayan calendar with its nine levels of consciousness. Or indeed you may be drawn to the nine interlocking personality types of the Enneagram, described and popularised by the philosopher G I Gurdjieff . . .

Suffice to say that nine is a big number. And the symbolism of concentric squares around a central protected square (or, if you prefer, eight identical squares around a ninth) reflects a very early order of thinking about the universe. The protected inner sanctum, the ninth square, is often depicted as the 'womb' in matrifocal cultures, examples of which can be found from around the world.

To travel from those pre-Christian times into the 20th Century, and hope to produce a clearly linked progression from ceremonial dance to the frolics of morris dancers at a modern folk festival, is impossible. It is a long and winding road, which in places has suffered from rock falls and subsidence or the natural erosion of millennia. Yet there are very obvious markers along the route about which we can be confidently conclusive. Like ley lines, the evidence of the road is clearly there if you look for it.

For instance, our transition as a species from nomadic hunter-gathering to settled farming precipitated an acute awareness of the seasons and the effects of climate on the growing of crops and raising livestock. The earth cycle became central to this, as we celebrated the midsummer and midwinter solstices, the spring and autumn equinoxes and the four cross-quarter days in between. Fire was an important element in these celebrations. The four quarter days, which came to be called *Imbolc*, *Beltane*, *Lammas* and *Samhain*, were the most significant community fire festivals, the most important of which was Beltane, coming as it does at the beginning of the most potent part of the whole cycle. Now translated into contemporary May Day celebrations, it still carries the power of spring, a life force that is irrepressible even to modern, disconnected, self-centred and destructive *Homo sapiens*.

Beltane in its more contemporary form celebrates the fertility of Mother Earth and the potency of the life force, honouring the symbiotic relationship between female and male energy, represented by the Horned God and the Fertile Goddess – the Great Mother. The spring cross-quarter celebrates rebirth, with earth energies at their most active. Fire at this time always had a special significance. To symbolise rebirth, all fires were doused on the eve of Beltane, and fresh fire – known as the 'need-fire' – was kindled to honour the returning light of the sun after the dark days of winter. To quote from the work of the legendary scholar, E K Chambers, "To achieve sunshine, a fire must be lit, or some other representation of the appearance and motion of the sun devised."

A great fire was built and lit, and those present were required to come into direct contact with it, either by standing in the smoke, leaping through the flames or by smearing their faces with the burnt wood. Or quite possibly all of the above. Ashes from the fire were also spread on the fields as an essential aid to fertility. Dancers, led by their Fool, would be present to add extra dynamism to the proceedings. Nowadays, the Fool, and indeed other characters that appear alongside morris dancers, are all seen as comic peripheral figures, but to our Celtic ancestors, the Fool held a central role, the symbol of sexual virility strutting his phallic stuff with his dancers in tow. Nothing short of the destiny of the whole community is what was at stake in the enactment of these rites. Everything and everyone was touched by the purifying and fertile fire. The Fool and his dancers had faces blackened by the charred wood, and the purpose of this can now be seen in sharp focus in the context of a celebration of fertility – wood ash, carbon and fertility are synonymous.

In Scotland, the *Bel-tein* fires were lit on the central ninth of a ninefold square cut into the turf. The historical record also shows that in Scotland the "need-fire was kindled sometimes by nine men and sometimes by nine nines of first begotten sons." In Scotland, Wales and parts of Scandinavia, the Beltane fire was made with nine sticks collected by nine men from nine different trees. Perhaps our nine morris men of the board game represent these rekindlers of the flame. Nine really is a big number.

Let me point out at this stage that what I have said in the above paragraphs is a very brief appraisal of a huge subject about which many great books have been written. A quick search on the internet will reveal how vast and complex the subject is, and all I have done is to try tracing the roots of morris to what might have been its most ancient ancestor in the re-enactment of hunts in a magical, mysterious shamanic way. It is a great pity that Dave Jones did not get this far in his research, but no blame attaches to him; his focus was on the dances themselves. His prime objective was to collect sufficient contemporary material to put together a number of 'collected' dances, so that his new Border side could put on a performance of dances exclusive to the Welsh Border. To put his efforts into context, however, his book, *The Roots of Welsh Border Morris*, was published in 1988, based on research conducted before the internet age. To discover that his suspicions about what we now call morris dancing were uncannily accurate would certainly have vindicated his resolute assertions about its origins and purposes. It would also have given him more than enough material to describe in detail those ancient 'pagan ritual male fertility dances' that occupied his thoughts. Even without this, however, Dave Jones still managed to change radically the understanding of morris and the way much of it would be performed in the future.

Part 2

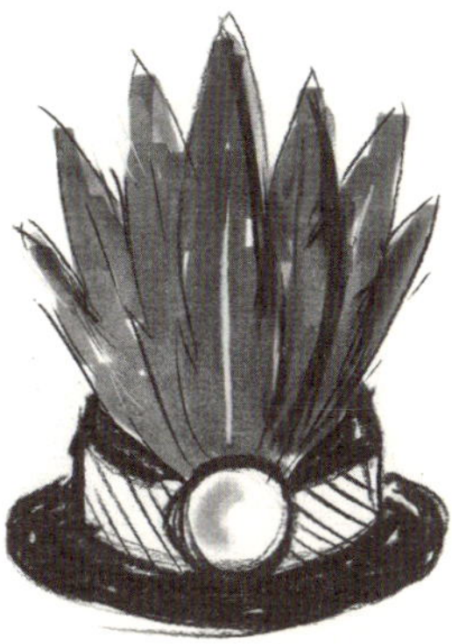

Chapter 3
Dreaming of a Black Christmas

• • • • •

"Oh, to plough and sow,
To reap and mow,
And to be a farmer's boy-o-oy,
And to be a farmer's boy..."

I bet you thought that was the end of the history lesson. Well, I've got some great news for you – it isn't! And if you have read this far you're obviously hooked. Or on a desert island. Just a teensy bit more then, okay?

So, enter Silurian. Back in 1969, this was nothing more than just another Cotswold side, but the Founding Father, Dave Jones (Jonesy to most people) had very definite ideas about morris even then. He accepted that Cotswold was just the ticket if you wanted to put on a performance of any length – and, in Jonesy's notion of performance, length was the operative word – but all the while he was gnawing away at the Border bone like a hungry dog. He knew he was onto an older tradition, and therefore a forerunner of Cotswold, so he unearthed little fragments of history and local knowledge and gradually pieced them together until he had a Border framework, something he had already achieved by the time he split from Hereford Morris. On this framework he hung the Boxing Day Tour.

From its birth in 1969, this was always a 'black job', a phrase coined by the inestimable Dave Smith (more on him later), because one of the undisputed details regarding Border Morris was that the dancers always blacked their faces. Boxing Day was one of the days in winter when the dances were traditionally performed. I venture to suggest that, in the misty past, this particular celebration centred on the winter solstice, a fundamental point in the earth cycle. Being midwinter in the northern hemisphere, the burning of Yule logs was a central theme, and the fertility symbolism long associated with fire would have been vital. Faces would have been blackened with charred wood, whilst ashes from the burnt logs would have been used to fertilise the soil. Fast-forward to our modern world and the solstice means nothing to most people. Blackened faces are nothing more than a hint of what might have taken place in ancient times. Nowadays, Christmas is little more than a three-day binge, but Jonesy, whilst recognising this, had the side blacking up every Boxing Day as part of the festivities, and treating the audience to some local ritual dances.

Kick-off at Ledbury's old market house was around eleven o'clock in the morning, or at least as soon as the local hunt had performed its own little ritual. Riders and horses would gather outside The Feathers Hotel, the redcoats posing on their chestnut chargers, looking down their noses at all the dross milling around the horses' feet. After relieving the hostelry of a stirrup cup or ten, they would move off up the main street, the spotless red of the huntsmen's coats standing out sharply amongst the profusion of black hacking jackets and tweeds worn by the lesser mortals and hangers-on. As the mounted cavalry left for the killing fields, the spectators' thoughts would turn to the spirit of Christmas as they checked their watches for opening time, and they began to make what should have been a bee-line for the pub had it not been for all the piles of steaming horse muck they had to negotiate along the way.

Ledbury's beautiful market house building is a very well-preserved black and white structure of herringbone pattern, supported on sixteen huge wooden columns of substantial girth, creating an open ground floor area for trade, with an enclosed first floor space above. The open ground floor also makes a handy space for morris dancers to hide in. And, as the hunt moved off, Silurian would be safely ensconced in there, ready to create a rowdy diversion. This was a cunning plan to stem the flow of punters to the pubs, thus keeping the way clear for themselves. As I am sure you all know, it is impossible to put on a good show without constant lubrication – something I believe was always a vital part of celebration of any kind.

Jonesy, in his lilting Welsh accent, would attempt to grab the attention so recently given to the cohorts of the hunt.

"Ladies and gentlemen! We are the Silurian Morris men of Ledbury! And we are going to dance for you some traditional men's dances . . . !"

Mentally thanking us for this advance warning, the serious drinkers amongst the would-be spectators vanished from the scene like mist on a summer river. The Silurian boys, encumbered with the kind of post-Christmas inertia that might have overwhelmed Cecil Sharp back in 1899, shuffled about like guilty schoolboys as they tried to avoid doing the first dance. It's an undisputed fact that breaking into sudden exuberant movement on Boxing Day without liquid refreshment was guaranteed to bring on a headache of epic severity, so the precautionary principle was employed as the dancers tried to avoid Jonesy's eye. Some members of the audience, hoping that at the very least a squabble might break out amongst the ranks, stopped to take a closer look at the tinkling melee under the market house. Jonesy, a committed public entertainer, was having none of it, and soon marshalled six dancers to get the show going.

Visually, it was an odd look, as the dancers wore Cotswold kit but with their faces blacked in homage to their Border roots. The kit was Standard Mark 1 Cotswold (white shirt, black breeches, white socks, black shoes) with the addition of a rib-length sleeveless surplice adorned with long inch-wide ribbons (that's 25mm for all you decimalised youngsters) in red, white, yellow, green and blue. On the shins were bell pads with the same ribbons, to subtly represent the four elements of earth, air, fire and water – and a yellow one for the sun. In retrospect, my feeling is that Jonesy had an elemental side to him that he never really explored. But he was proud of his ribbon idea and thought it was jolly clever stuff. Most of the rest of the side hardly thought about it at all, except when the ends of the ribbons floated into their beer mugs, which was basically every time they were worn. Subtly setting off the whole primordial thing was the somewhat incongruous black face. This might be a good place to add a few more words about this quirky practice.

Returning to the time of Henry VII, there is evidence to suggest that at one time all morris dancers blacked their faces. In 1509, with Henry VIII on the throne, there is a reference to his Shrovetide banquet at which the torchbearers 'were appareyled in crimosen satyne and grene lyke Moreskoes, their faces blacke'. Other references from this time clearly establish the link between morris dancing and the idea of disguise, of which a black face was an accepted part. During the current debate, which has been running for decades, it has been suggested that the black face disguise is one possible source of the word 'Morris' and that the word was derived from 'Moorish'. But who were the Moors? Ostensibly, they were the inhabitants of that region of north-west Africa known as Mauretania, annexed by the Romans in the 1st century and then conquered by Arabs in the 7th. The term 'Moors' has no real ethnological value, and indeed has been used by Europeans since mediaeval times as a catch-all for anyone from 'over there', dressed like an Arab or claiming Islam as a religion. Thus the term might have been around for many centuries, at least since the Crusades, for example, when Europeans would have been fighting 'Moors'. Maybe our boys came back from the Crusades via North Africa dancing the *Mourisque*, picked up in the casbahs of downtown Marrakesh. Maybe they thought the *Mourisque* was a lot more fun than the old fertility dances, and thus it slipped into the number one slot in the dance chart. No one knows for sure, but I believe there is very little to be gained from getting hung up about it, except for those whose main preoccupation is academic debate.

In the late '60s, for Dave Jones, it wasn't that big a deal. All he was interested in was that research showed Border dances were performed with black faces, and he was determined to keep the tradition alive, even if it did look very odd with the Cotswold kit. The two ideas were incongruous, despite Jonesy's elemental ribbons, but it happened only on this one day of the year, so really no one in the side was that bothered about it or gave it much thought. They were more concerned with acquiring a pint of beer to ease the pain of the first dance.

With a stomach full of Christmas dinner and a head full of Christmas cobwebs, a slow start was inevitable. Once the first dance and the first pint were out of the way, however, the dancing went up a gear. Jonesy, our balding, bearded, sad-eyed and serious leader, was always quick to remind us that the dances needed to be done with 'lots of vigour, look you.' He really didn't need to. The Silurian men of the day were a proud lot and didn't want to put on a poor show, especially with local dances on their home patch. Even the Cotswold dances were executed with some panache. Black Joker, Bledington, to take an example, involved sticks being clashed left, right and across the set. Sticks and fingers would often crack and splinter. Heads occasionally got in the way and, on one memorable day, an unlucky dancer copped a smack on the skull that sent him spinning out of the set. Luckily he was pulled back into line by the man next to him and he completed the dance on autopilot. It took two pints of Marston's Best anaesthetic to get his eyes to coordinate again.

At any dance spot, a little battle of wills would always take place between the dancers and Our Glorious Leader. It was just a bit of banter, but with serious undertones. Jonesy loved the opportunity to treat the crowd to an exhibition of morris dancing and he would happily have run through the whole repertoire. The lads had a different take on proceedings. They understood that there was more to it than dancing. There was the drinking for a start. A pint on Boxing Day was something to look forward to, and a dance was useful to work up a thirst. Then there was the 'bag'. Here we have another morris tradition, whereby dancers expected to be rewarded in coin of the realm for their performances.

There are those who erroneously believe this idea goes back to a time when those out of work might seek solicited contributions from the public in order to keep body and soul in good fettle. Jonesy had picked up on a reference to this during his research, but it has since taken on a life of its own, provoking much inconclusive discussion. All I will add is that we should be wary of this idea, because there is also strong evidence (via E C Cawte) that the Church was involved in coercing morris dancers to collect money on its behalf to pay for candles, church furnishings and structural repairs. This practice was well established by the 1500s, but was severely curtailed by Edward VI in 1547. I think it is thus fair to say that soliciting money long predates anything to do with jobless workers. For Silurian, in common with most morris sides, collecting money was basically a means of financing excursions that might otherwise be beyond the pecuniary means of the side. I suspect 'twas ever thus.

However, we certainly believed in giving it our best shot – do a good spot and people might be more inclined to drop something in the hat (it could be the hat or a pint pot or any receptacle really, but it was still called the 'bag' and the man responsible for counting it up at the end of the day was the 'bagman'). So, optimisation was the order of the day, whatever Jonesy thought. Minimum number of dances for the maximum bag, leaving sufficient time to do a comparison of various ales as the day progressed. Even with the energy that went into the dances, the majority (i.e. everyone except Jonesy) felt that it was impossible to keep the Ledbury punters riveted for more than ten minutes, so we rarely did more than four dances. The British Camp Hotel, a very popular tourist spot halfway along the length of the Malvern Hills, was the second venue. Dancing in the car park attracted a large crowd, especially if the weather was kind, and the bag was usually quite a bit heavier by the end of that spot.

Both Ledbury and British Camp, however, were just practice runs for the real business of the day – the lunchtime spot, at an out-of-the-way pub in some deep and isolated part of the countryside, with a landlord whose attitude to the calling of time was, shall we say, accommodating. In the days before pubs were allowed to stay open all day, it was not easy to find a publican relaxed enough to risk a visit from the local constabulary. And the boys in blue were not to be messed with during the Christmas period. They were disgruntled and bellicose, having been deprived of their after-Christmas snooze in front of the box, and they roamed the byways like feral predators looking for someone to tear apart.

Somehow Jonesy always managed to sniff out the right kind of watering hole. He'd start looking months in advance and then spend time and money in there convincing the landlord that, after playing host to Silurian all day, not only would he benefit from free entertainment but also his coffers would be overflowing, thus giving him the excuse, and the wherewithal, to disappear to Tenerife for a week on the razzle. We would arrive at our secret destination highly focused on living up to the landlord's expectations, so that we could add his pub to our list of Boxing Day favourites for future years. The dancing would be brief, energetic and confined, as the space available was usually about the size of a couple of tablemats. The bag, having by that time of day taken on the legendary status of 'the lucky morrisman's hat', would be passed amongst the crowd, and shortly afterwards the lucky morrisman would get a smack from the bagman for trying to spend the hat's contents on beer.

We would usually end the dance spot with an overt little number called Fanny Frail. Like many of the collected Border dances, this one was suggestively phallic. The men faced each other in two lines, one line with their 15-inch sticks held erect from the groin, looking like a row of urinating clowns, whilst those opposite them gave the erect sticks a good thrashing. After a chorus in which the sticks were swung skywards in a ramming motion, there was a cross-over move and the other side had a go.

It was a common feeling within the side that this kind of phallic symbolism looked and felt much more like a fertility dance than all that pretty Cotswold stuff with the fancy footwork. Having consumed several pints by then, we entered into the spirit of the moment with exactly the sort of vigour that got Jonesy excited. The air was full of the crack of stick on stick and mock-orgasmic groans, whimpers and cries of pleasure. Certain members of the audience thought this was just the business – others were jamming the phone lines to the Clean Up Britain campaign headquarters. As far as the Silurian boys were concerned though, it wasn't worth putting all that black stuff on your face unless you were prepared to go out and have a good time, so that was what they were doing.

Fanny Frail was what we called a 'getting off dance'. Despite the vague sexual innuendo, it was nothing more than a dance that was used to leave the arena. It had a little ditty at the end which included the words, "I met my little Sally at the corner of the alley". While Jones the Folk was straining his lungs imparting this particular piece of trifling information to the audience, the lads dancing the round were all singing sotto voce about doing something else to Sally at the corner of the alley. Thus, on the black-faced Boxing Day tour, Silurian laid the first foundations of the devil-may-care reputation that would define them in future years. At the same time, and virtually undetectably, there opened up a small fissure of mischievous confrontation with Jonesy's traditionalist attitude.

With the dancing out of the way, it was time to test the landlord's ability to keep a good pint. Real morrismen of course drink real ale, not those fizzy tasteless factory beers or industrial lagers. As well as a decent pint, the potential pleasure of the rest of the day depended on the landlord's willingness to continue serving. Had he remembered what Jonesy had told him about the guaranteed profitability of the day and the week in Tenerife that would result from it? This was always a rhetorical question. Jonesy's ability to find an obliging landlord was consistently good, and the landlord indeed played his part. His unflagging dedication to the pursuit of wealth soon had him turning pints into cash at a rate that would have had Midas himself taking notes. Our beaming host certainly was – fivers, tenners, you name it, he was taking them. They were dematerialising at the speed of light, leaving behind a handful of coppers. But in exchange we had the beer. Some (the softies in the side) even had beer and food. Soon everything was right with the world and the bar had a happy face. Even an eruption of traditional folk songs failed to take away its smile. Inevitably it was Jonesy who initiated the singing. It seemed his destiny in life to reintroduce anyone and everyone to the Folk Songs of Olde England and, once someone is on a pre-ordained path, it is difficult to dent their resolve. If you can't beat them, you just join in on the chorus and, soon enough, most of the assembled company were bellowing through the chorus of *Farmer's Boy* and assorted sea shanties.

I have my suspicions that Jonesy learned to sing in a church choir when he was a lad, because he pitched *Farmer's Boy* in a key that many found desperately difficult to cope with on the harmonies. It's the usual situation with all those church hymns, which were obviously written in a key understood only by devout Christians, a cunningly contrived divine plot to show up the Births, Marriages and Deaths contingent. If you are a regular churchgoer, look out for them in dimly lit corners, either trying to brazen it out by miming and pretending it's the person next to them who's got the problem, or desperately throwing the voice around upper and lower registers in a bid to coincide with at least some of the notes. All to no avail of course. Either the voice dies away completely in the lower octave, like a grumbling grizzly heading down the back of the cave for a kip, or it was eye-popping facial contortions with vocal chords snapping like gorse pods in the sun. Jonesy wasn't bothered either way. He just carried on singing, working his way through his repertoire, accompanying himself on accordion or, for real entertainment value, on a beaten-up old guitar. It was just like the one you might see festooned with cobwebs down the back of the Oxfam shop, unnoticed and unloved until someone like Dave Jones comes in and takes pity on it. An inescapable problem with such an instrument is that it is never quite in tune. The Silurian lads didn't worry about that though. They knew he was doing a grand job and keeping the pub humming, which of course kept the landlord busy. So, even if said landlord had had second thoughts about Tenerife, he was moving far too quickly to notice the normal passage of time. Einstein could have pointed out the problem to him, but fortunately Einstein was drinking somewhere else.

Sometime in the late afternoon, when the landlord was well into the 'excess fine' portion of his serving after time, things would begin to wind down, prompted by the gathering midwinter dusk. Thoughts would turn to leaving. Some thoughts would turn to staying, and indeed there was one occasion when the landlord said, "You might as well stay here lads – I'll be open for the evening shift in half an hour!" A few years after that, another landlord in another pub made the same suggestion and he was taken up on it, but in those very early days Silurian were good boys. Or perhaps they just had less beer money . . .

A tradition began to build from those early post-Christmas tours that a member of the side would invite the lads back to his place for tea and sandwiches, so Silurian would all head off into the dusk, in a convoy of suspiciously meandering vehicles, to relax in the comfort of someone else's sofa. Driving after consuming a serious quantity of ale was a dangerous and illegal sport, then as now, but the laws hadn't yet reached present day severity – when you have only to sniff a pint of beer to risk being banned for twenty years. Plus the country roads were very much quieter then. So quiet in fact that we would rarely see another vehicle as we weaved our way cautiously to the tea spot, never more than a few miles away. So we just took our chances. Back then, we were more likely to be a danger to ourselves than to any other motorists, but we generally arrived without incident. Floating a few sandwiches and some bits of cake on top of the beer was inevitably a big mistake. Add to that the soporific effect of comfortable armchairs, hot tea and a warm room, and the lads would go down like skittles, happily leaving this world for the Land of Nod. Any attempt to get going again for an evening spot was pretty much doomed to failure and thus the annual black-faced outing was all over for another year.

Personal Reflection : 1

Old Folkies

• • • • •

"And it's no, nay, never,
No nay never, no more,
Will I play the wild rover,
No never, no more..."

Around the same time that Silurian first drew breath, Dave Jones had launched another folk-oriented project, the Bromyard Folk Festival, choosing this unspoilt Herefordshire market town as the ideal venue for a compact family-friendly festival. I joined Silurian in 1975, after my fourth annual visit to the festival. Over the next two decades I watched people come and go and, in particular, I observed several dozen regular punters change over the years from lusty, beer-swilling, long-haired revellers into harassed greying family men with kids hanging off every limb. Though this might be considered no more than the natural order of human progress, it was nonetheless an interesting observational exercise.

In the mid '70s, these guys would roll up on the Friday night on foot or in beat-up barely roadworthy vehicles, quickly erect their one-man bivouacs somewhere on the field and then promptly forget all about them as they headed into town for the Drink the Pub Dry competition. Their appetite for ale, chip butties and home-made pork pies from the local butcher was enough to sustain them all weekend. The whereabouts of their tents was simply of no interest, as sleep was the last thing on their minds – well, unaccompanied sleep anyway. Fuelled up and ready for anything, the other favourite festival haunt was the ceilidh marquee, guaranteed to be twitching with nubile foxy females, many of them rampantly uninhibited in the sexual rush generated by the dancing – 'fulfilled of lustynesse' as Chaucer once put it. Come the end of the ceilidh, our heroes would be trying their luck with random but clichéd phrases such as, "Aren't you a bit hot in that dress?" and "Are those buttons down the front real and do they work?" *So* last-century. One can only hope that in the 21st century and the age of the internet, something more original has been gleaned from web searches on what women actually want to hear.

It seemed no time at all, however, before these young blades could no longer cut it, their once-sharp edges rounded and blunt. You would see them saying to each other, as they sat out yet another dance at the Saturday night ceilidh, "God, I could do with some sleep!" What happened to the times when they would still be going strong long after the late night extra, maybe eventually crashing out behind the stage or in the dewy grass outside? Two decades later and they are slinking off long before the late night extra starts, heading for their caravans (towed in with the loan-financed Mercedes) or eight-bedroomed continental frame tents (with built-in kitchen and washroom), from which they will not stir the next morning until they have had a jolly good breakfast and a cup of tea.

As much as I think how wonderful life might be if I were half the age I am today, in other ways I feel grateful that I have lived long enough to have a good understanding of the changes that have taken place over the last half a century (writing that down, it looks like a *really long time ago* . . .). My observation of the transformation of those attending Bromyard Folk Festival over a couple of decades has taught me something about people, social mores, trends and comfort zones. It has made me wonder whether we are simply programmed to do what we do, carried along on some invisible conveyor belt to whatever destiny has been pre-ordained for us. What I was observing at Bromyard might well have been nothing more than a 20th Century Rake's Progress, but without the inheritance of wealth enjoyed by Hogarth's 18th century victim.

We see our modern Rake enter the scene in the late 1960s as a newly converted folkie, rebelling against the supposedly nonconformist, but media-driven, late '60s flower-power pop culture. The media and corporates had hijacked Californian hippie philosophy, brainwashed it, sanitised it and reprogrammed it as a serious pop money-spinner. Neatly packaged, it was paraded before a gullible audience through the medium of colourfully attired mum-friendly bands (sorry – *groups*) singing slushy songs about peace, love and flowers. Our hero – it could have been me or any number of my friends – was having none of it.

Flower-power spawned its own sartorial dress code, as does every other sub-culture. Even drop-outs and anarchists have their own uniform. The folk scene was no different. Thus, wearing the appropriate kit, that is to say, dressed like a 19th century farm labourer, our virgin folkie enters the world of folk clubs and beer. He is amazed. All the songs seem to be about drinking or sex, his two most favourite things in the whole world. Sometimes they are about an absence of both whilst enduring a harsh life at sea or as a conscripted soldier. He can't get enough of all this, feeling a strong empathy with those mournful balladeers and their tales of hard times past. Listening to the songs is not sufficient though: he needs more. Vicarious experiences are not the real thing. Our hero wants to *be there*, scything the corn, drinking the harvest ale, or 'listing for a soldier before returning, scarred by battle, to ramble in the new-mown hay with the girl he left behind him.

Dancing solves the problem for him. Everything he needs is right there. Music, beer and women, whose desire to live the past life is as strong as his own. In his teens, early experiences of dancing, as a means of contriving encounters with girls, fell well short of his imagination. Mostly these were limited to dingy youth clubs, where he and his school chums would watch small knots of girls gyrating silently and demurely around a small pile of handbags on the floor, feet glued to the boards, hips coyly twitching and arms gently flailing like the damaged sails of an expiring windmill. Now though, it's all hands-on, and he can grab girls round the waist, swing them wildly through a polka or two, showing off his prowess as a dancer and the unspoken manliness of his strong and protective arms. The girls are up for it too, flushed, excited and sexy, their female pheromones smacking him round the head in ways he had never imagined, let alone experienced. And he can dance with any number of girls, sometimes as many as six in the same dance! Poor lamb, he doesn't know what to do with himself.

At a ceilidh one night, his mate says to him, "You're a good dancer. Why don't you come along to morris practice with me next week? We practice in the back room of the Red Lion . . ." He doesn't need any persuasion. In his folk persona, being a morris dancer seems like exactly the right thing to do. And it means going out for a few beers on a week night. All seems right with the world. Until another incremental change occurs.

As if guided by an unseen hand, the dozy boy, now smitten with nostalgia for a time he never knew and lulled into reverie by the happy-ever-after verses of the more sentimental ballads, falls in love. It's probably a pheromone thing, but he doesn't know that and, frankly, he doesn't care. His head is full of songs, ideals and images of country cottages, stoneground bread and contented laughing children playing around his feet with the wooden toys he has made for them.

Marrying his dewy-eyed bride-o, he sets about building on his dreams, but they disappear nearly as fast as his money does, and the spectre of the rat race takes their place. Morris practice begins to look like an escape, somewhere to rest his head or anaesthetise his sorrows. The country cottage turns out to be a financial millstone, and he has to buy a car and a map just to get to the place. The stoneground bread tastes as if the stones are still in it, and the contented laughing children are actually sworn enemies, battling it out tooth and claw, whilst the unwanted wooden toys littering the overgrown flower borders are gradually being whittled down by the local woodlice. Transatlantic influence and the behemoth of American marketing has ensured that all kids, not just his own, respond positively only to grotesque plastic figurines depicting overtly warlike alien creatures and manic robots, a playground manifestation of American confrontational aggression. He abhors that kind of gun-toting Wild West culture, but here it is – right in his own home.

All this bothers our hero, but comfort comes in the form of nods of agreement from his morris mates, as they discuss life's problems over a couple of pints after practice. In the place where his dewy-eyed bride once stood, there now appears a somewhat harassed woman with a frown who questions him about how much time and money he is spending in the pub during the week, pointing out that he now goes out on 'practice night' and another night of the week 'to play pool'. He has to get a job with a better salary to maintain this idyllic existence. It's true about going out two nights a week and, what with everything else, he has unwittingly fallen into the trap of spending just a bit more than he is earning. It is of no comfort to him to understand that 90% of the working population is in the same boat. He gets the job and he now travels to work in the new company car, which in itself stresses him out as he develops car envy, traversing the country's motorway system in his Vauxhall and being overtaken by BMWs and Audis.

His old car becomes the second car, used for shopping trips and other low-key excursions. He has to keep up some kind of pretence, so travelling to social engagements is done in the company execmobile. During the week, he spends most of his daylight hours away from home, seeing his family only between returning in the evening and the children's bedtime, during which time they are still winding each other up and have been doing so ever since mummy picked them up from school (in the second car). Weekends are packed with activities he never knew existed, most of them clearly promoted by the school to subdue parents and load them with feelings of guilt and inadequacy if they have the temerity to suggest that the schedule is unsustainable.

On top of that, the flowery print dress that first beguiled him by hugging the torso of his soon-to-be-beloved now seems to be a universal fashion statement. Like the hippie culture before it, folk culture has itself been hijacked by the corporate greed machine, set on full throttle to milk it until it stops yielding profits. Even in his own home, our erstwhile rake is now surrounded by Laura Ashley fabrics, lacy cushion covers and country diary tablemats. On the plus side, it does help him to keep the folk myth going, even if he has moved to Ealing to be nearer the job. But the only real rake is the one in his hand during his annual battle with autumn leaves.

He felt comfortable as a young folkie so, as a rapidly ageing folkie, he still likes to pop along to the local folk club, where he might find an ever-repentant Wild Rover still apologising for his prodigal ways and misdemeanours. It helps our hero to understand that he is not the only one with a problem and, empathising with wild rovers everywhere, he can pull the comfort blanket around him and nurse a pint while he listens wistfully to songs that remind him of less troubled times.

'Comfort' is the key word at the local ceilidhs too. Shying away from the acid house ravings and mid-Atlantic rap tracks his kids are bringing home, our man prefers the reassurance of those country dances that long ago set his heart on fire. But gone is the passion, the risk, the sheer adrenaline-fuelled madness of it all. He still thinks he's strutting his stuff, but it is slower, less explosive, more . . . *contained*. He gets up confidently for Nottingham Swing or the Dorset Four-Hand Reel, because he knows all the steps and he can get through the dances without mishap. Not like that time in Bromyard in the mad days of youth, when the Cumberland Square Eight went at such a pace that he lost his footing and was trampled by the next couple, who were moving too fast to brake in time. He cracked three ribs, but laughed it off. He is more careful now and knows the dances so well that he moves on autopilot, the dancing too staid to take his mind off his problems. He cannot relax his guard, but is comforted by the thought that he is at least in control and is not likely to sustain any unexpected injuries.

Morris is the same. Gone are the verve and the athleticism. Its purpose now is to get him out of the house, and it's the best excuse he can offer for putting off the wallpapering – if you are part of the team, you can't let the others down, can you? He has developed a sense of responsibility, though his long-suffering wife can, off the top of her head, present a succinct thesis on the variations of the word 'responsibility'. Of course he does feel a bit of a prannet these days, dressed in those silly clothes, but he is eager to promote team spirit and, more importantly, he can enjoy having a few pints without feeling guilty. Folk is still his thing and he is still living the part, albeit at a much slower pace. And he still has the waistcoat and tankard.

Every social and/or musical revolution spawns a culture which thrives in the devotees who are its very essence. They feel at home. The folk scene is no exception, but what is difficult to understand is the chimeric nature of such cultures. Essentially they are no more than fads and fashions, living briefly and changing rapidly, leaving the unwary caught in a time-warp, anachronistic castaways on an abandoned beach. Twenty years after the heyday of punk in the late '70s, I remember seeing one ageing follower of that fashion, complete with a chain of safety pins from nose to left ear and electrified clumps of coloured hair standing about on his head. Oblivious to his now antiquated appearance, he walked the walk despite his progress being severely hampered by the criss-cross assortment of strips and chains on his tartan 'bondage trousers'. From his enormous boots to his studded dog collar, he was a definitive example of Malcolm McLaren's contribution to the fashion carousel, but he was forty-five if a day, and he had obviously looked like that ever since wild-eyed and straightjacketed Johnny Rotten had spat and yelled his way through *God Save the Queen* two decades previously. Even teddy boys from the '50s never quite faded away, though the Grim Reaper has now carried most of them off. The beatniks of the same era hung on long enough for some of them to re-emerge, grey-haired, bespectacled and besandalled, blinking in the light of the shining new folk revival and posing as founding fathers of the new movement.

In 1968, the new converts to folk music came to Bromyard, harmonised to the new tunes and fell about laughing trying to do the dances. Those who became bored moved on, whilst those remaining became involved in their own perception of tradition, delving deeper and deeper into the archives to drag out more and more obscure songs – 'and this one was collected from Mrs Ida Bickerstaff outside her cottage in Dorset in 1854 . . .' – as a result of which even more became bored and moved on, following the instigators of change as the folk culture morphed into something newer and quite possibly untraditional.

A preoccupation with tradition, amongst those who had turned the revolution into a comfort zone, made it difficult for innovative young talent to enter the hallowed temple of the local folk club. Only those with a parental pedigree or a recognised talent as a new singer/songwriter were accepted as true exponents of folk culture. The rest were dismissed as too contemporary and were exiled to the outer fringes of the sanctum to wander in the long grass of the folk/rock undergrowth. The original young folk enthusiasts, having stuck it out through all this, were now rapidly becoming old folkies, seeking comfort, familiarity and stability as they reflected on the way their lives had changed, wondering where all the kids had suddenly come from. Thus did the old folkies get older, more middle-class-conscious and less rebellious, but they were not unhappy with how things had turned out. At least predictability and routine have a certain solidity. Many of them still played at being morris dancers, but they were in it for the clubby aspect of it all. They liked the ales, the feasts, the ring meetings and toasts to the Queen. The wives and children had to be catered for of course, but that was fine, as the festivals had become very family orientated, and certain morris sides were instrumental in organising their own family-friendly days of dance and other weekend events.

All became quiet and peaceful as festivals provided weekends of bliss and harmony. Health and safety became the new buzz words and everybody seemed to be into it. Healthy eating, healthy exercise, safe driving, safe sex – and safe morris. Just get your kit on, get yourself to the dance spot, do the steps to the best of your ability, have a beer or two and go home. Mind you don't upset anyone and don't make waves. Maintain the tradition and live your dancer's life by the Black Book.

Chapter 4
All Black on the Wight

• • • • •

"I borrowed a spade from the woman next door,
And I broke up the smoke that remained on the floor,
And I was shovellin' away 'til the closing of day,
Singing a smoke-shovelling song..."

The ferry had moved imperceptibly off the quayside and was cutting through the grimy swell of Southampton Water heading for Cowes.

"Well, this is exciting, innit?"

"Coo, look at the waves!"

"I've never bin abroad before!"

Had the residents of the Isle of Wight been warned that there was to be an imminent influx of unpredictable morris dancers with a puerile turn of phrase? I doubt it. Yet Silurian was aboard this ferry, disguised as normal passengers but buzzing with excitement at the thought of a trip away from the mainland, to join the island men by invitation to their ring meeting. The simplistic banter was simply part of the initial stages of the pre-dance psyching-up session.

"We'll show them buggers how to dance!"

"And play . . ."

"Shouldn't take too much doing – bunch of bloody Cotswold wasters!"

It was 1979, and I had been in the side four years, during which time I had witnessed a gradual deterioration of any respect we might have held for Cotswold Morris. Odd that, considering we still wore Cotswold kit. But our sorties as a border side had become increasingly frequent, rapidly moving away from the once-a-year Boxing Day bash. In 1977, at the Derby Ring Meeting, Silurian performed border dances exclusively all weekend. A rival claim to being the first full-time border side came from the Shropshire Bedlams, who had started up in 1975, but Jonesy dismissed that claim by pointing out that Silurian had been dancing border dances in public since 1969, albeit on only one day a year – and performing them as collected. Not like the Bedlams. As far as Jonesy was concerned, he pronounced these Shropshire boys 'impostors' and claimed they were making it up as they went along.

Derby was a turning point for Silurian, however. A bit nerve-racking really, dancing border all weekend, but it went down a storm. Inspired by the positive reaction of the Derby crowds, we thought we might try it again at the Ludlow ring meeting the following year, just to prove to ourselves that Derby wasn't a one-off. It wasn't. The Ludlow crowds were just as enthusiastic. We were impressed. Jonesy was plotting world domination. Border rules *okay*. Pausing to reflect, we might have agreed that any typical audience would probably have been suffering from an over-exposure to morris dancing by the late '70s, and therefore bound to react well to something a bit different. Even so, we had a point to prove and we were putting in some serious effort. This energy combined with the incongruous blacked faces was setting us apart.

We looked different, that's for sure, and the audiences responded well to that. Different is as different does. We danced; the audience cheered for more. The more they cheered, the more we wanted to dance. Our confidence grew. Although we definitely looked a bit weird with Cotswold kit and black faces, we really didn't care. We were in a minority of one – genuine outsiders. And we loved it. We became cocky and began to swagger when we came out to dance, but not in a bad way, just a confident one. Our judge was the audience. The general consensus within that audience was that we were one of the best sides around.

In making the ferry crossing to the Isle of Wight, it was just as well we had brought our secret weapon with us. He was sitting there amongst us, with an unassuming air, smoking, chatting and calmly surveying his surroundings through his thin-rimmed, gold-framed round glasses. Looking uncannily like John Lennon in his bearded hippie days, he seemed to be the one member of Silurian not particularly worked up or excited about the forthcoming weekend. He would be spending the whole weekend with 200+ morrismen, dancing, drinking and sharing the same cramped accommodation in a school hall, but he was clearly not bothered.

John (Willy) Williams was actually not the kind of guy to be fazed by anything. As long as he had access to his cigarettes, a good supply of ale and his trusty melodeon, all was right with the world. Equanimity and a sense of perspective may well affect the personality of someone who had spent time working with mental patients and deaf kids. Yes, you could still use terms like that in 1979. Everything in this life is relative and, however badly we think life has treated us, there is always someone worse off, and Willy seemed to understand this innately. Beyond that, the ability to play an instrument brilliantly also brings perfect calm to the soul. Something I wish I could claim personal experience of . . .

We were honoured to have him aboard. He had been around the folk scene for some time, and I had first seen him in a folk club in Malvern, wearing a 19th century red Royal Engineers jacket (all the rage in the late sixties) and singing songs by The Incredible String Band, a multi-talented, multi-instrumental alternative folk band who enjoyed a stellar career for eight years up to 1974. Willy's version of their *Smoke Shovelling Song* was as good as the original, even though there was only one of him. It set him apart as a musician and singer of rare talent. In hindsight, I can now fully appreciate what a pivotal moment it was when he joined the side, but at the time we were impressed just to have such a talented musician in our midst.

Not just a solo performer, Willy was also a member of a ceilidh band called Hodge's Dump, predominantly playing English tunes. The story, quite possibly apocryphal, of how the name of the band was decided is an indication of the anarchic attitude of its members.

One night when they were still practicing their repertoire, the accordion player, Roger Champkin, suggested that it was time they came up with a name. A brief period of brainstorming ensued but the name eluded them.

"Well, get the beer in," said Roger, "while I go to the bog. Back in a minute."

A round of drinks was purchased and Roger returned in due course.

"We've decided on the name," Willy informed him on his return.

"Oh yeah?" said Roger sceptically.

"Yeah," replied Willy, "Hodge's Dump."

"Hodge's Dump?"

"Yeah, well . . . Rodge is short for Roger; Hodge is another variation of Rodge, and you've just been for a dump . . ."

The name was adopted on a majority of 3 to 1. Practice night continued.

Hodge's Dump had a gig in Ludlow the same weekend as the 1978 ring meeting and, out of curiosity perhaps, they came to watch us dance. Our edgy rebellious style appealed to Willy and he accepted Jonesy's invitation to join the side. We suspected that Jonesy still saw himself as lead musician, but liked the idea of adding a fiddle to a line-up that often consisted of nothing more than Jonesy's accordion and maybe a small bass drum. What seemed to have passed Jonesy by was that Willy could pretty much play anything, and would not be content sitting in a box marked 'second fiddle'.

Willy and the Dump's drummer, Dion, had already been out with us a few times before this Isle of Wight bash, so we knew what to expect, even if our glorious leader didn't. Dion was not just a drummer, he was *The* Drummer. He knew all the drummer jokes (What's the definition of a drummer? Someone who hangs around with musicians . . .) and the drummers' ripostes (What's the difference between a drummer and a toilet seat? A toilet seat has to deal with only one arsehole at a time . . .). His ability on the drums was quite simply in another realm. Essentially a traditional jazz drummer, he was so proficient that he could faultlessly replicate the specific styles of his favourite virtuoso jazz drummers of the 1920s and 1930s. On the Cowes ferry with Silurian, he had just a snare drum with him, but that snare was as crisp as a flinty Chablis Premier Cru. If a freak accident had wiped out the whole band except Dion, we could still have danced all night just to the rhythm of his drum. The beat was so hypnotic, I believe it could have opened portals to a parallel universe or two. It was Dion's playing that made me understand how indispensable drum rhythms are to any kind of music designed to move the soul to a higher level – but the operative word here is 'rhythm'. Get the right rhythm going, and the dancers are entranced, transported, in another world. Add a hypnotic tune and the magic pot is stirred. Dion and Willy gave a strength to the band that charged us up, connecting us to the audience through invisible currents. And best of all, with their unkempt hair and bushy beards, they had a satisfyingly wild look about them.

Unsurprisingly, the music of the Cotswold morris tended to be played on traditional instruments. That meant instruments that were in general use up until the time that Cecil Sharp came along with his big tub of aspic. Fiddles and concertinas were in evidence, plus the occasional pipe and tabor (a three-holed whistle and little drum). The whistle was played with one hand with the drum hanging from the wrist of that hand. The drum was played with one drumstick in the other hand. This pipe and tabor combo goes back at least four hundred years, making it *very* traditional. I can't fault the music – the tunes are wonderful, even though they are mostly nineteenth-century pop tunes. It is stirring stuff to hear them played on those lovely instruments, and the intricate footwork of the dances accompanying them completes the picture.

But it doesn't work like that out there on the Welsh border. In that mysterious land of sheep and wellies, sleepy hollows and windswept misty hills, everything is a lot more basic and down to earth. The dances contain some obvious phallic imagery and work best if done with enthusiasm. Thus a noisy, percussive band is a bonus.

Since the Derby ring meeting, we had made some progress towards this ideal and, two years later on the Isle of Wight, we could muster two accordions, fiddle, snare drum, bass drum, tambourines and John Willy's melodeon when he wasn't on the fiddle. Willy's talent as a dance musician had not gone unnoticed by us, but on this particular weekend he went up another gear. The Silurian devil was in him and he had become a little impatient with certain musicians from other sides whose musical prowess was at the 'drying paint' end of the spectrum. He didn't say anything. He just got out his box and started playing. He and his instrument were as one.

After breakfast on the Saturday morning, the usual ring meeting agenda was rolling out. First: read information in order to locate and board coaches for a day tour of dancing at various spots around the island. Next: following instructions on map provided, proceed in an easterly direction, through underpass under main road, follow pathway around right-hand bend towards car park, where coaches will be waiting. Distance approximately 500 yards.

This was too much to take in for the two hundred morrismen that had spilled out of the overnight accommodation. They were having enough trouble dealing with the effects of a substantial breakfast working its way through an impaired alimentary system, still wobbling from the previous night's onslaught of a gallon or so of real ale. These unhappy fellows were milling about like a flock of sheep and making very similar noises. From their midst came the sound of a melodeon, notes tinkling out a steady rhythmic tune. The bleating subsided. The aimless meandering stopped. Eyes turned to John Willy. Slowly, in a daze of revelation, other musicians reached and fumbled for their instruments and soon there was a pretty impressive band on the go. Without saying anything and without missing a note, Willy turned in the direction of the underpass and marched off. The other musicians followed, and the rank and file behind them.

Reaching the underpass, Willy came to a halt, planting his feet slightly apart to gain the right balance, but he didn't stop playing. Everyone else came to a halt too, wondering what was going on. Willy glanced at them over the rims of his round glasses, perched on the end of his black nose.

"Acoustics," he said, rolling his eyes from right to left, taking in the span of the underpass.

A few nodded comprehendingly, and Willy's big band held fast. There must have been thirty or forty musicians in that underpass, bouncing the tunes around the concrete walls. Willy was in their midst, now stomping from foot to foot, accentuating the rhythm, notes tumbling from his melodeon like sunlit water on an upland rill. It was mesmerising. Willy had the band in his thrall, and no one looked as if they were likely to move for the rest of the day. All those watching, as well as those playing, were completely absorbed by this impromptu jamming, until the sighting of the Bristol Horse . . .

Many morris sides are accompanied by an animal character when they are out dancing. Theories abound as to the origins and significance of this practice, and there is as much confusion about it as there is about the dancing itself. There are those who will talk about witches and their familiars and those who lyricise about shapeshifting, animal spirits and the mysteries of the underworld. Then we have the *mari llwyd*, a Welsh version of the morris animal, complete with a real horse's skull, favoured by Dave Jones as a possible accessory for Silurian – until he realised that Silurian had no need of such accessories. For my own part, research by others has me convinced that certain central figures, such as the Fool, the man/woman Betsy and perhaps some sort of horse figure, be it *mari llwyd* or a hobby-horse, have always been present at ceremonial rituals since pre-Christian times. Indeed, if we follow the line right back to our hunting days, it was essential to the success of the hunt to become as one with the spirit of the animal. However, pursuing this subject inevitably descends into academic discussion, so I will leave it there. All we need to know is that nowadays these animal characters are generally made up of a papier-mâché or fabric head (horse, deer, dragon, bird, etc) and a shroud-like cloak that conceals the person inside. All these loopy animals seem to do is to run around attempting to scare the children and snapping their hinged lower jaws at everything and anything, especially canine hooligans that mistake them for trees.

The Bristol Horse, however, was in a class of its own, streets ahead of its nearest rival, and the absolute embodiment of the idea of becoming the spirit of the animal. Never had I seen such a life-like 'animal', and I have seen none better in all the years that have passed since. A bit like John Willy's musical daemon, this horse was its creator. Man and animal were as one, an extraordinary shapeshift with a cartoon quality. This beast's huge head had a genuinely equine appearance, and was in fact covered in a skin of brown suede. Eerily, strips of it were hanging off here and there, which gave it the gruesome appearance of having fallen victim to some mad muleskinner who had left the job halfway. The eyes enhanced this semi-skinned appearance by being made of ping pong balls supported on springs which left them protruding beyond the edges of the eye sockets. They were mad, crazy, comical eyes, giving the head an expression common to cartoon characters like Sylvester the cat or Wile E Coyote, the hapless pursuer of the relentlessly uncatchable Road Runner. The absence of a firm location in the sockets enabled these manically expressive orbs to dip and bob about alarmingly with even the slightest movement of the head.

There was such animation in this creature that half the time it seemed to be talking to itself, or smiling sardonically whilst its ever-mobile eyes took in the world around it, a world that it clearly viewed with some disdain. The cloak concealing the man within took on the appearance of a real body just by virtue of being attached to this amazing head, and the feet protruding below the cloak belonged very obviously to this beast and not to some human hiding inside. It was a real living horse, alien and bizarre in appearance, yet reassuringly sentient.

In the underpass, the music had been reverberating around the concrete enclave and commanding the attention of those morrismen not playing. They were riveted, but out on the fringe of the crowd something stirred. One by one, the attention of the watchers was drawn elsewhere. This distraction ran through the gathering like an unplanned Mexican wave, reaching the musicians in a matter of a few seconds. They themselves stopped playing one by one and turned their gaze in the direction indicated by the dozens of faces around them. Even Willy stopped. Music dying away like that was not something he was used to. In the ensuing silence, everyone now homed in on the figure up on the embankment.

It was the Bristol Horse.

This creature was all alone, having obviously ascended the embankment while the rest of the gathering was concentrating on the music, and there it was . . . having a pee. Realisation that it was being observed dawned at about the same time that Willy, the last musician, stopped playing, and it slowly turned around to a sea of two hundred grinning faces. Its bulging ping pong eyes darted about as it surveyed the scene. It said nothing. It didn't need to. But it was a cartoon animal and it was impossible to look at it without seeing the speech bubble forming above his head.

"Bloody 'ell! An 'orse can't even have a quiet leak these days wivout the whole world lookin' on!"

And with that thought it turned its back on the crowd and ambled off, leaving everyone in fits of screaming laughter.

In terms of high spots, the weekend could have ended right there. All we had to look forward to was lots of dancing, beer and food, fairly routine by comparison with the pure magic of music and disgruntled horses. Yet all those morrismen were here to dance and Silurian were here to show everyone else how to do it properly, but not in an arrogant way of course. There was morris dancing, and then there was Silurian, and we had John Willy and Dion. Their playing sparkled so much it pulled at the feet of the dancers, lifting them and moving them with the music, like some kind of invisible puppet master. The music was munificent, weaving through dancers and audience alike, embracing all. As each dance ended, the audience erupted in applause. Their appreciation made it difficult to keep our egos under control.

We had distanced ourselves from the Cotswold men and presented them with a disguised persona, a black mask from behind which we could watch their reaction to our debunking of the Welsh Border degeneration myth. Our rough band with its vibrant urgency and our short, energetic dances with their phallic suggestiveness, helped us stand away from the morris norm. Our belief in the pagan origins of the morris was strong and we were beginning to look down on our Cotswold counterparts with a mixture of haughtiness and sympathy, the former because we knew our dancing grabbed the audience by the throat, and the latter from an ever-growing conviction that the poor Cotswold boys had lost sight of the origins and meaning of the Morris. With the amount of interest and research that has been channelled into these ideas since then, the present-day debate around the subject has grown increasingly strident, which is something I will look at in due course. Meanwhile, suffice it to say, that back in 1979, Silurian were feeling increasingly 'other'.

Our blacked-up faces not only made us feel at odds with the clean and well-presented look of the Cotswold dancers but also, as if in unspoken acknowledgement of the adage 'cleanliness is next to Godliness', it made us uncomfortable in the presence of organised religion. Pagan roots and Christianity don't mix, despite the fact that Christianity could never have gained any traction amongst the sceptical populace unless it incorporated 'new improved' versions of the old beliefs into its format. An obvious sleight-of-hand that you would think no one would fall for, but there is no accounting for the gullibility of ordinary mortals, and the stunt was pulled off with startling success.

For those of you not familiar with the format of ring meetings beyond what has been mentioned in chapter one, I should add that the formalised and institutionalised Morris Ring cannot get through a weekend ring meeting without a church service on Sunday. Silurian abstained from this particular ritual. On the Isle of Wight, as with the two previous ring meetings we had attended, we were happy enough to join in with the procession to the church, but we tagged on the back, where our presence made the rest of the procession look like a bridal party walking through a sunlit churchyard with a rabid black mongrel snapping at its heels. On this occasion, as the procession approached the lych-gate, we veered off to the left and kept going. As luck would have it, there was a pub! Not that unusual of course, as churches and pubs are often in close proximity.

Not only was there a pub, but its doors were already open. We invaded the bar, tankards waving in front of us like piglets looking for the teat. The guy behind the bar was pleased to see us. We could only presume that it was unusual to have sixteen obvious real ale connoisseurs arriving en masse at opening time on a Sunday. Not that we were the only ones in there – the place was already busy with those locals for whom a church full of morrismen was a good excuse to go somewhere else.

Once we were comfortably settled, we started playing. Or, more accurately, Willy started playing and the other band members joined in. He was in command of an extensive repertoire of unusual little ditties, including some music hall numbers, and we felt it was commendable to offer the punters an alternative to Dave Jones's more traditional numbers. Of course, we had a duty to our host side to dance in the main dance display, featuring all the sides which were present. This was the highlight of the weekend for the public, allegedly, and another part of the ring meeting format, and we were happy to join in. But we would have been equally happy to stay in the pub and keep the locals entertained with our selection of tunes and songs. Still, all good things and all that . . . and before we knew it, we were back on the ferry bound for the mainland and already looking forward to the next event.

Chapter 5
Metamorphosis

• • • • •

"Oh, there ain't no hairs on our cat's tail,
There ain't no hairs on Tiny,
But I know where
There's lots of hair
On the girl I left behind me..."

There was something missing.

Gliding back through Southampton Water, with the Isle of Wight weekend already a fading memory, a few of us were on deck, the tinkling of morris bells still humming and jingling in our ears like that after-concert buzz.

Little was said, preoccupation having taken charge of us. As for me, I was involved with winking at the male passengers, putting to mischievous use the hasty de-blacking I had undergone, which had left me with mascara rings around my eyes. Very Robert Smith, but without the lipstick – I was a big fan of The Cure.

A couple of the others were in the same state, and we were sitting in a line on one of the deck benches like the three wise monkeys, reinforcing the effect of the kohled eyes with pouting, puckering lips. This was unnerving some of the men we targeted, who were anxiously checking their watches for arrival time, but we cared not. Being inventive on ferry crossings passes the time. An arcane, slightly merciless delight in unsettling people was showing itself more often these days. More usually it was when we were hidden safely behind our black masks, but it seemed that even a bit of eye shadow would do the trick.

We felt better with the full blacking, really very good in fact, but there was still something missing. The problem was, without question, the Cotswold kit. We knew that to be true, but we hadn't yet come up with an alternative. Jonesy was working on it, however, having gathered a lot of information on the various costumes noted in the Border area over the previous decades. One of our guys, Gordon Lilley, had been wearing a bowler hat over the weekend and this had got us talking. The consensus was that bowlers would look good with the style of costume noted in Upton-upon-Severn around 1930.

Over the next couple of weeks on practice night, the ideas for the new kit filtered down into: bowler hat, white collarless shirt adorned with multi-coloured rags, a shoulder sash tied at the waist, black trousers and black shoes. The bowler also had a sash to match the one over the shoulder. Each man had his own individual sash colours, which was a great help for anyone with an identity crisis. Having got the new cossy sorted, a time and place needed to be fixed to try it out in public. Where better than the Bromyard Folk Festival, where the side had first performed exactly ten years previously?

The festival site was situated on a few fields just below the town, with enough room for camping, toilets and event marquees. But what made it special was the way it spilled over into the town itself, so all the pubs could boast impromptu music sessions and the town's streets were full of people in festive mood. Right in the centre of the town was the Hope Pole Hotel, overlooking a huge square that was the ideal venue for dance displays. Silurian was one of the sides scheduled to dance there during the course of the Saturday.

Back in those heady days of the twentieth century, Bromyard was full of brilliant pubs, and one of our favourites was The Bay Horse on the High Street. Contained within a very atmospheric half-timbered building, the pub benefited from a jolly landlord and a jolly fine selection of ales. It was here that we chose to congregate and implement a quick change in the back yard, but not before we had sampled the beers to make sure they were up to scratch. There was no one called Clark Kent in the side and there was no telephone box in the yard, but we were planning a Superman transformation. The plan was to do it unnoticed and then emerge surreptitiously from the pub, all kitted out in our new colours: then to process down the High Street to the Hope Pole with much noise and gusto, in the hope that we would make an indelible impression in the minds of all those watching.

We changed in the outside toilet, taking it in turns to black up, applying the make-up and checking our appearance with the aid of a small hand mirror. There was a buzz of expectancy in the air. As each blacked-up, bowler-hatted man emerged to join the others in the yard, another cheer went up. An atmosphere of boldness and self-assurance was building, but something more important too – the sense of a common bond.

As we milled about in the yard, our new bells were making a satisfyingly different sound from the bells usually worn by morris dancers. In line with most sides, our original Cotswold bells were all of one small size and covered a pad about six inches square which was strapped below the knee. But now we had just five bells, two small and three large, attached to a band of the same material as the sash and tied under the knee. These bells had a harmonic resonance that produced a unique sound. From that day on, although it was difficult to recognise a Silurian man by his face, it became possible, even in darkness, to label him just by the sound of his bells.

Last to emerge into the yard was John Willy. We had expected him to come out looking just like the rest of us – but no. He appeared in his old Royal Engineers red tunic, no doubt picked up in the 1960s down the King's Road in Chelsea, at I Was Lord Kitchener's Valet, an emporium I revered but could not afford to shop in. His head was adorned with a homemade busby like an overgrown tea cosy, allegedly knitted for him by his wife, Sandie. A long pheasant feather sprouted from each side of this woolly black stack. As he walked, we heard the clanging of a bell. It was hanging from the rear of his belt, just visible below the red jacket. According to what I now understand about the ancient precursors to the Morris, the Fool was the wearer of the bells, as well as the principal wearer of the black face. And here we had our very own bell-wearing 'figurehead'. If we but knew it at the time, this was our Fool and we were his dancers. However, the idea of creating a Fool for the side had not been openly discussed. I believe that none amongst us truly understood the significance of the Fool's presence. There is evidence to show that historically the Fool was central and the dancers subservient. Whether by accident or design, Willy's costume gave him the Fool's authority, and he was indeed 'the man in charge' from that moment on.

As a speculative aside, I wonder whether a 25-year-old Matt Groening was in town that day and saw Willy's busby as the inspiration for Marge Simpson's hairstyle. He said Marge's hair was based on the beehive hairdo his own mother had in the 1960s, but you never know . . . he may just have been holidaying in Herefordshire that September in 1979.

Jonesy had a touch of the pursed lip at the sight of Willy's caricature of a guardsman, but he wasn't going to argue, particularly as Willy now suddenly looked about two feet taller, plus it was too late to squabble. Our scheduled appearance outside the Hope Pole was imminent. It was time to get out there. We headed for the street outside the Bay Horse and formed up in two lines. The band kicked in and we broke into the Much Wenlock dance that we had been using as our processional number for a couple of years. With our band at the head, we headed off for the town square. Dion's snare drum rang out like something from the Black Watch pipe band, while the extra percussion of tambourines, a triangle and a set of bones acted as effective fillers between Dion's drum and the melodeon and accordion. This was satisfyingly rough music, but note perfect for all that. We could see that we were stopping pedestrians in their tracks as far as we were able to see down the street, and we were dancing as if this was going to be our last day on Earth.

As we turned the corner into the square, the crowd melted before us like the parting of the Red Sea, letting us in and then closing up again behind us. The air felt electrified. Surrounded by people eager to get a closer look, we were in a space too small to perform effectively, so we finished the dance with a couple of full-tilt racing crossovers, roaring at the crowd, looking as if we were going to run right through them. With squeals and gasps, they melted before us again like snow against a blow torch. Now we had our space, and the crowd held back in wary anticipation. We brought the dance to a close and the crowd simply erupted, with deafening cheers, whistles and shouts for more. I know it's a cliché, but the hairs really did prickle on the back of my neck. It was the most emotional reaction to morris dancing we had ever seen. The whole side was now on a massive high – we could sense the adrenalin rushing through us.

Not giving the audience a chance to settle down, we started our set with the Upton Stick Dance, complete with its little introductory ditty:

"*Oh, there ain't no hairs on our cat's tail,*
There ain't no hairs on Tiny,
But I know where
There's lots of hair
On the girl I left behind me."

This was one of the few Border dances that had been hijacked by certain Cotswold sides and added to their repertoire, ever since the deservedly popular Albion Morrismen had featured it some years previously. Dave Jones had been particularly incensed by their version, especially as it was danced to a tune from Newfoundland

– *Newfoundland*, look you! He had spent the ten years since then showing everybody how it should be done. A dangerous attitude perhaps, and one which could easily have dropped us all into the Cotswold trap, where more emphasis is placed on the differences between traditions than on the spirit of the dance. I don't know what he was worried about though – the Cotswold boys danced it too coyly and without the little song, so we were already well ahead of them.

As we stood in our two lines of three, waiting for the signal from the band, anticipation was running high through the audience, and we were not going to let them down. We sang the little song and then burst into action. The first move of the dance is a circular figure known as 'rounds', the simplest of dance figures but full of portentous energy. In executing it, we took up all the available space, skimming the crowd. From that move, we would seemingly reappear in the middle of the arena in two lines again for some controlled but ferocious stick clashing, executed with what might be called 'naked aggression'. On the moves between the choruses, the whole set seemed to explode, filling the space again and touching the crowd. The dance finished on another rounds, climaxing with a jump into the middle of the circle and a shout of, "Upton!", "Up 'em!" or anything else we could get away with.

With that shout, the crowd erupted again, cheering, clapping, yelling for more. We gave them the White Ladies Aston stick dance, which was implemented with such energy that the dancers were blurred by a kind of snowstorm flurry of wood chips as the sticks began to split, feather and disintegrate. This was morris with attitude and woodsmoke and the crowd couldn't get enough. They'd never seen anything like it. We had the audience in our spell, a spell we hadn't knowingly expected to weave. Unplanned and unrehearsed, it was more like spontaneous combustion.

Finishing our set with our farewell dance, Fanny Frail, with its suggestive posing and fast finish, we cut a new path through the crowd and danced right down to the next pub. From the roared chorus of approval in our wake, we knew we had left them wanting more.

"Follow *that*!" said one of our lads, on a euphoric high.

The audience really did want more. And a new sense of close-bonded identity was upon us. We had already grown accustomed to being odd, but the new kit really made us stand out as being very different, and gave us an unexpected status. No longer just another morris side, or even a morris side with black faces. A switch had been tripped with this display, making us instantly the leading exponents of Welsh Border Morris.

Changing the kit also changed our attitude, and we began to think about what it must have been like to dance a fertility dance all those millennia ago. Highly speculative of course, because we had no real way of knowing, but we just pictured ourselves as twentieth-century torchbearers for something very ancient. After this performance, it was certainly easy to imagine that dancers in pre-Christian communities might have put themselves on a higher plane, and out of reach of ordinary mortals, by clothing themselves in a particular way, introducing a de-humanising disguise and creating some wild dance routines. We understood in that moment how an enigmatic appearance might create mystery, how mystery touches people and moves energy and how energy might conjure magic.

For us, the magic had come from the change in our appearance. The black face made us different anyway and made us feel special, but the new get-up clinched it. It was difficult to recognise us individually with our matt black bearded faces, now crowned with black bowler hats. Most people really had no idea what we were all about. It seemed we captivated them and frightened them in equal measure, which helped to create the mystique. We became strongly unified, an effect no one could have predicted. We were already an established morris side, but on that day we transformed into an entity, shapeshifted into a form unknown, united by an invisible, telepathic bond.

Anyone who has read *The Old Straight Track*, an exploration of ley lines by Alfred Watkins (another celebrated Herefordshire man), might remember his description of what was effectively a transcendental moment of perception as his mind entered the world of prehistoric Britain. On reflection, I would describe our experience that day in similar terms. It was if we had stepped out of this world into another, slipping through the veil, as it were. None of us could describe what had happened, but we all knew that something truly primal had taken place.

Looking at the available research today, it seems clear that we may well have had much in common with those ancient Celtic dancers. There is strong evidence to suggest that morris dancing developed from sword dancing (the swords having long since been replaced by staves, except in certain areas of England) in which the Fool was a central character, yet at the same time a perennial wanderer on the edge, an insider on the outside. Though he circled the perimeter of the dance, the dancers were at his bidding. By some kind of spooky coincidence, Willy's kit had conferred upon him the role of the Fool, but without taking him out of the band. His sense of command from this position made him masterful, and the dancers were at his bidding. Jonesy was still in the band, but somehow he just faded into the background in the face of Willy's startling appearance and magical music. Without knowing it, we had quite possibly recreated an innovative version of what we had been excited about when Jonesy used to rattle on about men's pagan ritual fertility dances.

All this also gave our dancing a true purpose. It was a display for the benefit of the onlookers. That might sound like a glib truism, but it is not. Sadly, at that time too many morris displays seemed to be weak, ineffectual or introspective. Displays of dancing, or anything else come to that, are spectacles, shows for a gathering of spectators. People come to see the show, to admire the skill and artistry with which it is being performed. We felt that performers have a responsibility to at least put on a good show, but we also wanted to go further. We didn't want spectators. We wanted participants. It was important for us to involve the audience, to create a positive feedback loop – our performance animates the audience which motivates us to produce a better performance. Reciprocation, symbiosis, call it what you will, but its effect was electric. And we felt it at the Hop Pole that day.

That fanciful image we had of pagan dancers included this synergistic relationship. We couldn't imagine how any kind of ritual dance could work without the involvement of all present. And we understood instinctually that the whole idea would fail without a disguise, essential in setting the dancers apart from ordinary mortals. And painting the face matt black was enough.

Back then, in the twentieth century, the revival of Border Morris prompted much discussion about black-faced morris dancers, and the debate has continued to the present day, though it is now being closely scrutinised by the Thought Police, whose clouded vision sees racism in this innocent and simple mask. They say categorically that the black face is mimicking the old minstrel shows, but that is pure unfounded nonsense. Black-faced morris dancers, engaged in ceremonial agrarian rites of vital importance to their communities, were much in evidence centuries before those offensive minstrel shows, designed only to titillate an audience of American slave-owners. As far as the Silurian guys were concerned, blacking the face was just an easy and necessary disguise. Musing on pagan rituals, our feeling was that you would certainly need a disguise if you were in the middle of a dance designed to defy malevolent spirits. The last thing you want is to be zapped by some malign fiend who is thinking, "I *know you.* You're that guy from the village who drove me out last year. Well, here's where you get yours!"

The dance, designed to renew and sanctify the boundary around a community, had a twofold purpose. As well as warding off evil spirits away from the boundary, the dancers were protecting those within. A sense of ceremony would be implicit, and it's just not going to happen if the dancers simply stroll up in their everyday clothes. They would have to look the part. They would need a new persona. Dealing with energies and maybe other force fields is not to be taken lightly. A real sense of ceremony is essential for dancers and other participants alike. The whole community would be involved and the Fool and his dancers would need to be distinguishable from everyone else.

Above all, the dancers needed to set themselves apart whilst remaining part of their community. These ceremonies took place at one or more of the eight key points of the earth cycle, when all is on the threshold between worlds. The dancers would need to be there but not there, human but not human. There is no more effective way that I can think of to achieve this than by blacking the face. Originally, charred wood from the ceremonial fires would have done the job brilliantly, especially with the added significance of carbon (what we might call today 'bio-char') being a potent fertility conduit.

Speaking now as an ex-Silurian, I would say without hesitation that blackening the face is considerably more successful as a disguise than donning a mask. Beneath that blackness, the face loses its features but remains eerily real and animate, merely devoid of distinguishing features. A mask, by contrast, is static. It is deprived of expression as well as features, too puppet-like to be taken seriously, especially in a modern world awash with imagery and special effects. A black face, however (or a white face on a voodoo priest) is unsettling and potentially scary because you can still see the eyes. That gives the face a human quality in a de-humanised frame. And it falls in line perfectly with the idea of 'here but not here', in between worlds, in limbo, in the twilight zone. – exactly right for all those earth cycle celebrations.

Even now, in the twenty-first century, there still exist indigenous tribal cultures that perform ritual dances in which the dancers clothe themselves in outlandish costumes, with faces painted or masked, all designed to de-humanise themselves and turn them into beings who can make the crossover and walk in the spirit world. In such a dance it is essential to hide human frailty from the gaze of humans and spirits alike. All identity with ordinary mortals must be lost. If morris dancing really does have roots that go back at least two thousand years (and I believe it does), it is very probable that the dancers would have been disguised to camouflage their earth-bound human selves.

Though it is certain that both costume and disguise have changed through the ages, it is thought-provoking that the basic black face has never really gone away. Discussions and arguments as to when it first appeared are of little use beyond academic interest, at least to the men of Silurian. What is of more interest perhaps is that we actually discussed other options over a few pints one night.

"Why black?" someone asked, "Why not yellow – or blue?"

"Oh, *come on* – don't be silly!"

"We could just put paper bags over our heads . . ."

"How about ski masks – or tights over our faces?"

And so the banter went. But we all knew that blacking-up was what we were going to do, because we knew it had been done for centuries. Plus it was obvious to all of us that blacking the face was simple and incomparably effective, conferring upon us anonymity and a unity that would become a powerful force from that day on.

Chapter 6
Crisis Management

• • • • •

"Beer and strong cider
Are old England's control,
So give me the punch ladle,
I'll fathom the bowl..."

Four months after introducing the new kit at Bromyard, we were given a chance to dance in front of a different kind of audience. We were invited to perform at the Assembly Rooms in Derby for an event called Dancing England, designed to raise public awareness of the varied spectrum of traditional dances across England. Our invitation came as a result of being seen as leading exponents of Welsh Border Morris. It was here at this venue that everything that had come to represent Silurian combined to help us get through a day that could well have ended up as an unmitigated disaster.

A coach and driver had been organised for the trip, so we were able to relax on the coach, sing a few songs and play a few tunes. Although this was to be an evening event, the coach was scheduled to leave in the morning, allowing us to get there early and in plenty of time for a practice, at Jonesy's insistence.

On arrival, the first thing we spotted was a line of nine-gallon beer barrels set up behind a make-shift bar on one side of the dance floor.

"Firkin hell!" came a cry from one of our number.

"More like firkin heaven," another voice retorted.

It was about midday and we were in need of a drink, so we converged on the bar area and fished around in our pockets for some money.

Choice was always difficult for us, and this line of firkins presented a range of ales that banished the idea of choice to the far reaches of academic concepts. Dispensing with the notion altogether, we opted to try them all. By two o'clock, this tippling was having a predictable effect, raising the decibel level of the conversation whilst lowering the intellectual. We were relaxed and happy but not in a position to execute considered observational judgements.

Thus the benign atmosphere in which we basked was threatened when one of our number suggested that normal licencing hours would no doubt apply at the Assembly Rooms, and therefore the bar would probably be closing imminently. A sudden rush to the barrels ensued, with everyone clamouring for attention and ordering double rations to see them through the afternoon. Minutes later, there we all were, with a pint in each hand, much relieved at having beaten the deadline, when a passing stranger stopped, eyed us and our hoard warily and scratched his cheek.

"What's up with you lot, then?" he asked.

"Getting' the drinks in before they close, mate," he was told, in a tone which suggested that it should have been obvious.

"*Close*!?" he replied . . . "Before they *close*!? They're not closing 'til midnight – they're open *all day* . . . !"

We looked at each other. We surveyed the stockpile of pints we were jealously guarding. We looked at each other again. Someone looked at his watch.

"Oh shit!" somebody else chipped in, "I've already had five . . . or six . . ."

Some interesting thoughts were hopping from mind to mind like happy little tree frogs . . . two-thirty now . . . five or six pints . . . not dancing 'til about eight-thirty . . . six hours to go . . .

"We're going to have to take it steady, boys," came the even-toned Welsh lilt of Godfather Jones, reminiscent of Colour-Sergeant Bourne in the film, *Zulu*. He may as well have said, "Just stare into its eyes and the lion won't bite you." The brow of his balding head was beginning to shine, and his whole face was furrowed with worry lines, as he scratched at his beard contemplatively. His golden boys; his dream of putting Border Morris on the map at this auspicious venue; his aching desire to show the Shropshire Bedlams how it should be done – all about to vanish like a wraith at dawn.

That afternoon's practice did nothing to raise his spirits. In terms of effective crisis management, he would have done better to suggest a few hours' kip, but his mantra was, "Practice, practice, practice." Watching us crashing about and just not taking it seriously must have troubled him deeply, but still he was reluctant to resort to Plan B. By the evening, he had relaxed into a WTF mood, greeting the prospect of dancing with a smile like a beatific vicar. He seemed totally unperturbed during our blacking-up ceremony in the toilets, when we fell about laughing and banging into each other as we swayed around. Either he was absolutely inebriated, or he trusted us, or he had already opted for Plan C: winging it. As for his merry men, we had ditched the idea of staying sober some hours previously. Once the tipping point is reached, the sudden drop into a new paradigm is inevitable, and all that can be done is to deal with the new circumstances. That's where the trust came in. We trusted ourselves and one another to perform on demand. Having got the kit on, we were strutting about defiantly buying more beer, and mentally daring anyone to challenge our sobriety.

Once we were on stage, we got a bit more serious. Willy and the band galvanised us and we responded accordingly. Judging by the applause at the end of the first dance, we must have got through it without any glaring errors, much to everybody's relief and amazement. Okay, it could have been tidier, but being a bit rough round the edges was one of our defining qualities, and nobody was criticising. Next, we lined up for the Dilwyn stick dance . . . or it may have been White Ladies Aston. I was dancing opposite Mick Quinn, our stalwart self-proclaimed Celt, an assessment based on his Irish name, his Irish-Welsh parentage and his Brummy childhood.

"What're we doing, Mick – White Ladies?" I asked in an anxious stage whisper.

"Dunno. I thought someone said Dilwyn?"

"Oh, *not* White Ladies then. Are you sure it's Dilwyn? Maybe it's Pershore," I suggested brightly, but in mild jest. I was quietly confident of Mick's judgement. You can always trust a teacher, that's what I say

As it turned out, neither of us had a clue. But we started dancing as soon as the music kicked in. Probably the whole side was on autopilot, moving with the rhythm of the band. The beat was fine. It was just the tune we couldn't hear. Mick and I were furthest from the band, and musical volume was being lost in the spacious arena.

"Are you *sure* this is Dilwyn?" I pleaded.

"No," said Mick, "I'm not sure. Just keep dancing!" That's teachers for you – so self-assured and assertive.

With an increasing sense of unease, we were aware that the others weren't doing what we were doing, but still confident that we were quite possibly right. Or wrong, depending on how you looked at it. Okay, in the interests of impartiality, let's say Mick and I weren't doing what *they* were doing. Truth is, we were making it up, but we stayed in time and rhythm and brazened it out, looking defiantly as if it was all meant to be like that.

Before we could take these misgivings any further, a crossover move was upon us, during which a strange and totally unexpected red and black bundle rolled quickly down the middle of the set, throwing us completely. On the return crossover, it rolled the other way. This turned out to be a cartwheeling John Willy. *What the hell was he doing*!? He was supposed to be in the band! Now, you might think this all sounds like utter chaos, but everybody just kept calm, kept the tempo and did what they thought was right. We ended up with a hybrid dance that had never been seen or done before, plus a cartwheeling musician. Yet, to those watching, the whole thing had been executed with precision, vigour and panache – or at least that's what the applause told us. The audience didn't spot the join in the two dances and they didn't know that Willy's cartwheel was not in our normal repertoire. We were safe. We had plummeted over Niagara Falls in a barrel and survived.

Concerned that we might have assessed our own performance through the over-confidence of inebriation, we were reassured by the compliments of many who came forward to congratulate us once we'd left the stage. We thought we were winging it; they thought they had seen a terrific performance. My own observation is that our experience and discipline from the Cotswold days, our desire to do well and our indefinable sense of unity kept us going through what could easily have been a complete catastrophe. Even with the high jinks and liberal quantities of liquid refreshment we could still dance when we had to, and dance well. It was as though this was what we were born to do.

As for our acrobatic musician, all was revealed when we were back in our seats and questioning Willy's sanity. It transpired that Jonesy, nose out of joint with Willy's eccentric garb on 'new kit day' in Bromyard, had said something along the lines of, "If you are going to dress like a fool, you'd better behave like one." So, just before going on stage, Jonesy had issued a reminder and urged him that 'this would be a good time to be the Fool'. The cartwheeling episode was a spontaneous reaction to Jonesy's none too subtle persuasion. Thankfully, it turned out to be a very short-lived idea that in fact died a death shortly after its debut. Willy was far too valuable a musician for us to allow him to risk injuring his playing hands by spending some time upside down. We unanimously agreed that our future as a Border side was not going to include a Fool, not of that ilk anyway. What we hadn't spotted at the time of course was that Willy was the Fool in the original sense of the word, and always would be. It was just a marvellously happy accident of fate that he was also the Music.

Leaving for home, my clearest memory was the image in my head of the poster for this event. Drawn as a detailed pencil sketch, it depicted a black-faced morris dancer in a full rag jacket and hat, with bell pads on his shins. On his head, bursting out of the ragged hat, was a huge pair of curly ram's horns, and in his hand he brandished a long stave. Hidden amongst the rags at the front of his coat was a human skull. The picture showed him in mid leap, as if he was jumping over a fire. Whilst certain that Silurian was hitting the spot as far as performance went, I was a little unhappy with our costume, and this poster had me thinking we could have done better. However, Jonesy had favoured the idea of basing our visual appearance on an old photo from the 1930s. Personally, I thought the photo too contemporary. I would have preferred something a bit more primal, more like the figure in the poster, but Jonesy did not want us to wear rag jackets. He had earmarked this particular idea for something else.

"Well, see, the old Cradley Mummers used to wear rag jackets, and I want to be resurrecting the old mummers plays, look you – so we'll be having rag jackets when we do the plays," he told us. "And anyway, them Bedlam boys are wearin' 'em now, and we don't want to be like them, isn't it."

I needn't have worried. A time would come when positive comments would be made about the individuality of our kit, but more on that in due course.

Meanwhile, Dancing England had turned out to be a success and we hadn't let Jonesy down – his dream was intact. Mind you, he was as drunk as a skunk himself, so we wonder how much of the proceedings he had been taking in. But, with the invitation to Derby, he had proved his point about Border Morris. Not only was Silurian now seen as an authority on the subject, but we were still a Ring side, a notion which Jonesy loved. He was on a high, and the obvious next step for him was to host his own Ring meeting in Ledbury – a bit of an upwardly mobile move for a career folky. 1979 had turned into a year of new kit and tumultuous acclaim at two very important venues and, with a touch of *carpe diem*, Jonesy decided it was time to realise the next part of his ambition as he pencilled in July 1980 for the Ledbury Ring meeting.

Chapter 7
Wessex in the Raw

• • • • •

"Oh, the holly and the ivy,
When they are both full grown,
Of all the trees that are in the wood,
The holly tree bears the crown..."

Regarding Silurian and ring meetings, the curious thing is that most of us actually disliked going to them, but we somehow managed to get to one every year. We had an aversion to the clubby aspect of it all and the formality of the Saturday night feast, which was always a sit-down affair with waitress service and toasts and speeches. To us, it was a clear demonstration that morris dancing had been reduced to just another middle-class pastime. On the plus side though, a ring meeting did give Silurian an excellent opportunity to demonstrate Border dances to a captive audience of a couple of hundred morrismen plus larger crowds than usual. We could also see how we compared to all those other sides, and give ourselves marks out of ten for performance, entertainment value and the consumption of real ale.

Hosting our own ring meeting was of course a venture into unexplored territory. But we were unperturbed. Jonesy was driving the whole thing, with our brilliantly capable bagman, Keith Francis, acting as navigator and co-pilot. Also on the credit side, Ledbury is a compact little town with numerous pubs, many of which were superior watering holes. It was also our own patch, so Jonesy was selling it to us on the fact that no one would have far to travel.

"Except all of us that come from Worcester," Mick pointed out.

"Well, see, if you're that bothered about it," replied Jonesy, tetchy about the fact that his Ledbury side was not pure Herefordshire, "there's always the Worcester boys."

"No thanks . . ."

Nobody in Silurian wanted to join any Cotswold side, let alone a local one, so that was the end of that conversation.

Succumbing to mild coercion, we gradually warmed to the idea of hosting our own ring meeting and ultimately became convinced. Conviction precipitates a positive mental attitude, a phrase we'd borrowed from the management manuals of the time. Although geared up for the whole experience, right from the start it felt a bit odd. On the Friday night, instead of rolling up late, after hours of driving, Silurian would be there first, meeting and greeting people as they arrived. Come the end of the evening, after a bit of food, a bit of drink and a bit of spontaneous morris, we retired to our sleeping quarters. Located as they were in several places around the town (the Youth Centre, in my case), Silurian had to split up. Morris weekends invariably meant we stayed together. Parting company generally meant the end of proceedings. So on that Friday, it felt as if we should be going home to our own beds, not to locations around Ledbury.

Next morning, things felt much better. We were in kit. But, after breakfast in the Community Hall, we were split up again, segregated into pairs to act as guides on the various coach tours organised to the wilder parts of Herefordshire and Worcestershire. That was unsettling. No, not venturing into Worcestershire, although that is certainly unnerving – being separated whilst in kit. When we were in kit, we were an autonomous entity called Silurian, but broken up in that way we were nothing more than pairs of strangely dressed morris dancers with no band. It was not a comfortable feeling.

I was on the Worcester tour, and my partner in guidance was one Neil Malvern, whose zany contribution to Silurian was greatly missed a couple of months later, when he was lured to Bristol in search of more lucrative employment. Being with him on the coach gave me a chance to ask him about his surname.

"So why is your name Malvern then, Neil?" I asked, getting straight to the point.

"It's cos I come from Malvern," he responded, equally directly.

"Yes, I know. And I know that place names are used as surnames, but I've never met anyone whose name is actually where they are from."

"Well, my granddad was from Malvern too," Neil continued, adding as an afterthought, "and my dad."

"Okay, that all makes sense."

I felt this was going nowhere, so I went quiet, pondering my next question. Neil saved me having to ask it.

"Thing is," he said, "my granddad was found on the steps of Malvern workhouse, wrapped up and left in a basket. So they took him in and gave him the name."

"Oh, okay."

There was not a lot more I could say. Everyone has a story, and Neil's was unique in the ranks of Silurian.

So there we were, sitting at the front of the coach with not a lot to do. Two Silurian men on their own cannot do a Border dance, so we felt a bit superfluous. Our duties for the day included making sure the coach arrived at each scheduled spot on time and the dancers had access to a supply of ale at each stop – hardly a difficult task as most of the venues were pubs. Neil and I sampled the ales as we went along but, being unable to dance off the effects, results were predictable. As the day wore on, my recollection of events became increasingly patchy, until it finally blurred into oblivion in the jumbled memories of all the other morris tours I had ever been on. Of the coach occupants, I can remember only the Wessex men, genuine high-calibre 'scene stealers'. They simply dominated the day's proceedings and, with a confidence brought on by success, their performance – dancing or otherwise – became ever more determined. Neil and I saw them as serious rivals for Silurian in terms of entertainment.

As the coach followed its scheduled itinerary, which took us through Worcester and Malvern, Wessex were like wild dogs on heat confined in a huge mobile kennel. Inebriated, excitable and girl-crazy, they were leaping around the coach yelping and barking at the local female population. Their look-out man was giving them advance warning of any sightings from his vantage point near the front of the bus.

"Left! LEFT!! Coming up now on your left!"

"On yer right! Over there – by the chemist's shop . . .!"

"In that car – on the left! No, *left*! WOW! – legs up to her *armpits*!"

It was like being on a rickety old bathtub ferry during a storm-tossed crossing to Cherbourg. The coach was bucking, diving and rocking from side to side as the Wessex mob charged around in response to these instructions and observations. The weather was warm and Wessex were warmer, so they had opened up the little ventilation windows in order to communicate verbally their affectionate feelings for the fair damsels of Worcestershire.

"'Ullo, gorgeous! *GERREMOFF*!!"

Someone in the middle of this mayhem, who had remained seated and wasn't really getting a look-in, made his own point of view known to anyone who was listening, "I don't care what she looks like, as long as she's got *big tits*!"

This was instantly taken up as a battle cry by the whole of the Wessex crew, and they were soon shouting it up and down the bus and through the ventilation windows. After the last dance spot of the day, on the drive back to Ledbury, it seemed to Neil and me that we might not make it that far before some terminal calamity overtook the coach and its madcap passengers.

Wessex, as you can imagine, retained this mood of boisterous exuberance from the moment we arrived back at base camp, where they fell off the bus in a heap. Somehow they managed to get through the Feast without serious mishap, after which they decided it was time to explore the town's hostelries. Once again they avoided potential catastrophe and were still intact at closing time. However, there was more to come.

With the pubs closed, those of us who were being accommodated in the Youth Centre, including the Wessex 12-man party machine, made our way thither . . . good word, that. I must try it out again sometime. The Youth Centre was a two-storey building typical of the genre, with an angular, utilitarian look, lots of space inside and floor-to-ceiling picture windows to the first floor, where we would be sleeping.

On that Saturday night, the place was not inhabited by the usual motley collection of marginalised bored teenagers, taking out their grudge against society on the brashly-coloured pool balls, but by a sprawling mess of dishevelled morrismen, lurching, swaying or just lying about in various stages of inebriation and physical disorder. Most of the Wessex men were supposedly there, but the place seemed oddly quiet after the antics of the day. Neil and I were thinking that we must have mislaid them somewhere, when a sudden tinkling of morris bells heralded some activity in the far corner of the room.

"Christ! Who's this?" came a disgruntled voice from under a small table by the door to the toilets. "Haven't we had about enough dancin' today?"

Inevitably, it was Wessex. Evidently they had decided to put on an impromptu dance display for the benefit of those camping in the Youth Centre. With bells tinkling to the accompaniment of a melodeon, they danced into the room – six dancers and a musician. What you might call a perfectly normal morris situation.

Except for the fact that they were all stark naked.

Well, okay, not quite. They did have their bells on their shins and they were waving their hankies. But otherwise – not a stitch. Processing into the room to perform the dance, they carried it out with unbelievable precision and seriousness to hysterical acclaim from their enthusiastically receptive audience, most of whom were now more awake than they had been all day.

Being quickly overtaken by this unprecedented turn of events, it initially escaped our notice that this naked frolic was taking place in front of the afore-mentioned floor-to-ceiling picture window. But then we saw the reflection in the panes. As the dance came to an end, the whole scene was brought into sharp focus, for our shouts and whistles of appreciation seemed to trigger a huge echo from outside. As realisation kicked in, we saw that a rapturous crowd of late night fish-and-chip addicts had gathered outside to watch the performance, which of course showed up brilliantly under the fluorescence of the room. The dancers were clearly visible from their toes to their tousled heads. Despite the clapping, cheering, general encouragement and shouts for more, from outside as well as inside, this was to be a one-off. Probably just as well. Although the whole room was now buzzing, nobody could follow a performance like that. Wessex had brought the day's proceedings to a magnificent and astounding close. Impossible to follow, it left everyone too stunned to do anything but drift off to sleep.

The mood the next morning, for Silurian at least, was altogether different. Being Sunday, activities were to be centred on the town, so we were united once more, yet we were under a grey cloud of sadness. Dave Jones' wife, Sandra, had died just a few days before the weekend, after a long battle with cancer, and this had left Dave dispirited and bereft in a glorious moment of personal achievement. All Silurian could do was to stick by him and ensure we made this ring meeting one to remember. It was absolutely 'one for Jonesy'.

Falling in line with the norm, there was a church service that morning but, on this occasion, there was no question of Silurian dipping out and swaggering off to the local alehouse. We were going to stick by Dave in what had effectively become a memorial service for Sandra. Together this couple had ignited the fires of enthusiasm for the folk revival in Herefordshire, set up folk clubs and created the festival at Bromyard. In addition, Dave's persistence in researching the roots of Border Morris had been the inspiration behind Silurian, and there we were, his dream team at his own ring meeting, a huge reward for all his efforts. It seemed poignantly unjust that Sandra should not be there to share his triumph.

During the service we, as the host side, were to dance in the church, and we sat there in our pews, kit on and faces blacked, contemplating this new situation and waiting for the moment. It came after we had led the whole gathering in singing the slow-time Herefordshire version of *The Holly and the Ivy*, one of Dave and Sandra's favourite tunes, which they had performed regularly together over the years and which had become a standard number on Boxing Day tours. A church full of morrismen adding their voices to those of the usual congregation raised the emotional level rapidly, and we were all on the edge by the time we had to dance.

A Border dance in a church is a contradiction in terms, but this one was for Dave Jones. It was decided that we would do the Bromsberrow Heath stick dance – partly because it came from a village not five miles from Ledbury and partly because it was danced in a line of six, simple to accomplish in the aisle. It involved dancers weaving the line in a figure-of-eight 'hey' and then 'stick-clashing' with long staves on the chorus. Performed outdoors in our normal swashbuckling fashion, with the music getting faster on each chorus, the dance was wild and unrestricted. If we didn't break at least one stick, we weren't doing it right.

In the church that Sunday, the dance became a study in precision and calculated movement, as befitting the sombre and emotionally charged mood. This was dancing for a wake. As the tune, *Cock o' the North*, started up in slow time, I had to bite my lip. Echoing around the church, the tune had a haunting quality to it. I passed Mike Massey on the first hey. He was crying silently, setting me off too. Passing Mike Rust and Dave Smith, and seeing the glistening rivulets on their black cheeks, made it difficult to hold myself together. Dancing Bromsberrow Heath like that, slowly and meticulously, was unreal, but it was our homage to Jonesy. The rest of the world could have their Border performance later . . .

After the church service, all the morrismen, still in a subdued mood, made their way to the market house, where the lunchtime massed display for the public was scheduled to take place. The pubs being open by this time, it wasn't long before the dark clouds of emotion rolled away and our sunny mood came shining through. In the true spirit of the wake, we were focused on following that unique remembrance service with a display that Sandra would smile down on. We were going to dance, not just for Sandra, not just for Jonesy, but for the audience out there – his audience – and we were going to show them some real morris.

Crowds were gathering outside the market house and groups of morrismen, pints in hand, were warming up in anticipation of dancing . . . but a problem was encountered. An Austin Allegro was parked in the area reserved for the display. Obviously, it had to be moved, but the driver was nowhere to be seen, and the car was locked. So Silurian did what any sensible bunch of idiots would do – we picked it up and carried it to the side of the road. The crowd roared their admiration.

"Let the dancing commence!" said Jonesy with a flourish, and a nod of approval to his problem-solving team.

We beamed. We were only clearing the arena. It's not as if we were showing off or playing to the crowd or anything . . .

By the time it was our turn to dance, our emotional pendulum had swung away from the heart-breaking sadness of the morning and we were impatient to get out there. Since our last outing, our band had gained one more member, another conscript from Hodge's Dump, with a well-developed Jekyll and Hyde personality, albeit relatively benign. He played a tuba, had independently mobile eyes, a grin like a chimpanzee and answered to the name of Burco. His real name, Colin Robinson, did him no justice at all and made him sound like an accountant. Remarkably, he was studying to be one. According to those who knew him well, the job would suit him, as he was normally a quiet good-natured lad. Alcohol, unfortunately, had the same effect on him as that famous potion had on Dr Jekyll. Thus, after a couple of pints, he would turn into a raving madman, staring around with bloodshot eyes and hurling abuse at all and sundry. What an asset to Silurian. And his '*pom-pom, pom-pom-pom-pom*' made our band sound like no other.

On a high after finally getting a chance to dance at our own weekend, we set out to prove a point. As far as we were concerned, all of our guests had joined us to witness dancing at the epicentre of Morris. They were on our home patch, and we were going to show them how it was done. We wanted them to know that Jonesy was right about Border morris, and Cecil Sharp wrong. The dances were wild, uninhibited, but the patterns were all there. The moves were precise. The music was quick, but we were moving with it, in its spell. Bits of stick and chaff were flying, with the occasional whiff of wood smoke. No tears now, we were enjoying this. Fanny Frail ended in a perfect circle before snaking off through the crowd, and the noise and cheering behind us told us that we'd got it right. Men from the other sides were shouting and whistling their approval and admiration. As for Jonesy, his day was made when he was personally congratulated by the Officers of the Ring.

It had been ten months since we had ventured into the light in our new kit, and we were surfing on a wave of public acclaim. Dedicated to the cause of 'real morris', we were keen to demonstrate it to the inquisitive. At our own ring meeting, we were confident that we had delivered, not just a demonstration of our local dances, but a great weekend for all.

As the afternoon stretched towards early evening, there was little else for us to do except tidy up, checking for any drunken morrismen asleep in dark corners, and ensuring that everyone left Ledbury safely. Our ring meeting had gone well and we were satisfied that, despite the tragedy of Sandra's untimely demise, we had flown the Border flag for Jonesy. Though the shadow of her death had been there all weekend, we knew she would have wanted us to make that weekend a triumph for Dave, and we were sure we had done just that.

The last to leave, inevitably, were the Wessex pranksters.

"*We* are having a ring meeting too – maybe next year?" their squire informed us, "and you're invited. Come down to our place and we'll show you how to have a *really* good time!"

"Is that a threat or a promise?" we asked.

Chapter 8
The Wild Bunch

• • • • •

"I saw him, I saw him,
Hangin' on the old barbed wire,
I saw him.
Hangin' on the old barbed wire..."

There was no doubt about it. Our eccentricity was deepening. Becoming a Border side had certainly focused us, but it also exposed a latent waywardness in our individual personalities. Our unique style of dress had indeed brought us together as parts of a whole and, under the unifying effect of the black face, our separate identities became blurred to the point of irrelevance. However, our personal peculiarities roamed unchecked, fearing no rebuke or censure from a world which regarded Silurian as not simply barking mad but having a touch of Dagenham about it – three stops beyond Barking, as they used to say about Maggie Thatcher.

Since we had 'gone Border', which carried the same implications as 'gone native' or 'gone feral', we of course blacked up every time we made an appearance. The blacking was not simply part of the kit, it was the essential means by which we exchanged our human form for something altogether more intangible. There was an unspoken acknowledgement amongst us that to make an appearance in kit but without the blacking would be inconceivable. So we were either in full kit or not in kit at all. There were no half measures. I suspect most Border morris dancers today would identify with this but, back in the twentieth century, such discipline was unusual.

Many Cotswold dancers – then and now – proclaim their identity and allegiance to a particular side by wearing sweatshirts or other tops with the name of their side emblazoned across the front. At ring meetings and other such events many, when not actually dancing, don these garments over their morris kit in order to keep warm or to feel less dressed up. Some even allow themselves to be seen in a sort of 'half-kit', where perhaps the bells, baldrics and hats are removed when not dancing, allowing the wearer to walk about more casually and less prominently. It has to be said, however, that standing around in white shirt and white trousers (or black breeches) with two white hankies hanging out of your belt loops doesn't render you inconspicuous. It will not help you blend into the crowd, so you might as well opt for the full regalia.

As far as we were concerned, any kind of half-kit was just not taking it seriously, displaying a lack of comprehension about the nature of the morris. These other guys may well have been happy as members of some morris club, but we saw ourselves as Dancers of the Morris, with a desire to cultivate and preserve the anonymity and mystique that properly belongs to it. Out of kit we were just ordinary blokes; in kit we were that strange many-faceted entity called Silurian. We took the idea of ritual dancing seriously, although the evidence for any history of this was exasperatingly elusive. Though the dancing itself may have never had any sacramental significance, the concept of rite or ceremony was still there for us, even in the dressing up.

On a typical weekend away we would arrive on the Friday night in ordinary clothes and wouldn't think about the kit until the next morning. Only then, with a performance imminent, would we dress up and black our faces. We would all stick together during this 'ceremony' until the last man was ready and then, completely attired – bells, hats and all – we would go to breakfast en masse, and we would stay together until crashing out at the end of the night. All this was much more spectacular than mooning about in smaller groups sporting costumes in various stages of assembly. We looked as if we meant business.

It all helped our growing reputation as outlaws. Other morrismen were learning to expect the unexpected, and we thrived on the unpredictability. After our own ring meeting, our wackiness had been stamped with the Morris Ring Seal of Approval, especially by the new Squire of the Ring, Father Kenneth Loveless MBE (awarded for his services to morris dancing), more usually known as Reverend Ken. He was a bit of a rebel himself, with an interestingly chequered personal history, which had taken him from being a sailor to virtuoso concertina player to becoming vicar of the somewhat papalist parish of Hoxton, where he wore his biretta and preferred to be known as 'Father'. His enigmatic and eccentric personality found favour with us, and he in turn admired our style of anarchy. And he was presiding over the ring meeting we attended a couple of months after our own, down in sunny Bristol.

Father Ken was hobnobbing with the other ring officials when we turned up on the Friday night, so we didn't get the big welcome from him. Instead, our Bristolian hosts greeted us with mischievous smiles, knowing looks and whispered asides. It soon became apparent that something special had been planned for the Saturday night feast, but no details were forthcoming. Predictably, we were thinking along food lines. We hoped it might be a carve-it-yourself whole roast ox, or thrushes' tongues in honey or a naked woman lying on the table covered in food that we then had to eat off her body. But it was not to be. No imagination, some people.

On the Saturday dance tour, we prised a little more information from our tour guide. It turned out that the Bristol boys were planning some kind of 'silly morris competition'. We thought that a ring meeting was in itself a silly morris competition, so we were a bit baffled. More details emerged as the day progressed, and it turned out that it was to be an after-dinner entertainment, whereby each of the twelve sides present would have to stage some novel interpretation of morris. Funny thing – but we thought we had already cracked that one. Yet we were still being pressed to come up with something else.

In typical fashion, we didn't really take this too seriously, consequently reaching the end of the day with virtually no coherent ideas. Serious debate on the matter did not commence until just before the feast, proving once again the maxim that, if it wasn't for the last minute, nothing would ever get done.

Burco, for reasons known only to himself, had brought a gorilla mask with him and, to help him concentrate whilst groping for ideas, he put it on. Nobody noticed the difference. For all we knew, he had been wearing it all weekend. He took it off again. Still nobody noticed. By way of historical footnote, as we found out later, Burco had initially introduced this handy little accessory when he was still called Colin and had a white face. He tried the mask on one night at a ceilidh where he was playing with Hodge's Dump. Willy had said, "You prannet! You look like Erco from *Planet of the Apes*, but you're a berk, so . . ." The name was soon spelled 'Burco' in homage to the little metal water boilers once popular in village halls. Don't ask me why.

Accompanying us on this Bristol weekend was our bagman, Keith Francis, (who was now known as Wilf, to distinguish him from Keith Close, who had recently joined the side, presumably as an antidote to the responsibility of his day job as a primary school deputy head teacher). Wilf was ostensibly quiet and unassuming, yet he emanated a real presence in the side. Whereas most of the men were 'bearded like the pard', as Shakespeare once put it, Wilf was clean-shaven. Yet he had a look of authority about him that might deter anyone from asking why he wasn't a paid-up member of BeardsЯUs.

Whilst we were wrestling with the dilemma of what to do for our after-dinner cameo, Wilf quietly chipped in.

"It just so happens," he said, "that I've got a few skirts with me, and I thought that we could perhaps . . . um . . .wear those . . . ? Oh, and there are some headscarves."

Got a few skirts with me?? *Headscarves*?

We all looked at Wilf. Our sensible and efficient bagman. Tall, well-spoken and well presented. A Classical scholar of some note and lecturer in Ancient History. A stabilising influence on us all – who just happened to have a few skirts with him.

"And I've got these balloons," he continued, "and I thought we could perhaps do something with those as well . . ."

Skirts *and balloons*?

Someone started scanning the floor for the marbles Wilf had obviously lost.

"Wilf," said Willy, whilst Wilf met his gaze with an expectant beam, "it's brilliant!"

If Willy thought it was brilliant, who were we to argue? The spark was lit, and we all gathered around to fan the little flame into life.

"Knowing the general feeling regarding women doing morris dancing," continued Wilf, still beaming and expanding his ideas, "I thought some sort of skit on that would go down well."

The idea was certainly going down well with us, especially coming as it did from such a respected member of the morris fraternity, so that was a promising start. Once enthused by something, our creativity kicked in.

"So it's skirts all round and balloons under the shirts, is it?" queried Andy, one of the more unassuming but totally indispensable members of the side, partly because of his cartoon mentality.

"Oo-hoo, great!" murmured Dave Smith, more to himself than anyone else, his eyes dancing wickedly above a lecherous grin. David Harvey Smith, to give him his full title, was more commonly known to us as Smudge, on account of his prowess as a screen printer, one of those skills long since outmoded by the advance of technology – unlike Smudge himself, who was (and still is) immune to any outside force that might attempt to make him obsolete. His distinct accent indicated Herefordshire roots, and his lascivious mutterings betrayed a one-track mind. If he couldn't put a sexual slant on any thought in his head, he simply dumped it for something more productive. Now here he was drooling over the prospect of a bit of cross-dressing.

Meanwhile, Wilf was prepared to reveal that his collection of skirts was nothing more than old theatre cast-offs in plain cotton, either pale green or mauve. But, as to how he came by them or indeed why he thought it might be a good idea to bring them along, no further information was forthcoming.

"Bags me a mauve one," said Mick, as Wilf pulled them from his bag, "it'll match my sash." His sense of colour coordination was admirable, considering what a plonker he was going to look, with two balloons stuck up his shirt front and a headscarf framing his black face, emphasising his Hobbit-like eyebrows.

Burco was back in his gorilla mask . . . or was he? He also wore a hairy black jumper with his pale green skirt, completing a very effective topless gorilla look. Content that this was his image for the stunt, he was off in the corner of the room practicing a few notes on the tuba.

"So, what have we got then?" asked Willy, summing up like a magistrate. "Skirts, headscarves and inflatable boobs – is that the lot then?"

"Well, there are some long balloons in here too," said Andy, rummaging through the bag. "We could use them as sticks perhaps."

"And we could black our bums!" Wilf suggested.

"Bloody hell, Wilf!" somebody remonstrated.

"No – bloody good idea!" corrected Willy. His face took on a thoughtful appearance as he looked up to the ceiling for further inspiration. Then, peering at us over the top of his round glasses, he said, "How about we have one black bum, one white bum alternately round the set?"

How's anyone going to see that, unless we lift our skirts?" came the obvious question.

"Exactly," said Willy.

And so, when our turn came to grace the arena of the dark, oak-panelled ancient school hall where the feast was being held, we took to the floor in our skirts, head scarves, black faces and long balloons in our hands. We minced our way through Fanny Frail, our beribboned shirts stretched over impossibly large and matronly busts and, with a flourish at the end, we bent over and flicked up our skirts, revealing our cheeky two-tone display. The room erupted, and uproar ensued. Many of the onlookers were in the grip of hysterical laughter, and many of Silurian were in the grip of the onlookers, being dragged off to the darker corners of the room, presumably for some one-to-one social intercourse. Judging by the expressions of delight on certain Silurian faces, the subject of adding this dance to our repertoire was going to be up for serious discussion come next practice night.

Our little offering had gone down well, but it was nothing compared with the highly original vignette from the Broadwood men. They had come in as six frock-coated pallbearers with a coffin on their shoulders, accompanied by an eerie little morris tune that seemed to come from nowhere. It was only when they put the coffin down that it became clear the music emanated from within. The lid of the coffin was opened to reveal their musician, looking suitably cadaverous in his shroud. He sat up like the creaking ghost of the old squire, playing his concertina while the pallbearers did an appropriately slow dance. On completion of this mournful tribute, they laid their musician to rest once again, closed the coffin, lifted it back onto their shoulders and solemnly walked off to the same ghostly muffled tune.

The judges awarded equal first prize to Broadwood and Silurian, a decision we disputed. We thought Broadwood should have won outright. However, the joint win helped our confidence enormously and kept our reputation for originality on an upward curve. Increasingly, we were receiving invitations to other events. Although ring meetings gave us the chance to demonstrate our own brand of morris to other dancers, the specialist events put us in front of different audiences. After the Bristol meeting, we received our second invitation to Dancing England in Derby.

It might be said that our second visit to Derby was conducted with substantially more decorum than the first one, though that is not saying a lot, considering the marked absence of decorum first time around. On this occasion, however, we were accompanied by our wives and girlfriends, a move instigated by Dave Jones, who believed in involving family members whenever possible. By no means was this a unanimous view, and careful observation at the time would have revealed a number of dark thoughts on the back seat of the coach forming themselves into a Bone of Contention.

Bearing in mind that one of Jonesy's personal triumphs was the establishment of the family-orientated festival at Bromyard, it is not difficult to see that he was just a typical example of Folk Festival Man, *Homo festivalus*. He was certainly well into all things Folky, but the majority of Silurian had no such aspirations, not even musically – our combined musical tastes varied from The Sex Pistols to Wagner. As for the dancing, Jonesy simply had an axe to grind. He wanted to prove himself to the Morris Ring, but we were interested only in proving something to ourselves, and to enjoy the spell that Jonesy had inadvertently cast to bring his Border side to life.

As Silurian, we shared a common psyche. Each of us was slightly unhinged, out of step with convention, and that helped to unify us. Like any other groups of people who are emotionally close, mood swings were contagious. As a side, we could be aggressive, depressed, playful, mischievous, exuberant or indeed in any mood, depending on circumstances. At Dancing England Take Two, we were cocky. We'd been before and we knew the score. This time we weren't going to do all the dances we knew at the same time. This time we weren't going to get completely legless. Well, of course we weren't – we were surrounded by our female minders. We loved them to bits, but their presence was like putting a governor on an engine, which became apparent when it was our turn to dance.

The dancing was adequately executed, but certainly not spectacular. This time around, we saw the arena for what it was, a stage on which performers simply entertained a remote audience in the surrounding shadowed tiers of seats. That wasn't enough for us. Still feeling cocky, despite the suppressant of a clinical performance, we were looking for more. Call it pack instinct, but we began to look predatorial as we became aware of the number of females in the Assembly Rooms that night. The governor was about to be disconnected.

"With any amount of luck, they'll all be at the ceilidh later on," ventured Chris Mulvey, plastering contractor of note and fame, as well as storyteller and folksinger with an eclectic repertoire of fine songs. His Irish genes made him a natural troubadour.

"Oo-hoo! Great!" interjected Smudge with his usual opening line. He was already salivating at the thought of a room full of nubile maidens.

"Pr'aps they'll get hot," added Burco, grinning his simian grin, "and then they'll have to get their kit off . . ."

"*Huh! Huh! Huh*!" Smudge, out of the corner of his ever-present leering smirk, was putting Burco's thoughts into words, in his own inimitable way.

As a member of Silurian, Smudge was in his element. Since coming out as a fully-fledged Border side, we had seen women from a different perspective, essential perhaps to our development as purveyors of ancient rituals. Smudge had picked up on this idea and seen it as complete authority to peddle his own brand of licentiousness, liberated as he was by the unshakeable impression that women had been put on this Earth for his personal pleasure. Most of the rest of us, however, taking our cues from all the speculation about Border Morris being rooted in pre-Christian male fertility dances, understood that such rites would be meaningless without reference to the female. There were those amongst us who privately yearned for the reinstatement of the Goddess in our imbalanced patriarchal society, but mostly we just saw women as an obvious and vital part of anything to do with fertility. Trouble was, although we were trying not to make it up as we went along, conjecture led to improvisation. Seeing ourselves in an overtly male role, performing dances laden with phallic reference, women came to be seen as essential protagonists in the Great Rite – in a symbolic way of course, rather than participatory.

In the early days of blacking up, we had discovered that the blacking rubbed off all too easily on the smooth skin of a woman's face. Trying it out on any female member of our Boxing Day entourage met with less resistance than expected, thus encouraging us to expand our ideas. Since the change of kit, the blacking up of women had been taken up as a serious sport by Silurian's lunatic fringe, that is to say, Smudge, Mick, Burco, Andy, me and a few reinforcements when needed. Some of our more cooperative victims loved all the stuff we were giving them about the 'luck of the Morris', the mystery of the fertility rite and the fact that they would be guaranteed long life and good fortune if they were kissed by one of us. Some found that a smudged cheek was the answer to the question, "Why do you black your faces?" Most of them thought we were simply off our heads. Which in a way we were, intoxicated by the Border drug.

The blacking up of women was fast becoming part of the proceedings. They had become metaphorical goddesses, and their smeared faces were an indication to others that they had been to the altar and participated in the rite. It was also the one part of Silurian lore that did not require us to adhere to the pack instinct. For this part of the ritual it was more successful to work in pairs. Let's face it, sixteen or so black-faced loonies in a bunch, with ribbon rags fluttering and bells jingling, are about as inconspicuous as a runaway

Scania truck. Splitting into smaller groups was therefore essential.

By the time the ceilidh was under way, we had already set up base camp around some tables between the bar and the dance floor. Guarding our territory for us was our female contingent, all of whom were quite safe from us, having long since been through the obligatory face-blacking. Having been thus initiated and part of our inner circle, they were content (at least, we persuaded ourselves they were content) to observe our antics from where they sat, which enabled us to roam freely. Andy, Burco, Smudge and I were swaggering about and strutting our stuff. Like Sam Peckinpah's infamous anti-heroes in that grisly little Western, *The Wild Bunch*, we looked as if we owned the place. We liked to think we had the outlaw image, but in reality we were no more than social untouchables, mildly unstable but reassuringly benign. Well, that was the impression we were trying to cultivate during our encounters that night. Hitherto, we had not been in an environment so heavily populated with nubile females, and we were making the most of it. We were amazed to find that the more we accosted, the easier it became. There was something quite unexpected going on, but it was clear that those women who were still white were beginning to adopt a 'what's wrong with me?' attitude. By the end of the evening they were practically queuing up.

There would come a time in the future when, intrigued by this phenomenon, I would become involved in some correspondence with a certain young lady from Cheshire, in order to gain some insight into what was going on. But, at the Assembly Rooms that evening, I just went with the flow. By the time we came to leave, there were what seemed like dozens of girls with smudgy black faces and a slightly dishevelled appearance. As well as these obvious 'tribal marks of honour', some of them also proudly sported badges acquired from us as trophies. These had been designed by Andy, the Quiet One, and depicted, in a kind of déjà-vu moment, a girl with a smudgy black face and a slightly dishevelled appearance, under the caption 'Silurian were here'.

Andy worked as a commercial artist, illustrating technical brochures for military hardware. Isometric views of the interior of Challenger tanks, for example. But this was just bread-and-butter stuff, helping to pay the bills. His real talent was his ability as a cartoonist. Like all the best cartoonists, he had a slightly warped mind, an amazing eye for detail and an infinite capacity for seeing the humorous side of any situation. The latter probably came in very handy on our first trip to Dancing England, because we managed to leave him in Derby.

Maybe it was his quiet nature (which he employed to good effect when tracking down women to black up), or maybe we were suffering from what was undeniably an excess of ale, but we really didn't notice his absence until we were nearly home. Chris Mulvey had been giving us the benefit of a selection from his repertoire in the back of the coach, and was in the middle of *Hanging on the Old Barbed Wire*, that cynical little anti-authority favourite from the First World War. He had worked his way down through the army ranks, from 'if you want to find the Colonel' (he's in Paris on 7 days leave) to 'if you want to find the private' (he's hanging on the old barbed wire), and now he was on to the passengers on the coach . . .

"*If you want to find old Andy,*
I know where he is,
I know where he is,
I know where – !"

"Where is he then?" asked Willy.

"Eh?"

"Where *is* he then?" Willy repeated, "*I* can't see 'im!"

Well . . . he's . . .he's . . ."

"He's NOT HERE – *that*'s where he is!"

And sure enough, he wasn't. Nowhere on the coach, not even under the seats or chatting to the driver.

We only found out – days later – that, at the same time as his absence was being discovered, he was hitching back from Derby at one o'clock in the morning in full Silurian regalia. So much for sticking together. We were going to have to have a sharp word with him. His experience was not without incident, as you can imagine. One lift was cut short when the West Indian driver became perturbed by the realisation that his passenger was not wearing gloves, as he had assumed. Uttering something along the lines of, "Don' kom ridin' in heah no mo' wid dem white hans!" the driver pulled up and politely asked Andy to leave.

We weren't going to lose him again, so the end of our second visit to Derby saw us prioritising the rounding up of Andy and bundling him on the coach, followed by a quick head count to make sure no one else was missing the bus. On the way back, the usual post-mortem of the event took place as we relived the high spots, knowing that our next outing, to some charity fete out in no-mans-land, followed by an Ale two weeks after that, wouldn't even come close to the Derby experience.

Personal Reflection: 2

Fete Worse Than Death

• • • • •

"This is it,
And that is it,
And this is morris dancing..."

Don't get me wrong. I've got nothing against fetes as such. Or indeed Ales, come to that (note the use of capital 'A', to make the distinction between a kind of beer and a formal occasion where a lot of beer is available, but only to those who come dressed as morris dancers). But neither fetes nor Ales are much to look forward to in Silurian terms. The former is attractive only in that it usually commands a fee, thus helping to swell the side's funds, whilst the latter is a wincingly introspective miniature version of a ring meeting. In other words, an evening of morris dancing, ale, food and more morris dancing. The kind of thing you go to only if your favourite drama series on the telly has just come to an end.

We generally had two main sources of income. One was 'bottling', an obscure term applied to the passing round of the lucky morrisman's hat whenever we danced in public, and the other was by charging a fee for a public appearance. Bottling was naturally somewhat random, but a pre-arranged fee was something that could be marked up in a double-entry ledger with some confidence. Thus, although most of us were reluctant to dance at fetes, we generally accepted invitations that dangled the financial carrot in front of us.

A typically quirky English institution, the Garden Fete works best as a summer phenomenon. Steer well clear of any fetes that are held in November in the parish hall, because these will turn out to be nothing more than a kind of car boot sale with tea and biscuits on the side. The genuine article, still enjoying a peak of popularity in the 1980s, blooms in high summer and most properly takes place at the local vicarage or on similarly sanctified ground, a location necessitated by the all-important presence of the vicar.

Dress code is important . . . for the vicar at least. A proper vicar should appear in dog collar, black shirt and sand-coloured linen jacket, squinting helpfully though gold-rimmed spectacles just visible under the protective brim of his panama hat. Demonstrating an impeccable sense of colour co-ordination, grey trousers, grey socks and brown sandals should complete the look. Beware the trendy vicar who presides over his fete in a jogging suit, with colourful socks and trainers where his brown sandals ought to be. Such attempts to gain street-cred for the Church and its officers rarely work. A vicar who wants to be 'one of the lads' usually ends up being called Vic, and having his back slapped a lot. The good shepherd cannot do his job by donning a sheepskin coat and bleating with the flock.

The genuine garden fete has stalls, usually in the charge of the more senior female parishioners, selling home-made cakes, jams and chutneys of indeterminate colour and content, as well as home-grown vegetables and plants in pots. In the heyday of fetes, you could also find a tombola stall (what exactly *is* that?) and various try-your-luck games, such as skittles or bash-the-rat. The selection of prizes for these distractions is incomplete without a bottle of cheap fizzy apple juice – today that would be industrial Belgian perry – and a small tin of Crawford's shortbread.

Under the mellow heat of a summer sun, and before the decline of fashion to its current nadir of unflattering tops, big shorts (short shorts for the girls) and flip-flops, there would have been floaty cotton frocks and rolled-up shirt sleeves, with people nodding and smiling benignly to each other. Teas, which of course would include cakes and sandwiches, were usually available, often in the cooler climes indoors, and a plentiful supply of ice cream and lollipops would keep the kids reasonably quiet. If entertainment was laid on, there was usually an area set aside for the purpose, often on the main lawn, with a row of chairs down each side. These would be sparsely occupied by a number of old biddies, half asleep, knees apart and swollen feet squeezing out over their shiny best summer shoes, bought forty years previously and worn only for such occasions. Some are accompanied by their once-dashing paramours, now overdressed in their one and only suit and stout black brogues, the older ones still with watch-chains dangling across tightly stretched rotund waistcoat fronts, and generally looking very hot and mildly annoyed.

In this still life of English genteelism there is no place for Silurian. To me, it seemed unjust to the point of malice to unleash upon such an unsuspecting audience a dozen or so black-faced desperados, clinking pewter tankards that were clearly not receptacles for tea or home-made lemonade. However, they were there by invitation and under a financial obligation to dance, so dancing is what took place, often doing untold damage to the vicarage lawn in the process. The scattered chair-bound audience, suddenly awakened by a few bass farts from the tuba, give each other accusatory looks before realising that something is happening in front of them. Nonplussed by our wild appearance, they watch the performance uncomprehendingly from behind polite fixed smiles. Some of them don't seem to notice us at all, and a few simply go back to sleep.

As each dance ends, an uncertain ripple of clapping murmurs through the gathering, with a slightly more positive demonstration of enthusiasm as we dance off and out of their sight at the end of the performance, perhaps to be confronted by the vicar, blinking uncertainly at us and self-consciously trying not to wring his hands.

"Thank you, boys. That was . . . er . . . yes, *um* . . . yes . . . *splendid*. Splendid! Tell me – why do you black your faces?"

"So you don't know who's dug up your lawn."

"*Lawn*? Oh! . . . yes . . . ha! ha! Very good. *Dug up my lawn*! Yes . . . splendid, boys, *splendid*! Anyway, do help yourself to some tea, won't you?" And, indicating the general direction of the refreshments with a vague wave of the hand, he bids us 'good day' and wanders off in search of some less challenging conversational partners.

Before leaving the scene of the crime, our bagman would usually pick up the fee from either the vicar's wife or the parish council's chief matriarch.

"I did *so* enjoy your show," she would say, all smiles, twinset and pearls. This of course is Fêtespeak for, "If I'd known it was going to be like that, I'd have gone to see my sister in Bournemouth."

From Jonesy's point of view, fetes were good, because they swelled the funds. Ales didn't – they depleted the coffers. But Jonesy loved them too.

The Ale is as quirky a phenomenon as the Fete, but it has no pedigree. It is merely a mongrel whose heredity can be traced back to a parentage of the Harvest Supper and the Men's Club. Even casual observers will have noticed that men have a penchant for clubs. It's a gender thing. Men have to gather in gangs to cover up their own inadequacies in the face of the undeniable superiority of the female. From schoolboy gangs to the boardrooms of multinational corporations, Man the Hunter gathers in groups to fend off rivals, vanquish his enemies and trap his prey. Those men out on the local fairway who say, "I just come here to play golf," are fooling themselves, or trying to fool the competition. Men are inherently competitive, and the club culture is the ideal medium for the generation and growth of this urge.

We live in a complex society, yet we are reassuringly animal beneath the glossy veneer of societal niceties. Trouble is, our innate instincts have been smothered by the unreal world of civilisation. The once benign and protectively responsible leader of the wolf pack has turned into the self-important captain of industry who protects nothing but himself and the profits of the company. Lauded by a society that promotes this kind of behaviour, the new 'civilised' leaders of the pack are imitated by every male gang and club, from Church to cricket, that dominates modern human culture. The lesser members of the gang, though maybe not born leaders, are happy enough to be part of the pack, able to heap scorn and derision on their rivals from the safety of their own numbers.

Morris dancing is not immune to such competitiveness and rivalry. We have only to look at the dances collected by Cecil Sharp to see it in action. Original performers of the ritualised dance were probably at one time shadowy, mysterious figures, hidden from the mortal world by impenetrable disguises. Today, however, in Cotswold Morris, we see an abundance of brightly coloured, easily identifiable group uniforms, displaying the exclusivity of each side. The disguise and mystique have virtually disappeared, retained only in the bizarre animal characters accompanying some of the sides, and the dances have gained more showiness and embellishment than is necessary for some ancient ritual invocation.

Great emphasis is placed on the differences between the 'traditions', named after the villages where each group of performers had its base, which of course is an idea that has very deep roots in the protection of boundaries, but which today is unknown to the average morris dancer. Because 'maleness' has taken the place of masculinity, intense rivalry now thrives between peer groups – our gang is better than *your* gang – thus the differences between the many styles of morris are appreciated best by the performers themselves. Consequently, a need arose to have regular gatherings to demonstrate, observe, discuss and appraise the variations. Any such get-together, if it is to be successful and friendly, will benefit greatly from the provision of food and drink, again something which has always been important at times of celebration, but which can easily become abused in an all-male environment. The harvest supper principle, however, whereby the rich landowner and his family would share a meal with his poorly paid workers, is applied wherever rivals meet under a truce. From the office party to international councils of war, this meal-sharing show of non-aggression reflects yet another of our primal instincts.

And so the Morris Ale has evolved. The venue is usually a village hall or similar, a space big enough to accommodate up to perhaps fifty people. The host side invites two or three representatives of a dozen or more different sides, and they converge at the chosen spot with tankards in hand and tongues lolling. The Vanishing Beer Trick sets the tone until all guests are gathered, whereupon food is usually served. The quantity, quality and presentation of the food vary enormously, but it disappears quickly enough, such is the effect of what used to be called 'the beer munchies'.

With liberal quantities of beer and food now sloshing about inside everyone, causing many a button-stretching paunch to swell up over the belt, the time has come to while away the remainder of the evening in quiet contemplation.

So what happens?

Tables and chairs are moved out of the way and the space is cleared. Somebody starts up a tune and on cue there are a couple of dozen potential heart attack victims out there on the floor, moving it and grooving it like men possessed. Dances follow each other as quickly as the pints still being consumed by the participants, and the huge back catalogue of Cotswold morris is plundered, giving everybody a chance to do dances from unfamiliar traditions. This is Manic Morris at its most insane. These guys are here to dance, and dance they will, putting on an overtly macho demonstration of stamina, agility and capacity for alcohol. They keep going like this for a couple of hours or more, with nearly as much moisture escaping through their pores as they are pouring down their throats. Inevitably, the beer finally runs out and the insanity with it, bringing the revelry to an end.

As with the fete, there is no place for Silurian here. The dancers that frequent these Ales, and the dances they do, are Cotswold biased. Occasionally a Border dance might be included, but only as a bit of fun. Two or three Silurian men at one of these dance-fests do nothing more than stand around looking spare, or at least looking at the Cotswold boys doing their thing. Our thing was to dance with an audience, trying to weave the spell. We were not interested in demonstrating steps and moves to each other, or even to a collection of other Border dancers. We tended to steer clear of Ales, although we did sample a few just to find out we didn't like them. Our derisive attitude to Cotswold should have disqualified us from ever being invited. Indeed, on the basis that it is a mistake to give mischief makers time on their hands, it was dangerous to request our presence, as we shall see later.

Chapter 9
Folk On The Tyne

• • • • •

"Oh weel may the keel row
The keel row, the keel row.
Weel may the keel row
That my laddie's in..."

Mick wasn't looking too special.

Understandable, of course. After all, we were at the Wolverley Folk Festival and he had stayed up all night, along with the rest of the Silurian wild boys. The rest of the gang was pretty much okay, but Mick was in poor condition. Maybe it was the beer – a bit keggy, and certainly not a prize-winning example of the brewer's art.

Or maybe it was the frog.

There had been much talk of frogs that morning, as we sat about on the grass of the campsite, Smudge, Mick and I, chatting to the bass drummer from the Earlsdon Morrismen, the guys who had organised the weekend. Following the lead of our man from Earlsdon, the topic of conversation had moved quickly from the previous evening's entertainment to the subject of frogs. Don't ask me how. He may have been a herpetologist, for all I know. You can never tell with morrismen; their day jobs are often out of the ordinary.

Up to that point, it had already been a bad morning for Mick, but he just about had the situation under control. However, with all this talk of frogs, he was rapidly losing his grip. His couple of hours sleep in the pre-dawn stillness had evidently been deep and blissful, if loud. It being a family weekend, I was sharing a tent with my wife, Dizzy, next to Mick's humble bivouac, and we could see his snores rippling through the outer fabric. We could imagine him in there, crashed out on his back, mouth open, arms and legs spread-eagled like a stranded starfish.

As the sun came up through our tent, painting everything with an eerie blue glow, another vision came into my head, that of Mick's face, half its blacking gone in the flow of perspiration generated by the previous night's ceilidh. With the remains of it clinging firmly to his eye sockets, eyebrows and beard, in that ghostly light he must have looked as if he would have been perfectly at home ferrying departed souls across the River Styx.

Answering a predictable call of nature, I writhed into some clothes and nipped out of my tent. It was a serenely still summer morning, with the earth still drowsy under its dewy cloak. All was well with the world and I was lost in the beauty of it all, strolling around the field, thoughts lost in the sparkling silver-beaded cobwebs.

CRASH! *BANG*!

Mick's tent seemed to be under attack. Invisible hands were wrestling with the entrance flap, to the accompaniment of muffled curses. Suddenly, out tumbled Mick, his face death white under the patches of blacking. He seemed to be having serious trouble with his legs, those once-reliable means of perambulation, now gripped by an obvious inability to carry the rest of his body in a perpendicular plane. Like a sleepwalking trick cyclist with four knees, he stumbled and staggered to the edge of the field, punctuating his meandering with violent retching. Though not an appealing vision, it did have the makings of an innovative little dance – one, two, three, *bleaaaagh*! one, two, three, *bleaaaagh*! –

but the timing needed sharpening up a bit. I made a mental note to discuss the finer points with him later, and headed over to offer my assistance.

I was just seconds too late. As I reached him, the contents of his stomach dive-bombed into the long grass. A startled frog leapt from the spot as the deluge hit the ground.

"*Urrrrgh*! I don't remember eating *that*!" groaned Mick, releasing his grip on lucidity as his hands moved to his stomach.

The thought of it was too much to take, and he was promptly sick again. Trying not to think about frogs, he tottered back to his tent, no more than peripherally aware of my presence, and there he sat, face like an accident on a barbecue. He didn't move for the next hour. The rustle of a sandwich being liberated from a paper bag by the Earlsdon drummer activated Mick's post-sickness munchie mechanism and stirred him into giving life one more go. He came to join us on the grass.

"Cheese an' pickle," muffled drummer boy through a mouthful of sandwich. "Should have 'ad 'em last night."

"If I'd known you weren't goin' to eat 'em last night, I'd have had them for you," Mick reassured him, thinking about his quietly gurgling stomach.

"You'd have only wasted 'em," Smudge pointed out, having heard the frog story by then.

"Anyway," said the drummer, "I hear you prefer frog sandwiches . . ."

Mick muttered under his breath and fired a Mephistophelean look at him.

His tormentor, drum now propped against his knees, began tapping out a 4/4 12-bar blues rhythm with his hands, before breaking into the opening verse of Bob Dylan's *On The Road Again*.

"Well, I wake up in the morning, there's frogs inside my socks . . ."

Drummer boy was clearly a mischief maker. His looks were a dead giveaway. With an ear-ring, pony tail and facial hair that made him look like a Victorian colour sergeant, he may as well have had 'desperado' tattooed on his forehead. He too was aware of Mick's early morning inspection of the field margins, and he was taking great pleasure in steering the conversation round to frogs. Such mild cruelty was uncannily Silurian in style. Though dressed very differently from us, he and the rest of his side were as much morris outcasts as we were. No black faces here, and no rudimentary phallic displays, however. Earlsdon Morrismen danced Northwest clog morris with style and panache. But, to do so in the English Midlands, not far from the fertile collecting ground that kept Cecil Sharp busy for years, was to invite opposition, opprobrium and ostracism, big words that boil down to the same thing – they were outlawed.

Northwest Morris in its modern form came out of the industrial revolution, chiefly around the cotton mill towns of Lancashire. The costume evolved from the working clothes of the time but morphed into something very colourful, with a kind of carnival feel about it. Earlsdon wore white shirts, black knee breeches, sky-blue socks and iron-shod clogs, but all this was enhanced with crossed sashes (one sky-blue and the other maroon and dark blue zigzags) and pale blue bowler hats topped with huge creations of flowers and vegetation. As if this were not enough, they also wore numerous strings of beads around their necks. They danced in multiples of four, with what looked like short, knotted lanyards in their hands, or short sticks painted in stripes like miniature old-fashioned barbers' poles. The tunes included military marches, played with suitable crispness on a variety of instruments, but always including bass drum and snare.

Up north, this form of dancing survives vigorously to this day. It is very much part of the social scene, being performed on 'high days and holidays' and other such festive occasions. It does not suffer from overkill and enjoys a popularity not often found in its Cotswold counterpart, which is frequently met with bored indifference. Down south, by contrast, the Northwest stuff was a bit of an oddity, like Welsh Border. To set up a Northwest side in Coventry indicates a certain attitude, and this came across in their dancing. Add to that an impressive band with a huge bass drum, plus the sound of twenty pairs of iron-shod clogs marching down the street, and you've cracked it. Heads will turn.

We identified with this show-stopping ethos and the desire to engage with the audience. What we really needed to do was to travel up to Lancashire or somewhere to see this military morris in its own back yard.

Later that year, 1981, we did indeed travel north, but ended up in the Northeast in Newcastle-upon-Tyne, as invited guests at a big festival of international dance under the suitably foreign-sounding title of Folkmoot '81.

Chris Mulvey, demonstrating the kind of problem-solving originality vital to survival in the building trade, came up with a bright idea. "No need to worry about hiring a minibus from one of them expensive hire places – they've got a Transit minibus at the old school. I'll go and chat 'em up, look."

Never trust a builder, even if he is a specialist plastering contractor.

When we went to pick up this vehicle, it certainly had the name 'Transit' tacked to the bodywork, but 'minibus' would never have been on the list of words to describe it. In essence, it was no more than a standard Transit van with a bench seat down each side in the back. No windows or any other features that might steer one towards picturing it as a bus. It was like riding in a shipping container. Naturally, Chris became the target for a serious amount of abuse on the journey up, particularly as he was occupying the padded driving seat, with panoramic views of what would eventually become spectacular scenery. Volunteering to drive did not exonerate him from blame as to choice of vehicle.

After an agonising journey of what seemed like about eight days, we had to stop at a motorway services for tea and a pee.

One by one, we fell out of the van and hobbled across to the dull and soulless 'Self Service Restaurant', helping each other up the entrance steps like a squad of walking wounded. Coming back to some form of life after a reviving cuppa, we were surprised to find we'd actually been in the van for less than two hours. Discussing this strange time warp, we came to the unanimous conclusion that it was going to be another two hours before we even considered getting back on board. Our driver had other ideas.

"Come on, lads – drink up," he suggested, coaxingly. "Long way to go yet."

"Piss off, Chris!" said one of the casualties.

"We'll never make it at this rate," answered Chris. "We're only just past Birmingham, look!"

"Some of us ain't going to make it at all if we have to get back in that heap!"

"You'll be alright," said Chris, in that reassuring tone of voice he used when sending his plasterers out on their next Mission Impossible. "Anyway, I'm going," he added. And with that, he headed for the door.

Chris wasn't taking any more chances with us, so the next time he deigned to stop we were off the motorway and just past Scotch Corner. This time, despite the fact that the van was now in a pub carpark, nothing happened when Chris opened the back doors. We were like those ashen figures from Pompeii. We had to be stretchered out in a sitting position and each injected with two or three pints of the local bitter to anaesthetise us sufficiently for first aid and physiotherapy to be administered, after which we stood some chance of getting as far as Newcastle.

On arrival we again limped and staggered from the bus. Two hundred and forty miles in a tiny shipping container – we certainly knew how to live it up. Fortunately, our hosts, the Monkseaton Morrismen, were there to guide us towards the much-needed refreshments, which included more hop-and-barley-based palliatives, a pure natural remedy essential to a quick recovery in these circumstances.

By the time we all unwound and took in our surroundings, we saw that we were in the large hall of a local college. There was music in the air and some lively impromptu dancing out on the floor. It may well have been a ceilidh, but not as we knew it. Fringe events were also in evidence, which we sat and observed as the evening unfolded. The liquid analgesic had washed away our pain, but certain symptoms of overdosing became evident. Burco, whose eyes had turned red as he relaxed into his simian alter-ego, was becoming animated, energised by some of the less familiar music on offer.

"Gimme the keys to the van, Chris," he said, eyeing him from two different angles.

"Why?"

"Just – *gimme the keys*!" responded Burco belligerently.

"What for?"

"I want me tuba!"

"Your tuba?"

"*Yeess!* – what are you? *Deaf*!?"

Sensing that Chris wasn't seeing the light here, he added, "I want to play in the oompah band, don' I?"

The keys were handed over and Burco swayed out of the room.

Having retrieved his tuba from the van and dutifully returned the keys, he loped off to join said oompah band, who were playing for an Austrian folk-dance troupe by the name of Volkstanzgruppe Pram. When we first saw this name on the publicity posters, we hadn't really sussed it was the German for 'folk dance group', so naturally assumed it was some kind of VW toddler's buggy.

Later on that evening, we spotted Burco with the Austrians. He seemed to have fitted in well with their wind band, but looked a bit out of place wearing a formal black morning coat. He and Dion, following John Willy's lead of musicians wearing different kit from the dancers, had decided to add black morning coats to their sartorial ensemble. On this occasion, there was also the added advantage that his unique attire helped us to spot Burco from a distance.

Which made it all the more obvious when he wasn't there.

Towards the end of the evening, when it looked as if things were winding down a bit, we checked the oompah band for signs of our volatile brass player. But it was clear that he was no longer with them. A search party was quickly organised, but no trace of him was found. We were being accommodated in the homes of the Monkseaton men, and there were indications that it was time to head off, so we gave up on Burco, trusting that the man who was putting him up would eventually locate him and escort him to his sleeping quarters. With that, we went off in our separate directions under the guidance of our hosts.

Next morning, we all met up in the college car park and waited for Chris to turn up with the van. When he arrived he looked terrible. His haggard face betrayed a sleepless night.

"Morning' Chris!" beamed Willy. "How's your accommodation?"

"Don't ask," said Chris darkly, shooting Willy a fiery glance.

"Well, I *am* asking."

"Well – don't. Okay?"

But he knew he couldn't keep the lid on it. He knew we'd all hassle him until he gave in. His laconic wall of resistance quickly crumbled into capitulation.

"Oh, all right then," he said, "if you must know, I spent hours driving around lookin' for this bleedin' address I'd been given – couldn't find it anywhere! Finally I decide to kip in the van. But of course, it's freezin' in there and it comes on to rain, and the bloody rain is rattlin' on the roof like dried peas in a tin, so I didn't get much sleep, did I?"

"Well, there's a spot of bad luck," lilted Jonesy with an ill-concealed snigger.

"Hang on! Hang on!" Chris continued, holding up a hand to quell the imminent mirth, "I may as well tell you the rest. When I woke up this morning – there I am, right outside the bleedin' house I've been lookin' for!"

Jonesy's snigger burst into a peal of merciless laughter, echoed and chorused by the rest of us.

"Where's Burco?"

Chris's question cut through the manic cackling, which died swiftly. He wasn't laughing, because he knew the joke already. Whilst we'd been chortling, he'd been doing a quick head count, and realised we were all present apart from our wayward tuba player.

"Dunno – haven't seen 'im," offered Smudge, who could be counted on not to see anything that didn't look like a woman.

"Anybody seen him since last night?"

Various replies in the negative confirmed that nobody had spotted the errant little toad since he had been experimenting with the VW Pram. The last of the previous night's rain was still drizzling out of the greyness above, as we reflected on how the day might pan out in the absence of a vital band member. We discussed our next move, which included subjecting the little sod to some of the more entertaining torture routines employed by the Spanish Inquisition.

A shout from the other side of the car park diverted out attention.

"Hel*lloow*!"

There was Burco, dishevelled, bedraggled, with his thinning hair stuck to his forehead and drops of water hanging in his beard. Everything about him was damp except his spirit, whose ever-present buoyancy was indicated by a wide grin and cheery wave.

"Where have you been??" we all tried to say at once.

"Huh! The buggers tried to shove me under a table!" came the reply.

"What *are you on about*?"

"They shoved me under a *table*!" Burco repeated, a note of exasperation creeping into his voice, "but I escaped. And then they tried to lock me in a cupboard – but I escaped from *there* as well!" We thought he had just been playing in a brass band. We hadn't reckoned on him getting involved with the local mafia.

"So what happened then? Where did you sleep?"

"In the car park!" he said, adding, "Well, I didn't *actually* sleep. I managed to get out of the building, but then I couldn't get back in, and I've been wandering around here ever since, in the rain!"

He was unable to elucidate further, and it was only later that evening that we finally found out, from the Austrians, what had really happened to Burco. Apparently, as Friday evening progressed, he became increasingly inclined to fall asleep on the dancefloor so, being good safety-conscious European citizens, they had put him out of harm's way under a table. As for the cupboard episode, no one could give us any information on that at all. Another entry in the Silurian Book of Mysteries.

Saturday's entertainment was very colourful and bursting with pageant, processions and displays, but not the ideal vehicle for a bunch of Border hooligans. There were seemingly endless parades in various parts of Newcastle, with all the people we had met on the Friday night doing their thing, all dressed colourfully in their national costumes. As for Silurian, we seemed to have migrated quietly to the fringe of all this. Moreover, we also seemed to be spending far too much time working up a thirst and not enough time quenching it – an odd little weekend really.

In a few places, notably Whitley Bay, we were given the opportunity to put on a show, to smiles of recognition when our musical medley included that old Geordie favourite, *The Keel Row*. We took full advantage of these moments, trying to break some sticks, charging the crowds on the crossovers and generally making a lot of noise. With the ribbons fluttering and our black bearded faces, we looked pretty wild against the colourful but more restrained European teams, most of whom were probably wondering how they were ever seduced into letting Britain join the Common Market.

Their folk dances appeared sanitised, a bit twee and almost static in comparison to Silurian's energetic and virile display. We had always assumed that any kind of dancing, folk, morris or otherwise, should be charged with at least some sexual energy. This was not the case with these examples from across the continent. I might go as far as to say that they were so benign as to be a pretty effective form of contraception. They had lost the essence of dance and moved into something labelled 'traditional folk dance display', an embodiment of nostalgia recreating a perceived aspect of life long ago, diminishing these displays to little more than mobile museum pieces. By contrast, Silurian acknowledged the roots and history of morris dancing but were creating something original – a new version of an old principle. We needed to be relevant, to have power over the hearts of the crowd, to bewitch them. If we didn't cast a spell over them, we saw ourselves as having failed. We didn't want to project the two-dimensional quality of a film, so we ensured we made our presence felt. The other dance teams seemed suitably impressed, and the French team looked as if they had suddenly twigged why they lost the Battle of Agincourt.

On the Saturday night, there were further festivities in the hall in the form of a kind of international ceilidh. Spotting an opportunity, the Silurian boys wasted no time in getting amongst the women from the foreign teams, all of whom appeared to us to be stunningly beautiful in that enigmatic European way. One or two of us of course swore unmitigated and undying love for these sultry maidens. There was whispered talk about the possibility of smuggling them onto the bus, until someone pointed out the lack of seating in the back and the four-hour torture that was to be the trip home.

The Turkish men, though they let us steal their women, challenged us to dance as a forfeit. They were all about eight feet tall and built like air raid shelters – and they danced with big swords which they obviously knew how to use. Weighing it all up, we decided the best option was to accept their challenge, despite the very real possibility of decapitation. Chris Mulvey had a plan though.

"Tell you what," said he. "Why don't you put the swords down and we can teach you one of our dances?" A lifetime of dealing with belligerent plasterers was about to pay off again.

Through gestures, simple words and broken English, the Turks were persuaded to lay down their weaponry and pick up some sticks. Bearing in mind the principles of simplicity, we taught them the Bromsberrow Heath stick dance, but not the sedate version we had done in Ledbury church. This was the show-stopping version with the music getting faster on each chorus. Though their style was a bit ragged, the Turks got the hang of it soon enough – a figure of eight is simple to explain without the use of words. We conceded that they had won on points, with the score cards coming up at 3 out of ten for style and 14 out of 10 for vigour. Disappointingly, however, these energetic sword dancers decided that reciprocation by way of teaching us their dance was not going to happen. Silurian were obviously too random to be allowed near any long curved blades with very sharp edges. Good decision, all things considered.

Following this episode, Saturday night fell into a predictable pattern of boyish antics interspersed with visits to the bar until our hosts intimated that it was time to retire for the night. Sunday morning was relaxed, peaking during a relatively quiet lunchtime in a local pub with our Monkseaton hosts. I spent most of the time trying to think up ways of escaping the dreaded bus ride home. Return journeys always seemed to take longer, lacking as they do the anticipation of adventure, and this particular return trip, with the prospect of sitting for hours on unpadded wooden racks, filled me with anxiety. Failing to come up with anything that wasn't going to cost money, I resigned myself to the probability of pain and switched to thinking about how I was going to explain away the corrugated bum to She Who Waits At Home.

As it turned out, the journey was not as bad as I had imagined. It was far *far* worse. Only the banter and repartee enabled me to survive as we bounced and bumped down the motorway. I wondered whether it was actually worth running the risk of serious spinal injuries and a deformed pelvis for a few hours of fun. But, with Silurian in my blood, the answer was always going to be 'yes'.

Chapter 10

Light My Fire

• • • • •

"Come put your wine into glasses,
Put your cider into old tin cans,
Put Barleycorn in the nut-brown jug,
For he's proved the strongest man..."

Being a Silurian man was not just a simple matter of joining a morris side. Many potential dancers turned up at our practices, but few remained committed. To those who did, Silurian became almost a way of life. At the very least, Silurian reflected the way they thought about life. Its heart was kept beating by a handful of long-standing members, ready to welcome and encourage enthusiastic new recruits.

Like the police, it was a case of 'once a Silurian man, always a Silurian man', and those who had to leave the area rarely found satisfaction dancing with another side. Potential members soon knew whether they were going to like it or not. It wasn't a question of learning the dances, which were simple enough, and it was nothing to do with having an affinity for the morris tradition. Something else attracted them, some indefinable quality. Whatever it was, it didn't take a new member long to decide whether or not he was of the right mettle. If he was, he fitted in and was quickly absorbed into the fraternity. Once he was out dancing with the side, it was as if he had always been there. We weren't elitist (we just thought we were the best!) and anyone was welcome to join. Many came, but few chose to stay, and the membership numbers were never very high, but they were loyal and reliable.

This kind of solid commitment was reinforced when we became a full-time Border side. Of course, the new kit had an unsettling effect on certain 'Silurian wets', who quietly drifted off-stage. But, by 1981, we were attracting stronger personalities who seemed to slot in perfectly with Silurian's eccentric temperament. In that year, for example, we were joined by a couple of brainy boffins from what used to be known as the Royal Signals and Radar Establishment (RSRE) in Malvern, which has since morphed through a couple of identity crises to become QinetiQ, whatever that means. They may have been introduced by Andy, as he had RSRE connections, but he never let on. At a professional level, they answered to the names of Dr Jethro Hill and Dr Vasant Deshmukh, but they were less formal with us.

Hullo, Ah'm Jethro," said Dr Hill in a Northumbrian accent.

And I'm Vas," said Dr Deshmukh, not in a Northumbrian accent.

"Hi Jethro. Hi Vaz," said Bernie Smart, one of the Worcester contingent.

"*Vass*," said Vas helpfully. "Short for *Vas*-ant . . ."

"Oh, okay," said Bernie. Smart by name, smart by nature, but maybe not good with certain names. Though he didn't realise it at the time, he was destined never to get Vas's name right.

These guys were bristling with qualifications, with at least one PhD apiece. They were into nuclear physics and the brand new discipline of microchip technology, then in its infancy. We never knew exactly what they did, because I presume they weren't allowed to tell us, the RSRE being part of the secret underworld of military innovation. Round at Vas's house one day, I did ask him, and his answer was to show me what he was working on at that time, saying, "Read that. If you can understand it, you'll know what I do." I didn't even make it to the second paragraph. There were only about half a dozen words I could understand, but I'm pleased to be able to tell you that one of them was 'systematically'.

Despite their qualifications, these two were on the right mental wavelength and just as unhinged as the rest of us. They picked up the dances more or less instantaneously and were out with the side even quicker than that. By the time we made it to the Wessex Ring Meeting in 1982, we couldn't remember a time when Jethro and Vas hadn't been with us, such was their Silurian aura.

Jethro was a big, bearded guy about the size of a grizzly bear. Vas was a smaller bearded guy and nothing like a grizzly bear. Being mad scientists, the beards were standard issue, but useful embellishments nonetheless, as more beard equals less blacking and it helps enormously with the wildman image. These guys were so competent that they quickly became two of our main men and within a year Jethro had been voted in as bagman, so it fell upon him to sort us all out for the trip to Sherborne to see our Wessex friends.

We were to be accommodated in the main hall at Sherborne Grammar School, a fact communicated to us by Jethro one Monday practice night, during the interlude known as 'bagman's business' or, more usually, 'bagbiz'. Getting through the bagbiz interval was always the most difficult part of the bagman's job. He was generally subjected to more heckling than an unpopular parliamentary candidate, or else completely ignored. Either way, there was usually a general hubbub of noise from those who saw the interval as an opportunity to discuss topical issues such as the price of beer, the futility of practicing the dances and the injustice of having to pay to go to a ring meeting.

On top of all that there was Smudge.

A law unto himself at the best of times, this exiled yokel from Ross-on-Wye didn't think like the rest of the side. Come to that, he probably had no parallels anywhere within the vast human species. Those familiar with the writings of Edward de Bono might describe his thought processes as 'lateral', but a more accurate description would be 'tangential'. Thus Smudge's thoughts entered a discussion obliquely, momentarily touching the surface of the conversation before continuing on their pre-destined flight paths. Alarmingly, some of them would fall back into the discussion at some future point and explode like star-burst rockets on Bonfire Night.

On the occasion Jethro was giving us the lowdown on the Sherborne weekend. Smudge was there, ostensibly taking it all in. Jethro, dodging conversational flak, was spelling out the dos and don'ts for us.

"There is a swimming pool at the school," he informed us, in that mellifluous Northumbrian accent, "but, as far as you're concerned, *it doesn't exist*. It is totally *out of bounds* for the duration of the weekend, so you can put it out of your minds as from now."

Noises of dissatisfaction rippled to the surface of the ever-present hubbub. Jethro felt the need to cut any protest short to avoid any pointless argument.

"It's quite simple!" he pointed out, the Geordie in his accent becoming more pronounced as his voice became louder and his eyes more fiery. "There is a pool there, but it is *OUT-OF-BOUNDS*. Under *no* circumstances are we allowed anywhere near it. All you need to know is – IT DOES NOT EXIST!!"

An urgent little wave from Smudge caught Jethro's eye as it roamed authoritatively over the assembly.

"Yes, Smudge," he said in an even tone which clearly translated into, "Don't try anything – I'm not in the mood."

"I just wanted to know . . ." began Smudge, his brow showing signs of heavy thinking, "is it an *indoor* pool or an *outdoor* pool?"

"Is it a *wh-* ?"

Jethro's jaw hit the floor at about the same time as everyone's howls and shrieks of laughter hit the four corners of the room.

Smudge looked around uncomprehendingly. He couldn't see what was so funny. It seemed a perfectly reasonable question to him, the difference between an indoor pool and an outdoor one being sufficient to warrant the inquiry.

"Well, I jus' wanted to know what I was missin'," he muttered, half to himself and half to any sympathiser within earshot.

This was not the first time that a pronouncement from Smudge had reduced us to hysterics. These verbal nuggets were precious beyond gold and hoarded avariciously in the collective memory of the side. We kept them in a little box marked 'Smudgerisms', and I notice many of them have found their way onto the Silurian website. Yet, if you were to meet Smudge, and share with him your enthusiasm for his tangential perception of life, he probably wouldn't understand what you were talking about. He was always totally nonplussed by the mayhem he caused.

For the Wessex trip, a unanimous consensus to forego the luxury of Chris Mulvey's old school van meant that we were to travel down to Dorset in our own cars. Smudge, Mick and Mulvey (as he was more usually known by then) were coming with me in my old Austin Maxi. For all you 21st century readers, that's a bigger version of the original mini, but looked nothing like it. Being in a permanent state of financial distress as a result of being self-employed, the upkeep of my car often slipped down my list of priorities. Thus, on this occasion, I had to warn my passengers that my alternator was on the blink.

"It's no problem though," I assured them with typical male bravado. "As long as we leave in good time and get there before dark, and it doesn't rain, so I don't have to use the lights or the wipers . . . we'll be fine."

Overconfidence, assumption, living life on a roll of the dice – these are not attributes that guarantee positive results.

And so it was that unexpected delays meant we had to revise our Estimated Time of Departure and ended up driving in the dusk on fast-fading headlights about an hour from Sherborne. Negotiating a sharp left-hand bend that I couldn't really judge properly in the light of what had become a couple of pocket torches, the car stalled. With the battery in the grip of rigor mortis, a restart was impossible, so we pushed the car onto the verge and phoned the AA. Which of course, in those days, meant looking for a phone box and having the right coins to operate it.

"About an hour," said the voice in the phone, in estimation of when I could expect the big yellow van, adding, "or so" as a safety factor.

"Buggerit!" said Mulvey, casting me a reproachful look. "We're goin' to miss the crack and the free beer!"

"Sure t'be a pub round yur somewhere," chipped in Smudge in his Herefordshire brogue, "I'll go an' have a mooch."

He wandered off in the dark, leaving the three of us kicking the car and speculating on the good time being had by all in Sherborne. Terminal melancholia was averted just in time by a shout from the darkness and the rare sound of Smudge running.

"I didn't know you could move at that speed," said Mick, voicing his surprise as our recce scout staggered to a halt.

"Never mind that," said Smudge, brushing the comment aside, "I've found it! There *is* a pub yur – and it's got Royal Oak!" His face was a picture of triumph at having flown a successful mission.

"Royal Oak!" he repeated. "*On draught*! Give us yer pots and I'll go an' fill 'em up, and we can take it in turns to be beer runner."

We didn't say anything. Impressed by his sniffer-dog ability to home in on a pub, not to mention this display of latent organisational ability in masterminding the supply run, we were dumbstruck as we handed over our tankards. Smudge faded into the darkness again as he headed off to fill our pots with Royal Oak, the local strong ale – one on our list of favourites. No longer worried about the car, the ring meeting or anything else, Smudge was giving us all a lesson in living for the moment.

Needless to say, we were well into the 'or so' period by the time the AA arrived to sort out the car. The Royal Oak had done some damage by then. Our mood had become sunnily optimistic, even though an unsteady totter had affected our gait. Being the driver, I had been exercising a commendable degree of caution and self-control in my consumption of beer. But this brew was unexpectedly potent. I was feeling very fuzzy round the edges by the time we hit Sherborne . . . and the car hit a bollard which I hadn't seen in the car park.

Arriving at our school hall accommodation, we noticed our lads were there in force, putting themselves about in a manner which suggested they had taken full advantage of the free beer. We tried not to get upset by the memory of having to pay for ours. It turned out, however, that the others had also left a bit late and decided they wouldn't arrive in time for the free beer. They too had stopped off for a couple of drinks on the way down, and had in fact arrived not long before us.

Willy and Burco had clearly applied the 'one for the road' principle, which had affected their behaviour accordingly. Willy especially was in a dangerously mischievous mood, particularly evidenced when he hid Jethro's bag, knowing it contained some pills vital to Jethro's health and stability of temperament. He also knew that Jethro had a short fuse. He waited quietly for the fireworks to begin.

We were standing around in small groups, laughing, chatting and swapping stories about the trip down. Mick was talking at a Wessex man, demonstrating why he was known to some people as Mick the Mouth. No one had noticed Jethro frantically but unsuccessfully looking for his bag. In the midst of the chat and banter, Jethro suddenly loomed up, blocking out the light. A wild look was in his eye and anger in his face after his frantic and fruitless search. His Northumbrian voice boomed out.

"Right! Now listen to me, you lot!"

A small percentage of those present became aware of an angry bear in their midst. The rest of them were oblivious.

"Ah'm going to count to three," continued Jethro with low menace, "and if someone doesn't tell me where mah kit is, ah'm going to smack the person nearest me."

His black brows twitched, and he gave us all the benefit of one more manic flash of the eyes before slowly counting, "One . . . two . . . three . . ."

SMACK!

Mick, the person nearest him, was on his back and about ten yards from the spot his feet has recently occupied.

"What the *fuckin' hell's happening here*!?" he screamed as he got to his feet, face flushed with a look of such terrible anger that Jethro's seemed quite benign by comparison.

"Ah want me bloody kit!" shouted Jethro, undeterred by Mick's fury.

"Well, *I haven't bloody got it*, have I, you tosser!?"

"Ah don't know and ah don't care – ah just want it back! And me pills! Okay?"

During the ensuing attempts to restrain them, someone suggested they might like to talk to Willy as he may know something about the mysterious disappearance of the kit. Mick and Jethro stormed off to look for him. By the time Mick caught up with Willy he was in a murderous mood. With Mick's fists firmly gripping his lapels, the back of Willy's head made contact with the wall several times in quick succession, whilst Mick's cat-o'-nine-tails tongue lashed and whipped him into submission.

"And if you try to pull another stunt like that, I *will* fucking kill you!" warned Mick, the pugnacious Irish side of his character now in full view.

Jethro, meanwhile, had located his bag and the vitally important pills, which had inexplicably reappeared right next to his intended sleeping space. He'd had about enough for the night and was content just to bed down. The rest of us felt that perhaps the evening had come to a natural end, so we were all unfurling sleeping bags and making ourselves comfortable. Having narrowly escaped the jaws of death, Willy was now hiding under a table at one side of the hall, half-hidden by the paper tablecloth above and seemingly content to spend the night there.

Without warning, somebody switched off the lights.

"Chris'sake – put the lights on!" shouted Willy from under the table.

"No! Go to sleep!"

"I can't see a bloody thing under here," Willy grumbled.

Suddenly he could. The hall was lit up by the flames ripping through the white paper tablecloth above Willy's head.

"That's better," he said, putting away his Zippo lighter.

An impromptu chorus of *Light My Fire* had started up in the gloom at the far end of the hall, whilst a couple of volunteer firefighters leapt into action to douse the flames. Even Willy settled down after this, but Mick was still fuming, even as he dozed off, muttering to himself about how he was going to wreak terrible vengeance on 'that mad bastard' in the morning.

The tone for the weekend had been set.

Mick was still bellicose the next morning, glowering under a heavy frown. Willy, instinctually growing into his predestined role of the Fool, was unrepentant, happy in the knowledge that life is one big experiment into which one can inject random inputs in order to observe the results. Dave Jones was the one most damaged by the antics of the previous evening, clearly suffering a painful degree of embarrassment at the behaviour of his boys.

Wessex, unperturbed by it all, just wanted to see if we had mastered the Vanishing Beer Trick. To that effect, they had organised a pub crawl (with some dancing thrown in to justify dressing up) starting at the premises of one financially motivated landlord who was prepared to open up at 10 o'clock in the morning. We took up the challenge without hesitation, confident that we could drink and equally certain that we could dance. We saw no reason why these two disciplines should be mutually exclusive. Some morris sides are into serious dancing and will not allow the demon drink to mar their performance. Others use the dancing as an excuse to drink, with insufficient care being dedicated to the quality of the performance. Silurian's ethos was to deliver street theatre at its best and then to reward ourselves with a pint or so of good ale. As we have seen from the AA call-out service, the 'or so' factor is usefully flexible. But keeping it in check can be more difficult than walking a swaying tightrope . . .

We kept up with the drinking pace set by Wessex, but we also maintained the standard of dancing set by ourselves. At the end of the day, our reputation for dancing was intact and we were still perpendicular, except for those of us with a naturally crouching stance – naming no names of course. The side had suffered a number of internal squabbles during the day, little ripples that lapped the shores of the previous night's memories, but nothing too disastrous. At one stage, Willy emptied a plate of food over Smudge's new hat and, at another, Willy was frogmarched to a village pond for a ducking, but the perpetrators lost their nerve at the last minute. After all, a musician of Willy's calibre was not an asset that should be thus abused, whatever his shortcomings.

The Saturday night feast came and went without further incident. Unlike some ring meetings, the proceedings that evening were going at some pace, ending in time for a swift visit to the local hostelry before last orders. One of the Wessex men, convinced by then that we had mastered The Trick, promised to reward us by organising a raiding party on the beer stocks in the dinner hall after the pubs had closed and as soon as it was safe.

"You'll know it's me," he said, "cos I'll bring m' parrot with me."

Around midnight, always the right time for any nefarious goings-on, Mick, Mulvey, Smudge and I met our man from Wessex outside in the school grounds. He looked a bit odd. Was it the moon lighting up his bright-white knee-length socks? Or was it just the parrot on his shoulder? Closer inspection of his avian companion revealed it to be life-sized but made of plastic, frozen in mid-squawk even when his perch bent down to tie up a shoelace.

With appropriate furtiveness, we skulked down to the dinner hall like a gang of Victorian grave robbers. On arrival, our guide went round the whole building checking to see if anything had been left open, while we stood round conveniently merging with the shadows. We were still in kit, but had taken the precaution of removing our bells and donning black tailcoats, an increasingly popular new line in Silurian outerwear. We were thus virtually invisible. Our patrol leader soon returned from his sortie and informed us that the only way in was through the ventlight of the window in the ladies' toilet – and it was 'up there' about seven feet off the ground. We walked round to have a look.

"Right then, Chris," said Mick, "In you go!"

"Eh?"

"You're the man for the job," I informed him. "All your experience in the building trade – you know about windows and heights an' all that sort of stuff."

"Sod off!" he said, "I'm not going through that tiny hole. Whaddya think I am – a cat?"

"No. You're just thinner than the rest of us." And, with that, we yanked him off his feet, hoisted him up and stuffed him in the ventlight, deaf to his muffled protests.

Once inside, he groped his way to the back door, opened it from inside and let us in. Then we all fumbled our way to the kitchens where the barrels were set up. Reaching the kitchen door first, the Phantom Wessex Parrotman attempted to open it, but . . .

"Shit!" he cursed, "It's locked!"

I tried to think of something helpful to say.

"Lemme 'ave a go," volunteered Smudge, pushing against the door. "Oh – you're roight. The bugger's locked."

"Shit!" repeated Parrotman. He seemed a bit agitated.

"Don't blame me," I said defensively, "I'm only the triangle player!"

Mulvey extracted a small cigar from a packet of five and fretfully lit it up. He looked justifiably upset, his eyes lasering out of the dark and targeting the bobbing parrot and the human who was dangling from its foot.

"You mean to tell me that I've forced me way through that rat trap of a window, riskin' life and limb – and other bits – just to find this place *locked*!?" What's your game, eh?"

"Wass your game?" the parrot seemed to squawk.

"Hang on, hang on," Mick cut in, using his college mediator voice and demonstrating his Libran tendency to always weigh the alternatives. "Are you sure it opens that way?"

"'Course I am!" responded the irritated Parrotman, the confidence in his voice tinged with exasperation, "I put the stuff in there, didn't I?" The parrot was dipping up and down on his shoulder, obviously in total agreement. You could almost hear it saying, "Put the stuff in there! Eerrk!"

"Well, let me just try it," said Mick, patience personified. We couldn't argue with his classroom tone, honed to perfection during his years as a teacher. He turned the handle and pulled the door towards him.

"Oh!" said Parrotman.

"Violà!" said Mick in fluent French, demonstrating that opening doors was not his only talent.

"Come on then," Mulvey urged, "let's get in there! No point in standin' out here gawpin' at the door, is there?"

In silent agreement, we filed in, tankards at the ready, to enjoy what we considered to be a well-earned private drinks party until the early hours of Sunday morning.

During the *later* hours of Sunday morning, and indeed into the early afternoon, I spent the time sobering up for the long drive home, whilst my three passengers made up for my abstinence by drinking the beers I couldn't touch. As an academic exercise, we worked out from the money we had left how much ale we had consumed over the weekend. It turned out to be somewhere in the region of forty pints each, including the freebies. Thank goodness we hadn't been with Willy and Burco, otherwise we'd have been in real trouble – and no money left at all.

To some, this might look like nothing more than typical male bravado, but I can assure you it is not. It is easy to assess it with modern eyes and see nothing but the reflection of disenfranchised youth ravaged by the dystopia of 21st Century life, running amok in weekend city binges. But, to Silurian 35 years ago, it was simply part of the process. To tot up a weekend's beer consumption was not to put our name into some hall of fame; it was to reflect on the events of the weekend and evaluate our competence as performers. Whether by instinct or persuasion, we were aware that intoxicating substances were, and probably always had been, essential to the idea of important ritual ceremonies. We had sung *John Barleycorn* often enough to understand its importance as a homage to good ale, and there were those amongst us who grasped the deeper and ancient significance of the story. We clearly saw the metaphor of life, death and rebirth. The long roots of this universally popular folk song grew in the same direction as those of the morris.

For us, good real ale loosened us up. It banished inhibition, enhanced our edginess, buoyed our bravado. Quite simply, it lit our fire. There is evidence from ritual practices around the world that heady potions and mind-altering substances are ubiquitous in these ceremonies. We were being innately authentic. We didn't drink to get drunk, but to get 'high' – 'out of our minds' you might say – the better to execute the dance. Thus, despite this level of consumption, we had managed to maintain our acclaimed standard of dancing. Only Jonesy and a couple of the wets looked perturbed. But they needn't have worried. Our overriding sense of unity had carried us through a difficult weekend. That indefinable quality that kept us all under the Silurian spell was strong enough to put our squabbles into perspective and keep us focused on the performance, ready for our next appearance.

Chapter 11

The Boar's Head and the Bunny Girl

• • • • •

"Onward Christian soldiers,
Marching as to war,
With the cross of Jesus
Going on before..."

The week after Wessex, we were off again. Another visit to Geordieland, but this time in something actually resembling a minibus. For all its comfort, however, it was still a tedious journey up the motorway, and we had to travel a long way before finding any worthwhile views from the window.

As we traversed the industrial sprawl that fills the north midlands with too many pylons, buildings and roads, I became bored by the lack of external stimulus. My mind began to wander, humming to itself and peering into the dark caverns of my brain. Always inquisitive and always on the lookout for more information to analyse or problems to solve, my busy brain never kept still. I was known by some as a worrier, but the reality was I just liked untying knots. There is a certain satisfaction in being handed a jumbled heap of interwoven knots and conjuring from it an unbroken length of string.

Unable to find anything inspirational in the panorama of industrial wastelands, my mind dragged out a favourite old ball to play with. I found it in the box marked 'How to Run a Small

Business', a pursuit in which I had been engaged for seven years by then, and the box was full of tangled what-ifs, hows, whens, with-whats and yes-buts.

"Who do these bank managers think they are?" I thought to myself, my mind tugging at the first loose end it saw. "They are in the business of lending money – but they don't do that unless you can prove you don't need it."

We all know what banks are like, particularly in the first couple of decades of the 21st Century, but back in the 1980s you could still get to talk to a 'bank manager' rather than a computer screen. The main difference is that if you give a computer a good kicking, as you might today, nothing much happens, but if you gave a bank manager a smack on the nose, he started bleeding. Either way, the bank still sues for damages.

Bank philosophy hasn't changed much over the years. It's still a case of, "If you get to the top of the cliff, we'll lend you a rope." Or, in the case of an overdraft, "Here's an umbrella, but if it rains we want it back." In 1982, I had become painfully aware of this 'heads-we-win-tails-you-lose' ethos. Having invested a small amount of money in a good idea in 1975, the clothes manufacturing business this had generated had grown to a point where, to fund the bulging order book, its financial requirements had outstripped its available collateral. The bank informed us that they could "no longer see our way clear to extending our financial support without further security from yourselves." We were about to go bust even though we had a fistful of orders from some of the top shops in the country. Insane. According to our accountant at the time, this is known as 'overtrading'.

I was fretfully tugging at this cluster of knots when Mick's voice floated into my brain to bring me back to another plane of reality.

"I hope we don't get given any more of that whisky," he said.

"What whisky?" I asked, puzzled.

"You remember," he prompted. "When we stayed with that Monkseaton guy last time."

Instantly, it all came back to me. During the Folkmoot weekend, Mick and I had stayed with a Monkseaton man who was into classical music and serious whisky. On discovering that we too were partial to a wee dram of the Water of Life, he informed us that he had a spot of something special that we might enjoy. He placed on the turntable his favourite recording of Beethoven's 4th Piano Concerto and nipped out of the room. As we settled into the piano intro, he returned immediately with a suspicious-looking bottle devoid of labels or other identity marks.

"Try some of that," he said, pouring us a tot each.

Eyeing it warily, and sniffing for any clues as to its origin, I surmised that it bore a passing resemblance to some of the single malts I had in my cellar, but with an afterburn that prompted a mental note to keep it away from naked flames. Guardedly I took a little sip. Coinciding with the entry of the strings in Beethoven's 4th, something exploded in the back of my throat and fumes leapt through my nasal passages like paint stripper on a door.

"I've been sabotaged," I thought. By way of confirmation, the warm feeling at the end of my nose turned out to be a full-scale nosebleed.

"Back in a bobent," I informed the gathering as I jumped out of my chair and headed for the bathroom, fingers clamping my nose. Having mopped up the blood, I returned to the room and demanded of our host the suspect source of this lethal potion.

"Oh," he replied casually, "I got it from a friend of a friend who knows someone who goes fishing who knows someone else who works at a distillery."

"Oh, right," I said, as if this circuitous route was the normal means of acquiring a bottle of whisky. "So what exactly is it – *rocket fuel*?"

"No, it's . . . er . . . the stuff they take off the top of the still. They have to throw it away, and this fellow thinks that's a waste, so he brings it home when no one's looking."

"But it's illegal, isn't it?" questioned Mick.

"Well . . . er . . ."

"Because it kills people," continued Mick, who had inherited from his Irish family a clutch of stories about *poteen* and its effects.

Our genial host seemed unfazed, and pulled the stopper from the bottle again, moving towards my glass. Not wishing to appear impolite, I informed him that the stuff was 'interesting' but that I would regretfully have to decline his offer of a top-up, but that a new nose would be very handy.

"Yeah, I certainly do remember it!" I said to Mick. It was the only whisky that had ever caused me physical injury. "I'll just stick to the beer this time," I concluded, turning to the window to check our whereabouts.

"Are we there yet?" came a predictable voice from the back of the bus.

"Nearly," answered our driver, Mike Massey, ex-policeman and dependable member of the side, "only about three hours to go!"

"Aw, rats!"

Time passed, as it does. At the speed of light when you are enjoying yourself; painfully slowly when on a motorway in an industrial wasteland. But eventually we got there and even managed to find the right location, where we were greeted by our Monkseaton hosts.

What we had actually signed up to, in what might have been seen as an act of pure folly, was another Ale. Our justification, however, was that this one was in honour of Father Ken Loveless, who was coming to the end of his two-year stint as Squire of the Ring. He was such a charismatic character that he had become a favourite figure amongst the morris fraternity. With his aquiline nose, balding pate and close-trimmed pointy beard, his face was unmistakeable. His love of life, and especially morris life, showed up in his twinkling eyes. As an elder statesman of the morris revival in this country, he was invited to most get-togethers and could usually be spotted somewhere, cradling his concertina and sucking on one of his vast collection of Meerschaum pipes.

Although we 'adopted' him at our ring meeting, a great many sides had conferred upon him honorary membership, a phrase too formal for Silurian. Adoption implies something far more friendly, though Father Ken might have said that being adopted by a bunch of lunatics was an undeserved fate for a cultured and erudite man of the cloth. We did treat him with care and respect though, and never wound him up too far. Our pranks were mild by our usual standards, as exemplified by a little interlude on the Sunday at the Bristol ring meeting. All the sides had gathered for the procession to the church. All except Silurian, that is. Everyone, including Father Ken, was waiting for us. We had decided that the Reverend Loveless deserved a grand entrance from us, so we held back until the procession was ready to move, at which point we appeared stage left, slow marching to *Onward Christian Soldiers*, Mike Rust at the head of the band, holding aloft two sticks in the shape of a cross. We stopped when we reached Father Ken.

In his deep educated tones, the plum of received pronunciation moving easily around his mouth, he pronounced meticulously, "Oh, you Silurians – you are some wags!"

Little did he know then that our paths would converge in Monkseaton, where we were about to pull another stunt to commemorate his time as squire. With everybody present in the dining hall and the party about to start, Jethro, in his role as our bagman – and the only one amongst us with an accent that revealed his local roots – announced to the assembled company that, following our previous adoption of the good reverend, we were going to make him a Silurian man for the night, even though he was dressed in the Cotswold kit of Greensleeves Morris. Without further ceremony, and giving him no time to escape, his face was blacked up and a bowler placed on his shiny head. He accepted this mild molestation in good spirit and wore the blacking and the bowler for the rest of the evening.

The food was sumptuous. Forget the usual fare that typified these occasions – filling and uncomplicated. This was high class catering, undertaken mostly by the Monkseaton ladies. And it was not just the food that made the evening truly memorable.

When all the guests were seated, their hunger turning to anticipation of satiation, the last-minute babble, scraping of chairs and general noise suddenly died. All heads turned as one to the haunting electrifying sound of Northumbrian pipes, whose tinkling staccato notes danced into the room trailed by their hypnotic drones. Through the door the piper came, in traditional plaid and cockaded hat, escorting a glazed and decorated boar's head carried into the room on a huge silver platter. This was placed on the top table and, in acknowledgement of the guest of honour, was adorned with the Reverend's black biretta and one of his Meerschaum pipes.

The instrumentalist was no less an individual than the Duke of Northumberland's personal piper, one Richard Butler. It was instantly obvious how he had achieved this high status. As the evening proceeded, we were treated to many more tunes from this master musician, during which his transfixed and captivated audience uttered no sound. The notes just skipped out from under his fingers, stilling the whole room and bathing it in a spell of sound as the tunes ran freely into every hidden corner and crevice of the hall. As each tune ended, the sound of the last note ignited an explosion of appreciation, but all the clapping and cheering could never measure the depth of what we all felt. Music like this really does touch the soul. Played on an instrument hand-made with love and a deep understanding of the true essence of place, these tunes were full of the colour, the beauty, the majesty, the spirit of Northumbria. It is a musical language with a greater vocabulary than mere words. Those who dismiss such music as just a bit of folksy rubbish are missing something truly precious.

Music is a fundamental form of human expression that should be unencumbered by the restrictive practice of labelling and categorising. The dedicated rock fan who dismisses folk music as the stuff of the jumper-and-sandals brigade is denying himself as much as the classical pianist who dismisses all popular music as mind-numbing noise. To deny your soul access to the sparkling beauty of a simple melody played on an unaccompanied instrument, like the Northumbrian pipes, is to diminish the experience of life and remove much of its richness and basic human quality.

Richard Butler's presence and the piping-in of the boar's head were not the only surprises in store for us that evening. At some morris events, outside caterers can be called in to manage the food, and waitress service is often provided, so it is not unusual to see females at these all-male gatherings. I know I am at this point risking the introduction of all sorts of images of patriarchal dominance and the subservience of women, neither of which I subscribe to, but let's not go there. A whole book could be dedicated to that subject.

So, back in the dining hall that night, the Monkseaton WAGs were in charge of operations, which included serving the food. Anyone who has read *The Invisible Gorilla* will understand clearly that we imperfect humans often do not visually register something if we are not expecting to see it. Thus no one noticed anything out of the ordinary when the first course was brought in and a bowl of soup was placed in front of each man. It was only when the girls turned their backs on us to return to the kitchen that some of us noticed – they were all dressed as Bunny Girls!

Now, speaking for myself, I have a very limited tolerance of American culture and I find the cartoon image of the Playboy Bunny Girl particularly abhorrent. But that doesn't mean I am going to be the token killjoy when a group of women choose unanimously to dress up in a certain way, and I thought they did a brilliant job with this unexpected costume, adding something original to the festive atmosphere.

Smudge was so busy talking that he didn't notice the appearance of a bowl of soup, let alone a Bunny Girl.

I gave him a dig in the ribs. "Smudge!"

"What?"

I indicated the white bob of a tail on its way back to the kitchen.

"Corrr – *bloody hell*!" An interesting choice of words, considering that he must have thought he had died and gone to heaven. "Fishnet tights an' all!" he added.

With his eyes bulging but maintaining their concentration on the receding tail, Smudge picked up his soup spoon, no doubt thinking that a fixed stare would look less conspicuous if he was seen to be doing something . . . and having a spoon moving towards his mouth might help to explain the lolling tongue. Mechanically, he lifted his spoon several times to his pursed lips but, due to a technical malfunction, very little soup found its way to his taste buds. His spoon was upside down. Smudge was oblivious, his thought processes completely tied up with the problem of which chat-up line was needed to precipitate a close liaison with one of these scantily clad waitresses.

I nudged Vas and pointed at Smudge's spoon. This prompted a suppressed snort of laughter.

"Pass it on," I suggested quietly.

Within a few seconds, Smudge had become the focus of attention, and the volume of laughter was enough to break his trance. He looked around him and, realising he was the only one not laughing, deduced that he was probably the object of our mirth.

"What!?" he demanded. "Wossa matter?"

Gurgling laughter prevented anyone from saying anything coherent, but a lot of finger-pointing was going on.

"Eh?"

"Your *spoon*!" I finally managed to say.

"Eh? Oh . . ." said Smudge, looking at the utensil for the first time. "Well, oi was thinkin' about summat else, wasn't I?"

Well, of course he was. The summat else in question was never far from his thoughts. We knew (unlike the waitresses, to whom Smudge was just another black-faced morrisman) that any one of these women coming within grabbing distance of him was going to have a hard time shaking him off. Predictably, Smudge was on heat now and, in order to protect the waitresses, we had to talk to him like you might talk to your dog misbehaving in the park. "*No*, Smudge, she is *not* gaggin' for it, whatever you might think. She's just trying to clear the table, okay?"

The girls took it in good spirit, and in any case they probably predicted that there was going to be at least one lecherous lunatic in the room that night. I'm sure they all knew they would cause a stir anyhow, and it probably came as no surprise to them that, amongst other things, their fluffy white tails were soon being coveted as collectable trophies. I am honoured to report that Silurian was the only side to have liberated one of these prizes, and it was my own nimble fingers that did the necessary. Many times that evening was I offered big money for that tail, but it was not for sale. By the time I hung up my bowler in 1998, the tail was still fixed to the back of it, though it was in a pretty sorry state by then, after well over a decade of fair wear and tear. As I write this now, my bowler rests in a cupboard in my room, with what is left of that tail still clinging to the hat's sash.

It was actually the next day, with the risk of theft gone, that I fixed my trophy to the hat, travelling back down the motorway safe in Silurian company. I knew none of the lads would take it from me after I had personally captured it from behind enemy lines, so to speak. Each man's hat was a personal statement, and any decoration on my bowler would make no sense on someone else's.

As we travelled, we held the usual post mortem. We were pleased for Father Ken, whose obvious enjoyment shone in the beatific smile he wore all evening. We were unanimous in our praise for Richard Butler, though some of us felt he might have been a trifle warm wearing about forty yards of thick plaid cloth.

If he was, he didn't show it. As for the food and the waitresses who served it, we ran out of superlatives to describe the experience. Smudge merely mumbled a bit, gazing lasciviously into the middle distance and dreaming of what might have been.

Stories were swapped regarding the latter part of the evening, when the tables were stacked to make space for dancing. This was the cue for Silurian to meander freely until called upon to demonstrate a couple of Border numbers. Less dancing of course meant more drinking, with predictable consequences. Vas and I told our story of how, at about two o'clock in the morning, we had attempted to teach a six-man Cotswold dance to two Northwest guys. That represented a number of challenges. The two dancers had to attempt to be all six dancers at once and, in the absence of musicians at that late hour, I hummed the tune whilst Vas directed the dance. Such antics proved once again that alcohol, like advertising, will con you 'into thinking you're the one that can do what's never been done', as Bob Dylan told us all those years ago.

Trumping our story, Mike Massey prefaced his own with, "That's nothing . . ."

"I wasn't going to kip on the floor in the hall," he continued, "so I thought I'd sleep in the van. Nice bit of peace and quiet, comfy seats. So I settled down and pretty soon I was asleep."

He paused for dramatic effect. Inevitably, someone said, "So? What happened?" There's always one.

"So then," Mike continued, "I'm dreaming away, and I dream I'm out at sea and my little boat is rocking and the seas are getting higher, and I've got to start baling out. So I'm thinking about where the bucket is."

"Don't tell me – you pissed yourself," came a suggestion from the depths of the bus.

"No!" said Mike. "Then *I woke up*. And I'm lying awake and thinking, 'it's the van that's rocking, not the boat.' And then I hear this moaning from outside."

Another dramatic pause. Enough to get Smudge interested.

"Yeah. So?" he prompted.

"So I roll down the window and stick my head out . . . and it's a couple having it off right up against the side of the van!"

"Bloody Geordies!" said Smudge. "No bloody manners!" He went silent after this appraisal, doubtlessly wishing it had been him and one of the Bunny Girls.

"We know what you're thinking, Smudge," Mick informed him. We did know. And Smudge knew that we knew.

"Huh! Huh! Huh!" was his only reply.

Following Mike's story, silence descended for a while.

"Are we there yet?" came a voice from the back of the bus.

"Nearly," answered our driver, "only about three hours to go!"

"Aw, rats!"

Chapter 12
Frankenstein's Monster

• • • • •

"I am an antichrist,
I am an anarchist.
Dunno what I want,
But I know how to get it..."

We used to think it was only Jonesy who had kids, but suddenly it seemed there were kids everywhere. Even I had one. "It's a boy, and it's called George!" Dizzy had replied emphatically to all enquiries regarding her rounded midriff. Those people born under the sign of Aries invariably think they are right. And she was.

I welcomed this latest member of the Elliott clan most enthusiastically. Watching his daily progress in adapting to his new world gave me a warm feeling (especially when he was sitting in my lap without a nappy). Initial fears brought on by his uncanny resemblance to my brother were calmed when I remembered my younger sibling was in New Zealand and had been for years, not just the last nine months. So George was accepted as the rightful heir to all my worldly goods, including a moss green pottery piggy bank (containing fourteen and sixpence in old money) and a signed copy of *John Lee Hooker Plays The Blues* – signed: 'This record belongs to Adrian Cummings'.

On the Boxing Day tour in 1982, when the heir to the Elliott millions had passed his third annual milestone, the lunchtime pub stop looked more like a kindergarten tea party. There were small kids and big kids – kids inside and kids outside. There were toddlers immobilised in buggies, and others risking life and mobility by tottering across the flightpath to the dartboard. In dark corners, fretful mums were soothing crying babes or conducting a furtive nappy change. Everywhere the whiff of Johnson's Baby Powder mingled with the usual pubby smells.

New tricks had been mastered by Silurian, such as how to balance an infant in one hand whilst juggling a pint, a cigarette and a ploughman's lunch in the other. Up at the bar, frowns could be detected on blacked-up faces as increasingly long orders were being processed by brains accustomed to ordering in pints. The barman meanwhile patiently stood by, with a customer-is-always-right smile and thoughts of "why didn't I take up market gardening?" running around his head.

"Right, sir – that's your two pints. Anything else?"

"Er . . . yes . . . half a lager, please."

"Lager. Righty-oh. Stella, Harp or Carling Black Label?"

"Er . . . um . . . actually I think she said 'pills' or something."

"Pils? Okay. Löwenbräu or Holstein?"

"Oh! Ummm . . ."

"Holstein is the most popular."

"Okay, let's go for that."

"Thank you, sir. Is that the lot?"

"Yes, thanks . . . errm . . . I mean, No. Two bottles of lemonade as well, please. With straws."

"Thank you, sir. Two pounds thirty-nine then, please."

"Oh, sorry – just remembered. Two packets of crisps. Sorry!"

Customer-is-always-right smile vanishes. Replaced by pursed lips and frosty stare. Patient barman resists impulse to drum fingers on bar top.

"Two packets of crisps . . ." he says, eyes narrowing. "What flavour? Cheese and onion, Smoky Bacon, Roast Chicken . . ."

"Just plain, thanks."

"There you are then. Two packets of plain crisps. Thank you, sir. That'll be . . ."

"Could you make that *three* packets? Sorry – I forgot. The missis wants a packet. Oh, and could I order some food too?"

The barman wants to say, "Yes, as long as you order it in a café in the next town," but he doesn't. He needs a breather, so he settles for, "Can I just serve this lady first?"

Under the burden of complicated bar orders and the need to negotiate the obstacle course of small children across the barroom floor, a number of Silurian men were left with frayed nerves. They felt more like daft prats in fancy dress than invincible warriors guarding lesser mortals from the malice of evil spirits or helping to open portals to the other world. We were supposed to be awe-inspiring. We were supposed to unsettle women and children, not buy them lemonade and crisps.

Whilst some of us were mentally grappling with the challenges of reconciling the conflicting interests of Morris and Family, Dave Jones was quite happy to combine the two. It was all folk to him. Jonesy had survived as a widower with four children for a while and subsequently met and married the lovely Annie, who arrived with three children of her own. His inclination to combine his activities was therefore partly motivated by necessity. But he loved his 'family weekends'. All of his extended family had some musical talent, and Jonesy used to line them up to do a spot or two at these gatherings, many of which he had organised himself. Inevitably they became known as the Von Jones Family, an epithet he loved, but the idea of becoming family-orientated was not sitting well with some of us.

It had been less than a decade since the concept of Silurian as a Welsh Border side had first taken root in Jonesy's head. We admired his tenacity in tackling the smug devotees of Cecil Sharp. He was assertively determined to prove to them that Cotswold morris was a derivative of Welsh Border and that the latter was not some withered branch of this dance form, but a main root. His enthusiasm for the cause fired us all with the same resolve and we set out to prove Jonesy's point. We successfully rekindled the fire, putting life and energy into the Morris. We walked tall, with the air of victorious warriors. In our more fanciful moments, we saw ourselves as the original Silures, a marauding tribe of Welshmen who used to kick hell out of the English. Symbolically, we were doing the same thing. Yet our glorious leader was limping.

In 1984, marking seven years as a full-time Border side, we were gathering pace all the time, moving unknowingly towards a tipping point. Jonesy, however, preoccupied with a large family, Bromyard Folk Festival and other projects (not least of which was an ongoing extensive renovation of outbuildings at his home) seemed to have relaxed. He was absolutely content that Silurian was recognised as a Border side – to some even *the* Border side. Having reached this pinnacle, his main aim was to concentrate on keeping up the standard. This translated into: practice, practice, practice. It became a hard slog of endless repetition. Internal dissent was growing like a fog bank.

The whole thing was still very much the Dave Jones Show and he remained the main figurehead. It seemed that at any one time he was squire, bagman or foreman, sometimes occupying two of these positions simultaneously. This left little opportunity for keen new members to demonstrate any latent leadership skills, and it left most of the decision-making to Jonesy, who was thus a major influence on policy, including which events to attend. Though the wets were happy enough with this situation, we didn't put any store by their opinions, as a number of them had been virtually press-ganged by Jonesy into joining and never really became part of the Silurian corpus.

Those of us who felt strongly about the ideals, principles and ethos we had embraced, had very definite views on the direction we should be taking. We were not big fans of the family weekend and we didn't enjoy dancing at fetes, carnivals and Ales. They were fine for the usual sort of morris displays, but we weren't the usual sort of morris. Mystery, electrifying performances and receptive audiences were what we thrived on, which demanded total commitment to those ideas. It was impossible to achieve this if there was a family to look after at the same time. The lack of interest amongst audiences at fetes and carnivals was another depressant. Thus the radical element in the side looked to break new ground, seeking unknown venues and audiences. We preferred it if our reputation arrived before us. It gave us the challenge of defending our status.

Discontented grumblings were peaking as 1982 came to an end, but were put on temporary hold by the optimism that usually sweeps in with the New Year. Plus we had two bookings in Northwest Morris country to raise our spirits and move our troubles to the back burner for a while. Both bookings were technically family weekends, but we got around this problem by not taking ours.

All weekends away, whether good or bad, left memories which infused and expanded our own mythology. Our visit to Preston, the first of our Northwest destinations, proved the rule. Our hosts, the impressively named Preston Royal Morris Dancers, had organised a dance spot in the centre of the city in front of the war memorial, an imposing monument surrounded by a square of steps.

Adorning those steps as we approached was a random collection of Preston's punk element, sadly out of touch with the fact that, in the Deep South of England, punk had been swallowed whole by the rabid media at the end of the 1970s. Stripped of any commercially potent assets, chewed up and spat out, the punk movement in London was like the undead – walking wraiths with a lost cause. Not in Preston though. Here they were still built in the image of the Sex Pistols, fancying themselves as anarchic antichrists. They sprawled around the memorial, staking their territorial claim with a 20-foot radius of crushed lager cans, cigarette ends and chip papers.

Sewn up with safety pins, studded dog collars and chains, these punks began jeering as soon as we entered their domain. Their clothing was uniformly drab, except for the guy with the skin-tight red tartan trousers held together with an intricate system of zips. What they lacked in sartorial clout, however, they made up for with their spiky day-glo hair. Whilst we discussed amongst ourselves which dances to do, the heckling continued unabated. Indignant at our proximity to their own personal area of the city, they hurled abusive salvos over our heads, and colourfully worded suggestions as to what we might like to do with our sticks. For good measure they threw in some racially charged comments alluding to the colour of our faces.

Undeterred, we opened the show with an energetic number to set the tone for the rest of the performance. The punks all went quiet. Their taunting bravado vanished in the face of this onslaught of Wild Morris. As the performance continued, they became mildly receptive and then seriously attentive, responding passively to the banter we were now throwing back at them. We gave them Bromsberrow Heath with all the energy we could muster, smashing and splintering several sticks, before finishing with Fanny Frail, playing heavily on the sexual imagery. As we danced off, the punks stared in amazement at the splinters and broken sticks that littered the area. One or two of them, now completely docile, were gathered around John Willy, plying him with questions. In his guardsman's tunic and round gold-rimmed glasses, he was no longer a figure of fun but a fellow outlaw, and one to be admired. For these Johnny Rotten fans, Willy had become a real live antichrist.

Setting off for the next spot, the last thing we saw was two of these heavy-booted outcasts slide off the memorial steps and surreptitiously pick up a couple of broken sticks as souvenirs before slinking down the road, Mohican haircuts swaying stiffly in the breeze.

Our hosts were already retelling this story even before the weekend was done, and indeed it preceded us to Saddleworth Rushcart Festival a couple of months later, our second Northwest excursion that year. This traditional festival was a pure delight, put on for the benefit of local people rather than passing tourists. Also, in the north-west counties of England, morris dancing was simply part of the festival scene, not some fancy revivalist thing. The candid naturalness this bestowed upon the participants created a relaxed, friendly atmosphere – even when man-handling a heavy farm cart stacked impossibly high with a towering rick of rushes.

Essentially, the tradition was to venture onto the moors above the town, cut bundles of rushes and load them onto a cart for ease of haulage to the local church. Creating a festival out of this involved press-ganging a bunch of unsuspecting 'volunteers' to pull this cart literally up hill and down dale over a 10-mile route around five of the local towns, calling at various local hostelries en route for much-needed and well-earned refreshment. The devious and bizarre ideas grown men will come up with as an excuse to go to the pub always amaze me.

This little tour took up all of Saturday, but there was more to come. On the Sunday, the cart had to be pulled from its overnight resting place at The Commercial Hotel in Uppermill (the chief amongst the five towns) straight up the hill to St Chad's Church, a heart-pounding two miles. On arrival, the rushes would be spread out over the church floor as insulation over the winter. St Chad's was not remote as such, but there were only two other buildings close to it – the Church Inn and the Cross Keys, a fortuitous and not uncommon example of community care. Following the church service (for all except Silurian!), the rest of the day was spent meandering between the two pubs to catch the variety of events, competitions and dance displays taking place outside each of them.

With its beautiful location, its friendly atmosphere and the absolute lunacy of hauling a cart stacked with a 12-foot tower of rushes, to say nothing of a church snuggled between a brace of pubs, the Rushcart Festival was one of the best events we had ever attended. When we were invited to return the following year, we were ecstatic. But Jonesy lit the blue touch paper again when he suggested it would be a bad idea because of the danger of overkill.

"Well, you'd know something about overkill, wouldn't you, Dave?" came a sotto voce response when this announcement was made to us one practice night.

"Always hogging the spot," agreed another quiet murmur.

"Yeah – always doing about four bloody dances too many," chipped in Smudge.

He had a point. Even if we were asked to do only one dance at an event, Jonesy would still do at least one too many. The Silurian hardcore believed that our appearance should be sudden and our performance swift and spectacular, followed by a quick exit. We didn't want to hang around long enough for an audience to get used to us. Mystery and anonymity – surely that's what morris should be about.

We certainly voiced our opinions, but they were no more than water off the proverbial duck's back. The rift was growing, but it didn't stop Jonesy overdoing a performance. Even as far back as the dawn of the 1980s, this was already an issue, as illustrated by an incident on a 'local tour' in the Malvern Hills area.

Emerging from a tea shop after a mid-afternoon break, we made our way to the next scheduled dance spot. The location was deserted.

"There's nobody here, Dave," Willy observed. We only called him Jonesy when we weren't annoyed with him.

"Doesn't matter," replied our leader. "They'll soon come when we start dancin'!"

So we did a couple of dances. Nobody came.

"We might as well move on, mightn't we?" suggested Mulvey, "This is a dead loss."

"No, look you – there's somebody comin' now," Dave insisted.

"That's only Keith Close," said Willy. "He was thinking about joining us. I 'spect he's just come to have a nose."

"Well then," lilted Dave, "let's do 'im a dance, then he can see what we're about, isn't it?"

Three dances later, Keith was still the only observer and looked about as fed up as we felt. Unbelievably, after this demonstration of overload, he still joined – and became another committed member of the side.

"Just loike a bloody practice night in kit," Smudge muttered to himself as we finally left the spot.

"Exactly," I agreed, overhearing him.

It was true, and practice nights had become a study in tedium. Our full repertoire was only sixteen dances and we all knew them well. We also knew that they didn't really come to life until we had an interactive audience. For us, practice night was all about chatting or playing pool, with maybe a bit of dancing thrown in if we felt the need for some exercise. Practice night was Monday, and Monday is not a night for doing anything too energetic. Jonesy didn't agree with our attitude at all. By 1984, there were enough bones of contention to be able to construct a rudimentary skeleton. So that was what we did.

Just before our AGM that year, half a dozen of us got together to discuss the problem. We concluded we were in serious disagreement with Dave Jones on family weekends, practice nights, style of performance and the 'overkill' element. Other little niggles were aired too, for example Dave's obsessive concern with precision footwork, hand movement and the like. *Hand* movements!? That might have been the last straw. We saw all this as being a pedantically Cotswold attitude, one to be quickly suppressed in favour of putting on an electrifying performance. If the crowd was excited, no one was going to say, "Oooh, did you see that hand movement there? Needs a bit of work, I reckon."

There we sat, late into the night, discussing ways we could reduce, or preferably eradicate, the problem. With the AGM looming, we concluded that the only way forward was to break the mould by electing a new squire and bagman. Vas and I were asked if we would stand for election against the normally unopposed Dave Jones.

"Well," said Vas, "I'd be happy to be squire if Rob will be bagman."

I readily agreed and, following some canvassing up to the AGM, Vas and I were duly elected. Understandably, Jonesy was distressed. He thought it was some kind of plot. We tried to reassure him that Silurian would benefit from a change of management and expressed our hope that he would be prepared to take a back seat for a while and let someone else drive. Predictably, this was unacceptable to Dave and, within a couple of months, he had left the side he created, taking with him a number of good men and true, including the energetic and amusing Mike Massey.

Like Dr Frankenstein, Dave Jones had attempted to realise a dream that would revolutionise the world. Like that famous fictional physician, Dave had managed to create a new living entity from spare parts. He had energised it and given it life, only to suffer the same fate as the good doctor. His creation had seemingly turned into a monster and he had lost control over it. Breaking loose, it was now rampaging across the country, creating havoc and destruction. Jonesy saw us as 'biting the hand that fed us', refusing to accept the next stage in our development. Though still a ring side by default, we were the bad boys of morris, as well as Jonesy's monster. He was convinced that, without his guidance, we would sicken and die – and get thrown out of the Ring. We didn't agree. We believed that our graph was still rising, and we set out to prove that not only would we survive but also that the best was yet to come.

Part 3

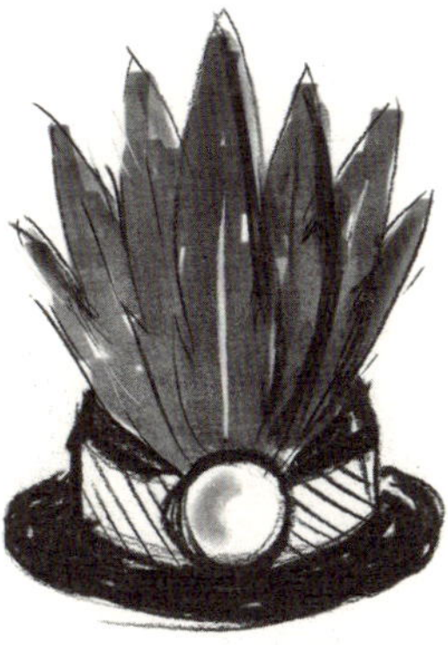

Chapter 13
Jonesy's Ale

• • • • •

*"Oh, when Jonesy's ale was new, me bo-o-oys!
When Jo-o-nesy's a-a-ale was new . . . !"*

"What are we going to do?" said Vas.

"I dunno," I said. "What do you want to do?"

Like those two wacky Liverpudlian vultures in Walt Disney's *Jungle Book*, we were at a loss, groping around in a fog of indecision. It had never been our intention for Dave Jones to leave the side, but he had. And he had taken some star players with him. The most likely reason was that he was not content to be just 'one of the boys'. Or did he disapprove of us voting in favour of attending events where there might be women's sides? Perhaps he felt that playing pool all night was no way to perfect the Upton Hanky Dance.

Whatever the reason, he was gone, and Vas and I were the new guys in charge. Yet we took our roles seriously enough to want to resolve the problem. As squire and bagman we were Silurian's new ambassadors, out there on diplomatic service. All the bucks stopped with us, as this one had.

"It bothers me," I reflected, brows furrowing.

"It bothers me too," agreed Vas, "I didn't want him to *leave*."

"Maybe it had something to do with Lassington Oak," I suggested.

"I'm sure it was," surmised Vas, "but that's not the whole story. I reckon Dave just lost us. We've outgrown each other and it's now a parting of the ways. And I don't think there is much we can do about it."

"Not so much lost us, but lost control of us," I said, "like Frankenstein and his monster. Still – Lassington Oak didn't help, did it? Could have been the back breaker."

Vas agreed again. The Lassington Oak in question was not, as might be supposed, some local variant of the mighty *Quercus robur*, but an event. An Ale, to be explicit. And Jonesy wanted us to be there. As mentioned previously, we didn't like Ales, but Jonesy had organised it for us just before the 1984 AGM, when he was still our bagman. It seemed he had a soft spot for the Lassington men, even though he was not attending the event himself. Anyway, he had confirmed the booking, Lassington were expecting us and we were all content to honour it. Not without a little rancour, however.

"Bloody Jones!" I said, peeved that we were having to fulfil a booking made by the previous bagman. "Bookin' us in for an Ale and then not turnin' up!"

For some reason, I just couldn't get the words to a certain well-known folk song, *Jones's Ale*, out of my head . . .

Kick-off, according to the invitation, was 6.30pm. Being the conscientious bagman, I made sure we all arrived on time.

"Hello boys!" said the man on the door. "You're very punctual. Anyway, now that you're here, welcome to our little gathering and help yourselves to the beer."

"Oh, ta!" said Burco avidly.

It had been a bit of a trek finding the village hall venue, tucked away as it was in deepest Gloucestershire, and the thought of a refreshing drink was most welcome. The wooden barrels were lined up by the door to the kitchen with their brass taps just asking to be turned on. So we queued up with our tankards and drew a draught. The beer was good. But, connoisseurs to a man, we double-checked the quality by having a second tasting.

About 7.45, the Faithful City Morrismen arrived from Worcester.

By way of historical interest, Worcester City's coat of arms bears the motto, *Civitas In Bello et Pace Fidelis*, which basically means 'The city faithful in war and peace', granted to them in honour of their support for the Royalists during the Civil War. So there we have a problem straightaway – in another age, Silurian would have been with the rebels.

They were our nearest local side and a friendly rivalry, falling just short of hand-to-hand combat, had existed between us since the early days. Whereas Jonesy had opted for polishing up Silurian into a Border side, Faithful City were content to remain as a Cotswold side that did some Border dances, thus leaving themselves undefended against the kind of heckling repartee we directed at all Cotswold sides. As they were just up the road from us, they came in for a lot of special attention. The banter between us was easily comprehensible. We thought they were unexceptional; they thought we were hooligans.

Mostly we kept our distance, and the status quo lapped like a languid turning tide until 1984. Earlier that year, prior to the Lassington Oak Ale, by way of a bit more history, a local day of dance had been organised by Faithful City to celebrate the silver jubilee of the Morris Ring, and we found ourselves on the same coach tour as the Worcester boys. We were up to our usual tricks, displaying our particular brand of swagger and producing an enviable interaction with the audience at each spot. The other sides on the tour were all of the Cotswold persuasion. They managed to raise no more than the usual polite ripple of applause from the onlookers, whilst Silurian were again grabbing all the attention. Whoops, roars and shrieks for more followed our performances, causing some of the other guys to fall prey to the green-eyed monster.

Feeling mischievous, and opting to cause a bit more of a stir than usual, we were working on a plan to smuggle a woman onto the coach. It was a non-starter really, as all seats were occupied. Limited space being something of an insurmountable issue, we ditched the smuggling option and set our sights a lot lower. Settling for a bit of token contraband instead, we boarded the bus with an empty carafe that had been 'borrowed' from the pub by two of our professional souvenir hunters. Not quite the same cachet as a real live woman, but at least it was a trophy. We were spotted by one of the green-eyed bus passengers and were shopped for our 'outrageous' behaviour. Outrageous? He seriously needed to consult a dictionary. The tour leader, predictably, insisted that the coach was going nowhere until the carafe was returned, which Smudge and I duly did. The surprised barman was mystified by the fuss, saying he was happy to let us keep our souvenir and offering us another so we could have one each. Declining his generosity for fear of further reprisals, we returned to the coach empty-handed, to murmured disapproval and other sotto voce grumbling from the Cotswold wets.

This incident was enough to increase the adjectival vocabulary of our more ardent detractors. Words like 'dangerous', 'dishonest' and 'untrustworthy' soon appeared in general use within the usual pejorative lexicon, endorsed by certain members of Faithful City. It was enough to convince them that we really were not just ruffians, but thieving delinquents too. The discontent simmered within their ranks, growing spiteful and turning into something approaching loathing along the way. Thus it came as no surprise that this contingent was spoiling for a fight when they arrived at the Lassington Oak Ale.

Like us, they were greeted by the man on the door and pointed in the direction of the beer barrels.

"Hey, this one's empty!" came a melancholy wail from the first man to reach the supply.

"Well," said the Lassington man blithely, "Silurian have been here since six-thirty!"

"Hrmph! Bloody typical! Greedy sods."

"Whaddya mean by that?" challenged Willy, looking very authoritative in his military jacket. He gave the surly fellow a gimlet stare through his Lennon gold-rims.

"Well – you Silurian lot! Selfish load of buggers! Always nickin' all the beer, without a thought for anyone else."

"Shoulda bin here on time, shouldn't you? It said 6.30 on *our* invitation," Willy replied tartly. "Anyway, you've got a pint, so what are you grumblin' about?"

With that, we left them to their mutterings and went to find some seats. Willy's eye had a dangerous glint and it was clear some mischief might be brewing. His fuse was short, and the spark that might ignite it was the Faithful City whinger at the beer barrel who seemed to be on some kind of personal vendetta, despite the fact that he was unknown to us.

"Where'd they buy *him*?" asked Burco.

"Must've been a free transfer from another side," Andy suggested.

"Another planet, more like," Willy said, adding ominously, "He'd just better behave himself, that's all."

However, behave himself he didn't, and we came in for some more verbal abuse next time our paths converged. So we sat in our corner and kept our eye on him for any further signs of belligerence. Willy was taking this personally and was immersed in thought.

"I know!" he said suddenly, pausing for effect and to light another cigarette. The rest of us leaned in towards him like a cabal of evil plotters.

"We'll spoik 'is beer," chipped in Smudge helpfully, a grin beginning to widen his face.

"Better than that," Willy continued. "We'll take his beer away. He keeps moanin' about not getting any, so we'll give 'im something to moan about!"

Nods of assent approved this as a justifiable punishment and one that required no need to cross the Rubicon into criminal activity, so we waited and watched. Our chance came soon enough. When our quarry got up to dance, Willy showed us what he had in mind. Getting up himself but heading in the direction of the toilet, he passed the table on which sat our target's tankard. Surreptitiously picking it up, Willy casually left it on another table on the far side of the room. Come the end of the dance, we were all sitting around our own table like inscrutable temple monkeys, observing our victim's predictable reaction to the disappearance of his pot. He found it again, of course. But every time he got up to dance, one of us would pull the same stunt. Our mirth increased along with his exasperation, but eventually he put two and two together and made 'Silurian'. What really bugged him, however, was that we kept doing it even after he knew we knew that he knew.

Meanwhile, there had been a run on the beer, with everyone in the room responding to the rumours by getting one in before Silurian emptied all the barrels – with predictable consequences. The beer ran out.

Realising they were still within licencing hours, the Lassington bagman suggested a whip-round for funds to dash to the local pub and replenish the stocks. As the collectors made their way around the hall, somebody from the Faithful City ranks shouted out, "Come on, Silurian! Cough up – this is all your fault anyway!"

"No thanks!" chortled Burco. "We don't need to make a contribution 'cos we're not having any more beer. We've had enough, ta!"

That just about did it for our Number One Fan. From his furious expression it was obvious that this feud was still on, and an earnest little tête-à-tête was forming around the Offended One, presumably to plan their strategy for future conflict.

Like all such incidents, the rumours emanating from it grew exponentially, liberally spiced with fictitious detail and specious embellishments. By the time it had got back to Dave Jones, the story was like an account of one of Genghis Khan's raiding parties. Our founder was not amused. Lassington Oak, on the other hand, were very amused. The story had put them on the morris map, so to speak, and they were not displeased with that outcome. It would not have surprised us if they had had some tee shirts printed with 'We hosted Silurian and lived!' splashed across the front.

As the new bagman, and taking my responsibility seriously, I made our apologies known to all concerned, but it didn't help our case as far as Faithful City or Dave Jones were concerned. They simply saw us as the spawn of the devil and they expected us to burn in hell. For a long time after that, possibly even to this day, for all I know, these disgruntled individuals muttered and ungraciously talked about the whole incident like a gaggle of old allotment owners recalling the time when 'the new couple' arrived on their hallowed ground.

Chapter 14

Cutting Loose

• • • • •

"Touched her on the toe,
That's my share,
That's my toe-a-tapper
And you can play there..."

Jonesy, treating us with the contempt he believed we deserved, refused to be associated with us after The Lassington Oak Incident, preferring to put his efforts into creating a new Ledbury-based side. He considered that too many Silurian men were from the badlands of Malvern and beyond. As a result of this attitude, he couldn't bring himself to come with us to the Thaxted ring meeting in 1985. That was when we knew we had assuredly lost him, because all sides belonging to the ring wanted to appear at Thaxted, and for Jonesy it would have been another personal triumph, another fulfilled ambition.

After Vas and I had been elected to run the side, Jonesy had predicted the death of Silurian. Feedback from Faithful City may have prompted his comments, as we knew he saw the Lassington fracas as a glaring demonstration of our uncontrollable lawlessness. From his viewpoint, we had gone over the edge and were sliding rapidly towards a self-inflicted demise. He couldn't see how such a band of brigands could survive the authority and strict adherence to principle set out by the Morris Ring, and thus I am sure he thought we would be laughed out of court at Thaxted, derided and buried by the other ring members on this hallowed ground, the Holy of Holies of the traditional morris world.

But Jonesy was forgetting that we still had Wilf.

Anyone who had done a stint as an 'officer' of any ring side was eligible as a nominee in the election of ring officers. And Wilf had been proposed and elected as Bagman of the Ring in 1984. The other ring officials knew him by his more formal title of Keith Francis, and he was in attendance at Thaxted in 1985. His cultured presence, his rank and his inescapable touch of Silurian lunacy helped to bestow credibility on the rest of us. All the rumours, stories and gossip that flew into town before us, like harbingers of doom, were stopped at the gates by the reality that one of our number had achieved high ring status. Thus we were given leave to prove that all we were doing was performing the dances of the Welsh Border to the best of our ability.

An aura of mystique and reverence had grown up around Thaxted, since it had hosted a meeting every year since the inception of the morris ring. It was always over-subscribed and those attending felt honoured to be part of such a prestigious showcase of English tradition. We felt the same, and we were going to show why we deserved to be there. I am sure no one who saw us that year would have been disappointed. We cut loose with undeniable enthusiasm, determined to prove something to ourselves, to Jonesy and to all the mischief makers. This was Thaxted, our best team was on display and Wilf was there, in his uniquely original Silurian kit.

Around the time we opted to add black tailcoats to the kit, Wilf had said, "I don't have a tailcoat, but I do have a Victorian frock coat." We agreed that would be fine, and we weren't disappointed when he first appeared in it. He had set it off a treat with an undertaker's top hat, complete with a wide band of black silk hanging down behind. Tall, straight and clean-shaven, Wilf was a commanding figure, and every inch as unsettling in appearance as the rest of us.

Though some said he looked as menacing as Doctor Death, to us he was almost like a father figure protecting his wayward children from the potential wrath of authority.

Wherever we danced that weekend we were congratulated and encouraged. We were on a real high, flying on a potent combination of adrenalin and alcohol. The mixture was just right and, on the Saturday tour, Silurian was running like a finely tuned machine.

Our sense of unity had never been stronger and we distanced ourselves from the ordinary mortals around us. It's not that we adopted a haughty attitude – we needed them. They were part of the process. We were indeed there for them, not as entertainers, but in the capacity of disguised sacred dancers, to perform the Morris in something approaching a ritual sense. We had no need of historical reference, academic research or the blessing of peer-reviewed postulation. Driven by instinct, and with no formal strategy, we set out to deliver what we understood ritual dancing should be like at an elemental level. We didn't need to talk about it. Perhaps we were in tune telepathically. If we got it right we would certainly appease the gods and banish evil spirits. Instinctively, we felt unique, not in the same mental space as anyone else that weekend. On that auspicious Saturday, our dancing started off at such a pitch that, by the time we peaked, at the lunchtime spot, we achieved heights we never knew we could reach. We may well have been on the top of the bell curve that day.

We began that spot with the Upton Hanky Dance, the closest we ever got to Cotswold. But this was what we might have termed Welsh Border Cotswold. In modern parlance, it would be described as seriously sexed-up. A Border dance with hankies performed with more vigour than a typical Cotswold dance with sticks. We had plenty of room to dance, so we made the most of it by starting with a 'wide set' – about six feet between any two dancers, just able to touch fingertip to fingertip. With three facing three, we were cued in by John Willy, looking impressive and commanding in his red tunic. The sun glinted on the rims of his glasses and the pheasant feathers in his misshapen busby bristled in anticipation, as he breathed life into his melodeon and released the tune from its confinement.

The notes twinkled into the space between us and asked us to dance for them. We leapt into the first move, the rounds, racing around the perimeter, pushing the crowd back with our flicked handkerchiefs. The circle was at least twenty feet across. As the music pulled us into the chorus, we were right in formation again, two lines of three, almost perfectly equidistant. Next came 'three tops', a double three-man figure-of-eight that split the set diagonally. On the call, the set exploded as we formed such a wide pattern that it might have been difficult to tell who was where, but then suddenly we were formed up again, three facing three. Just when the crowd had accustomed themselves to this simple geometry, we broke into three tops for the second time. Two crossovers and two heys brought us to the final rounds, which again skimmed the crowd and pushed them even further back. From that perimeter, we ended the dance with a warlike shout and a leap into the centre of the circle. In hindsight, I am amazed I could jump that far. But we all did, and it was a stunning finish. At the risk of sounding fanciful, I believe we were at a different level of reality during that performance, hypnotised and spellbound by the magic of the music.

With that last shout, the crowd erupted like an active volcano. As earthbound reality kicked in, we couldn't comprehend what we'd just done. It was almost as if we were part of the audience, watching ourselves dance – a communal out-of-body experience. We felt about ten feet tall, buoyed aloft by the energy of the crowd. My heart seemed to be clocking up about four hundred beats a minute. I could feel it pounding in my head, but the adrenalin blocked out the pain.

Later, we danced an eight-man Brimfield Stick Dance, normally done with four. The chorus move was another figure-of-eight, whereby the two outside men in each line of four move to their right, charge each other to cross in the middle of the set, round the far man and come back to place after crossing once more in the middle. Dancing with eight meant that the moves had to be done in close parallel to avoid looking disjointed. Yet we still did them over a huge distance of ground, with murderous shouts and at full tilt like mediaeval jousters. Vas, in his repartee with the crowd, said, "Well, at least you now know where the Red Arrows learned all their moves!" The audience loved it and supported us at every spot.

It is customary at ring meetings for all the participating sides to join in a procession on returning to base camp after the Saturday coach tours. There was at that time only one Border ring side, and that was us. Not wishing to interrupt the cavalcade of other sides, Silurian tagged on the end of the line. The parade, in time-honoured tradition, worked its way up the main street to the top of town, with bands playing and dancers joining in with the processional dance. At the destination, each side danced a quick number before leaving the arena. Silurian, at the back of the queue, were busy with their own processional dance to the accompaniment of their raucous band thrashing through *Yankee Doodle*. Our reputation was still travelling before us, and people further up the street were craning to see where this new noise was coming from, rather than watching what was going on in front of them. It was like the entrance of the Queen of Sheba.

After the day's efforts, we relaxed. For us, that meant taking over the corner of some popular pub, filling our tankards and keeping the punters musically entertained until closing time. When in kit, we remained exponents of multi-faceted street theatre. A costume that involved blacking out individual facial features had the effect, not just of uniting us, but of keeping us functioning as a unit throughout any given period. Thus it didn't feel right to try to act 'normal'. We were 'Silurian' – the word had taken on a special significance for us. We were enigmatic dancers, but we were musicians and singers too. So long as there was a catalyst in the form of a receptive audience, we danced, played and sang for them. Even at breakfast, we entered the hall as a full side, with Willy at our head, playing his melodeon, which he continued to do as we queued.

Once we had the kit on, we were performers, all day, or even all weekend – it was that simple. We empathised with our audience. If we didn't please them, there was no energy exchange. Thus, in the pub sessions, we were keenly aware that not everyone is happy to pop into their local for a pint only to find some finger-in-the-ear folk singer doing his thing. Our remedy was to vary the musical menu for them, making sure we also played tunes the other musicians could join in with. The whole mix was spiced with songs that were not strictly 'folk'. Willy was the driving force and our touchstone on these occasions. Having found a pub we were happy with, we claimed a corner and brought out the instruments.

"What shall we give 'em then, Willy?" Burco asked, attaching the mouthpiece to his tuba.

"Better let 'em know we're here," replied Willy. "Let's do *Mickey's Son and Daughter*. You ready, Soopy?"

This question was directed at a tall, thin, bespectacled fellow with an accordion strapped to his chest. He displayed a unique design in perambulatory appendages (they were too advanced to be called simply 'legs') which saved on hip space by being joined directly to his waist, giving him an inimitable stance and the kind of eccentric look that was an essential element of the world of Siluria. He arrived with the name Steve Glennie-Smith, but was quickly crowned by Willy as Super Steve, or Soopy for short, when Steve had played the wrong tune and our red-coated pied piper had reacted sardonically.

"Ready John," confirmed Soopy, in an educated accent which probably came in the same starter pack as the double-barrelled name. However, anyone whose day job involved designing stabilisers for helicopter rotor blades was inevitably going to be just a little bit educated. And a little bit off-the-wall. He and Willy were very different, but they were both Silures at heart. And Soopy was a real hero for opting to stay with us rather than fleeing with Dave Jones.

"Okay then," Willy said, "let's do it."

We launched into *Mickey's Son And Daughter*, a classic 60s number from the Bonzo Dog Doo Dah Band. In belting this out, Willy and Super Steve held their own against a cacophony of ancillary percussion. Soopy's accordion was built like a battleship and it added so much volume to the melody that we were able to add percussion without fear of stifling the tune.

When it comes to musical ability, I was in the 'leave-it-in-the-box-son' category, but I had discovered I could play the triangle. Without any arpeggios, scales or keys to worry about, my musical hypertension melted away and I was at one with my simple instrument. It had been made for me by Dion from a piece of reinforcement steel picked up on a building site, and tuned by pitch-perfect Super Steve. I played it with two six-inch nails, one for the rhythm and one for the drone. Sadly, Dion was hardly putting in an appearance by 1985, due to complex health problems, so we were without a snare drum. Mick, however, had arrived one day with a miniature bass drum, quickly spotting that a drum was essential to the band, and he who plays drum dances not.

Many of our favourite songs were trotted out that night. Willy's personal repertoire ranged from military marching songs through pop favourites to music hall monologues. As much as we enjoyed folk standards like *Farmer's Boy* or *Pleasant And Delightful*, we felt this might not apply to an average pub audience. A sudden burst of Tom Jones's *Delilah* or *I Do Like To Be Beside The Seaside*, however, was enough to keep them wanting more.

One of our more outrageous interludes was a little number called *Touched Her On The Toe*. It involved kidnapping a likely looking nubile female from the audience, standing her on a chair in full view and surrounding her with a ring of Silurian men to prevent a hasty escape. We then sang the praises of her anatomical construction (with hand movements), going through the verses from 'toe' to 'head' via all the more interesting bits along the way. The victim that evening was an American girl called Jessica, apparently accompanying a morris side visiting from New England. What an opportunity to teach her a hitherto undiscovered ritualistic practice from Olde England.

Jessica was wonderfully voluptuous, with an overt sense of fun and zest for life. Before the evening was over, secret vows were taken to seek her out later on and engage her in further conversation . . . which is how Willy, Burco and Andy came to be roaming the campsite at four o'clock in the morning, still in kit of course. After the pubs had closed, we had been invited to a party. When the drinks ran out there, the party ran out of steam. Looking for Jessica's tent seemed to be the obvious next move.

Moving with the stealth of a three-legged warthog on marijuana, our renegade trio banged and crashed their way around the campsite, unzipping tent flaps and shaking guy ropes, demanding repetitively in loud whispers, "*Jessica!* – you in there?" At one point they were startled by the sound of a zip opening nearby to reveal a bulky form obviously answering an urgent call of nature.

"Quick!" hissed Burco urgently. "Pretend you're a tree!"

While this silhouette happily watered a patch of ground not ten feet away, our heroes were standing motionless in the gloom, arms out and bent awkwardly at the joints, like three storm-stunted bog oaks. The sleepy camper saw nothing, and shortly disappeared inside his tent. In the lightening dawn came the understanding that the likelihood of finding Jessica was becoming increasingly remote, whilst the possibility of an early breakfast had gained in appeal. The hunt was abandoned. It's always the same when you stay up all night – that little empty feeling hits you about half five in the morning.

Lunchtime on Sunday saw us all back in the pub after the morning dance display. The place was packed. Everybody in Thaxted seemed to be there including Jessica, the Horwich Prize Medal Morris Men, the local bikers and a stunning German girl sporting a miniature Tina Turner wig discreetly tucked into each armpit.

We had first met Horwich in Saddleworth. Another colourful Northwest side, they wore dark red velvet breeches, dark yellow sashes and tassel-topped schoolboy caps in matching red with gold piping on the seams. And clogs. You can dress in any way you want if you are wearing steel-shod clogs. No one will argue. The Horwich boys had brought their mascot and leader with them. He was about seven feet tall and answered to the name of Glyn. On a lanyard around his neck, he wore a referee's whistle, an all-important accessory for Northwest sides, as its piercing shrillness can be heard over the noise of a big band and many pairs of clogs. Only with the aid of such a whistle is it possible to guide the dancers through the set moves.

With the noise level in that pub, the whistle was also the only way that Glyn was going to tell his dancers it was time to 'fall in outside, men'. Next to Glyn in that tightly packed bar were two bikers, all leather, denim and studs, talking Harley Davidson. They hadn't noticed Glyn, despite his size, until he blew his whistle. The strident blast penetrated the nearest biker's shaggy mane of hair, hit him full in the left ear and stuck there in his eardrum, quivering and humming like a crossbow bolt in an oak plank. With pain and wrath struggling for supremacy on the biker's features, he wheeled round, fists clenched, ready to provide the perpetrator of this rash and foolhardy deed with a free but painful demonstration of why the Hell's Angels inspire fear and submission wherever they go.

One hundred and eighty degrees – and half a second – later, the injured party's progress and vision was blocked by a huge expanse of white shirt and red velvet waistcoat.

"What the f— ?"

Looking up to see how far this obstruction might extend, he saw Glyn's smiling face about three feet above him, the offending whistle still clenched in his teeth.

"Er . . . very nice whistle," pronounced this terror of the streets in a voice a lot smaller than his mighty motorcycle boots.

Still smiling, Glyn reached out, picked up the biker by the shoulders of his oily leather jacket, planted a big kiss on his cheek and said, "Oh, ta! I'm so glad you like it."

This seemed to set the tone for the afternoon, which was spangled with memorable incidents. Our impromptu Hokey Cokey, for instance, triggered by John Willy unexpectedly playing that tune instead of White Ladies Aston. Our dance spot was no more than a token display, however. Willy was more inclined to hold musical court back in the pub. By closing time, we had run through most of our favourite tunes and songs, which included that old rugby club favourite, *Sunshine Mountain*, set in motion by Burco. For those unfamiliar with this bit of nonsense, it goes like this:

I'm climbing up the sunshine mountain,
Where the little breezes blow.
I'm climbing up the sunshine mountain,
My face is all aglow.
I'm turning my back on sorrow,
Reach up to the sky,
We're climbing up the sunshine mountain,
You and I.

On the last line, the singer points at someone in the room, who is expected to join in as the song is repeated. The process continues until the whole room is pretending to climb the invisible cliff in front of them before turning their backs on sorrow and reaching up to the sky. It's the kind of aberration that can be appreciated only through an alcoholic haze. Soon everyone was climbing and reaching up, including the hirsute mädchen in her sleeveless top, a bonus for those men in the room who preferred natural women – which a later poll revealed to be the majority, a fact that might surprise most women today.

Those members of Silurian not directly involved in singing or playing were moving surreptitiously through the gathered throng offering the females in the room the traditional greeting of rubbing faces. By the time the fun came to an end, most of the women had a smudgy visage, the German girl being no exception. Stopping by for a quick drink in 'ze kvaint Englander pob, ja', she had found that playing cricket and drinking hot brown water with milk were not the only inexplicable customs practiced over here. Also, Jessica discovered things about the English she definitely wouldn't tell Mommy, and those people in the pub who expected morrismen to sing drinking songs were taken by surprise when we gave them *My Baby Has Gone Down the Plughole*, and *Jerusalem* with hand movements.

As we headed for home, we felt we had left them wanting more. Though we may have shocked some and outraged others, we knew that most people had been uplifted by our dancing and entertained in the pub sessions. Jonesy's predictions had not been realised. Quite the opposite, in fact. The side without him had fledged and taken wing as a new confidence established itself.

Chapter 15
Dinner For Two

• • • • •

"Of all the world's great heroes,
There's none than can compare
To the tow-row-row and the row-tow-tow
Of the British Grenadiers..."

It was raining.

Occupying our usual Monday night corner at The Horse and Jockey, our practice venue, we listened to the rain lashing the windows and the wind moaning mournfully under the eaves.

"Mucky night," observed Chris Mulvey, in response to the wind's noisy shaking of the ancient Xpelair window vent.

"Cosy in here though," Willy pointed out. "And the fire's nice, just for a change."

"The beer's crap," said Smudge, glumly.

"Buck up, Dave," admonished Mick, "I'm not having you moaning all night. Ansells is Ansells. If you don't like it – get yourself a Guinness or something."

"The Guinness is crap too."

"Bloody hell, Dave! Get a grip!" I said. "Anyway, I've just struggled out here in the pouring rain and wind, so *I* am going to enjoy myself. If you can't buck up, Smudge – buck off!"

"Hmph!"

It was indeed a somewhat inclement night to be driving

anywhere, but it was the middle of winter, so it was only to be expected, as was the poor turnout for practice. As bagman, I felt duty bound to turn up, despite the 12-mile drive from Worcester over the Malverns to Colwall. Along the way, I had picked up Mick, Smudge and Bernie Smart. Entering the bar, we noticed Willy, Mulvey, Andy and Vas were the only others in there.

"Evenin' Vaz,"said Bernie.

Vas gave him a withering look. "*Vas*," he reminded him.

"Oh, yes – sorry!"

This would not be the last time this scenario played out.

Eight was barely enough for a sensible practice, so that idea was not even mooted. We preferred the cosiness of the bar to the Antarctic conditions in the practice room, and anyway we were still recovering from Jonesy's overkill era. He thought 'practice makes perfect', but he was obsessed with lines and pretty footwork. Of course these were important, but we believed it was all about putting on a dynamic performance which would strike fear into evil spirits and audience alike. And if Jonesy had seen us at Thaxted, he might finally have got the message. Two hours every Monday night doing the same few dances quickly dulled our edge.

We needed to be psyched up for a performance. An important part of the process was sitting around our favourite table, chatting and reminiscing about past triumphs. It helped in working ourselves up for the next sortie. On that cold, wet, windy night, we were doing just that. Listed on the agenda that evening was an invitation from a women's Northwest side, from Mossley, up Manchester way.

Unlike many diehard Cotswold traditionalists, the majority of us had no problem with women doing morris and we were happy to share a spot with them – or a whole weekend. As for mixed sides, we could take issue with that, but only because we could see that mixing male and female energies in that way was unfavourable to both. Overall, we felt we could dance as well as anyone, male or female. So any other side was part of the audience for us, rather than a rival. During bag-biz, I had established that we could expect a turnout of 12 or 13, with eight or nine dancers and four in the band. This was just about enough to put on a good show, despite the fact that Dion and Burco would not be there, leaving us without snare drum and tuba. It was to be our first outing with a women's side, so we wanted it to be memorable, and we had to make up for the absence of two valuable band members. As we sat in that cosy bar we speculated on the potential of the Mossley outing to produce a weekend to remember.

"All those women to black up," drooled Andy, a faraway look in his eye.

"Just think," said Smudge, taking up the theme and talking through one side of a lecherously leering mouth, "they'll be on a coach with us. Trapped. Nowhere to run . . . Huh! Huh!"

"Won't bother you much," said Vas. "Two pints and you'll be asleep!"

A chorus of laughter followed this shrewd prediction. We had all seen the damage a couple of pints could inflict on Smudge's ability to stay awake. It never stopped him dancing though. Even if it was necessary to stand him in position at the outset of a dance, as soon as the music started he'd be off, going through the moves automatically, like a programmable electronic toy.

"Don't worry," he assured us, "Oi'll pace meself!"

More howls of laughter greeted this suggestion. We actually knew Smudge better than he knew himself, so he was the only one in the room who didn't understand this as a pious hope rather than a statement of intent. I had a question for him.

"How can you pace yourself when you keep forgetting you have a pint-and-a-quarter pot?"

"Oh, yeah. You're roight. I do keep *forgettin'*! Sure t'make a difference, I s'pose." He lapsed into reflective mood, mentally grappling with the arithmetic necessary to work out that he was consuming five pints for everyone else's four.

The conversation moved on without him for a while, leaving

him pulling thoughtfully at the spiky fringe of his receding hairline. Thinking about women had prompted him to check his coiffure, just in case it had been tousled by the wind. Smudge had always been proud of his hairstyle but, ever since some woman had told him it made him look like Clint Eastwood, he had become a bit precious in his care for it. Of course he didn't look a bit like Clint Eastwood, but that didn't stop him thinking he did. Fortunately, his dialect made it impossible for him to say with any kind of authority, "Go ahead, punk – make my day." So that was something to be thankful for.

Cossetted in the cosy warmth of the fire, rumination turned to reverie and Smudge's head began to slump.

"Wake up, Smudge!"

"Eh?"

"Mossley, Dave," Mick reminded him. We all called him 'Dave' when we needed him to pay attention.

"Yeah? Wot about it?" said Smudge guardedly, thinking his imperfect hearing had caused him to miss something vital.

"We were just talking about the women, Dave," prompted Mulvey, "and what we could do for them on this Mossley weekend."

"Huh. Oi know what oi could do for 'em," muttered God's Gift, half to himself.

"No, no, Dave," said Bernie in an avuncular tone, patting him on the back in feigned affection. "We were just wondering if you could do some printing for us."

"*Print*in'?" Smudge was wary, looking for the wind-up.

"Yes," said Bernie, "printing. It's what you do for a living, remember?"

"We were thinking, while you were asleep – " began Willy.

"I was *not* asleep!"

"As I was sayin', when you were asleep, we were wondering about having some cards made," Willy explained. "You know – so we could give the girls marks out of ten, like the Olympics."

"Oh, you mean loik the ol' nine point three an' eight point nine jobby?" said Smudge brightly, confident he was now tacking with the wind.

Someone suggested that six point nine might be more appropriate.

"Eh?"

"Six point nine, Dave."

"Wot?"

"Sixty nine, Dave," said Bernie, doing his friendly uncle thing again.

"Dinner for two," added Andy, quoting the old Chinese menu joke.

Catching on suddenly, Smudge laughed long and loud, eyes shut and tears rolling. Infected by his sheer exuberance, we were all soon rocking and gurgling around the table.

The seed was sown. Smudge had come up with the goods by the Monday night before the Mossley weekend. With a flourish, he had displayed the results of his efforts, stealthily carried out at work whilst the boss was out.

"Here y'are," he said, placing a few on the table, "all sixes and nines!"

"Oh! How did that happen then, Dave?" someone asked.

"Just what we need to make up sixty-nine though," someone else observed.

"There's more," pronounced Smudge, mimicking the Irish comedian, Jimmy Cricket, who had made that phrase famous, "Oi've done the backs as well!" He smiled proudly, flashing an incomplete set of teeth.

"You mean they're *reversible*, Smudge?" queried Bernie.

"Wot? *Ninety-six*?" He looked positively startled by this concept. "No! They've got rubbish on the back."

No reaction. We all looked blank. Smudge looked

disappointed. Rejecting verbal explanation in favour of a practical demonstration, he shuffled through the cards and, with surprising speed and dexterity, laid the lot out along the table's bench seat. We all craned to inspect the result. The cards spelt 'R-U-B-B-I-S-H-!-!-!' in big black letters.

We were seriously impressed.

"See?" beamed Smudge. "We just stand in our line, hold up the cards, one in each hand, look – six point nine, six point nine and so on. An' then we just turn 'em round and there you are – rubbish!"

"It's going to take some engineering," said an unfamiliar voice in the corner. It was Stuart Watts, our most recent convert to the faith, from over the border in Gloucestershire. Although zany enough to be a Silurian natural, his inherent practicality enabled him to spot trouble a mile off. It had taken him no more than a few seconds to understand the hazards involved in getting five excitable lunatics to synchronise with each other as well as coordinating both hands and then turning them through 180 degrees. A couple of trial runs provided sufficient evidence that Stuart was right. Despite this, we agreed to adopt an 'it'll be all right on the night' attitude, and the cards were put away until needed.

The weekend came and we were soon travelling up the motorway, wedged in the back of yet another minibus between the sleeping bags and musical instruments. It was a camping weekend, so space in the bus was further restricted by an assortment of tents and other gear. Quick to notice the largest single space in the whole vehicle was the driver's seat, Willy said, "I'll drive." He was in there like a rat up a drainpipe, setting a course for The Billy Goat in Mossley.

On arrival, our first observation was that the campsite was what one might call 'unfit for purpose'. A campsite is not a rocky outcrop of bleak moorland protected from human trespass by fearsome guardian winds howling horizontally over and around the boulders like banshees playing tag.

"I'm not camping there!" Willy announced emphatically, staring morosely through the window at the impenetrable murkiness of it all. "Let's head for the pub and sort somethin' else out."

Once inside the pub, we set Smudge in motion to apply his Standard Beer Test, whilst we waited edgily for his verdict on the suitability of the local brew for Silurian consumption. It was a thumbs-up. "Luvly pint," he informed us, licking the froth from his top lip.

"Better than Ansells then, Smudge?" Mick suggested, a broad grin breaking through the bushy blackness of his beard. We were all bearded apart from Smudge and Bernie. With the latter it was simply personal preference; with Smudge, however, other factors came into play. For instance, his beard was of a strange orangey-red hue, giving him the appearance of an orang-utan at a fancy dress party. He was quite capable of getting himself into serious trouble without people thinking he'd escaped from the zoo, so clean-shaven he remained.

A couple of pints into the evening, Willy announced, to nobody in particular amongst our Mossley hosts, that we had nowhere to sleep.

"Yeah, and we brought all that camping equipment and everything," observed Smudge. "And the back of the bus was like being in a cattle truck."

"It's all right. You can stay with me," came a quiet female voice from behind us.

"What, *all* of us?" said Willy in disbelief.

"Yes," confirmed the voice. "I've got room."

She introduced herself as Kathy, one of the Mossley Rose and Clog dancers, and reiterated the affirmation. What she must have meant was, I've got *a* room. Or, more accurately, I've got *a* room but no spare space! It turned out she lived in a well-appointed, but nonetheless standard, two-up-two-down terraced house with no obvious area to accommodate a dozen extra people. Someone made an observation about swinging cats.

"Reminds me of a joke," Willy remarked, "talking of swinging cats."

"We thought you were talking about the accommodation."

"I know a joke about that too – but anyway, there was this blind bloke," continued Willy undeterred, "He goes into this shop with his guide dog. Next minute, he picks up the dog by its tail and swings it round his head. The manager comes rushing up all concerned and says, 'What's going on? Why are you mistreating that animal??' 'It's all right,' says the blind bloke, 'I'm just having a look round!'" Another John Willy gem for the Silurian joke book.

We piled into Kath's compact house and unfurled our sleeping bags wherever we could find a bit of floor space. Our benefactress was soon having to pick her way carefully through the growing heaps of jetsam, as she bustled back and forth with cups of tea in her hands. She had that slightly starry faraway look in her eye that people get when they think their boat's come in. However, we were not about to add Interference of a Single Lady to our list of misdemeanours, so Kath may have been disappointed when we all retired peacefully for the night as soon as we'd finished our tea. On the other hand, she may have been relieved that we were so docile.

It was a different story the next day of course, after the usual transmogrification – a word I first heard in Sunday school as a kid, and haven't had a chance to use until now. Silurian was unleashed again, complete with the special pack of cards. Mild harassment of unwary females was also on the agenda, as ever. We were, as Smudge had correctly predicted, on a Saturday coach tour with the lovely ladies of Mossley. Their men were with them too, but we soon had them separated, banishing the men to the front section of the coach whilst we jealously guarded their ladies in the back rows.

At the first dance spot, as the Mossley girls danced in their pretty red and white costumes, Silurian had surreptitiously formed themselves into a line in front of the encircling audience. Black tailcoats were now an essential part of the kit, giving us a unique and offbeat appearance amongst the morris fraternity. In some odd way, it often made us inconspicuous, and we lurked there unnoticed like a squabble of roguish vultures. We waited for our victims to finish their dance. As the audience broke into applause, up went our cards. The applause changed to laughter as the cards were sighted, but not by the dancers, which left them bewildered. Not for long though. They instinctively homed in on the Silurian front line, with bewilderment turning to comprehension in a confusion of blushes and just in time to see the cards reversed. Renewed laughter deepened their colour, but they acknowledged our mischief graciously. However, they didn't want to sit in the back of the bus with us anymore.

It was only the first stop of the day and we had already blown our cover with the Mossley girls. Segregation was difficult to maintain thereafter. We had chosen to reveal our new card trick at the first venue before we became too inebriated to execute the slick changeover from 69 to RUBBISH!!! But we may have peaked too soon. For some inexplicable reason, the Mossley men saw something more than just consistent marking on our score cards, as did several of their ladies. Though it was difficult thereafter to entice more than a few of the braver ones to our lair on the back seat, the card trick had been taken in good spirit, and executed with precision.

"I'm glad I didn't put money on that," said Stuart, referring to the seamless transition from numbers to letters. "I didn't think for one second we would ever get those cards in the right order!"

"Yeah, but we haven't had a drink yet," Keith Close reminded him.

This bespectacled duo, Stuart and Keith, looked very similar in their blacking, but standing together highlighted their difference, as Stuart was about a foot taller than Keith. Keith was also a deputy head teacher and Stuart was not. But he made up for this lack of academic achievement in other ways – checking his CV might have revealed the word 'ventriloquist'. He didn't bother with all the usual dummy-in-a-suitcase stuff though. He did telephones and dogs. All day long we heard phones ringing and dogs barking, but only when Stuart was around. It took us far too long to make the connection.

"You bugger!" said Mulvey, finally getting it, "You had me goin' there – I thought it was the bloody Hound of the Baskervilles or something!"

As the day progressed, we became merrier, the cards became more random, the girls became friendlier and their faces became blacker. And, by the end of the evening in the Billy Goat, it seemed that phones were ringing constantly and everyone was doing dog impressions. I remember noticing that the landlord was serving after time, but then things became a little hazy. The next memory was that of Keith cooking scrambled eggs in Kathy's kitchen and Andy coming into the room, fresh from his Sunday morning sortie, something he did every time we went away for the weekend.

"Eeergh! I hate Sundays!" came a muffled mumble from the dark recesses of a sleeping bag crumpled on the landing. My suspicion that it was no longer Saturday increased. A chunk of my life had gone missing. Thirty-eight years old, and already the brain was crumbling, no longer able to grasp simple chronology. Senile dementia at my age – where had I gone wrong? Would I ever retain enough sanity to see my kids grow up? Perhaps in three years' time I wouldn't even recognise them.

So lost was I in this introspective reverie that I hadn't noticed that the rest of the morning had vanished too. A tug at my sleeve and an insistent voice asking, "Do you want a pint, or wot?" brought the world back into focus, a world in which Keith was no longer cooking breakfast and no sleeping bags were to be seen anywhere. We were in a pub in the midst of a windy stretch of moorland, and I had no recollection of how we arrived there. I accepted the proffered pint in hope of the comfort it might provide.

Two pints later, I was reliably informed that it was time to dance. We gathered outside, formed the set and put in an adequate performance. It was a typical laid-back Sunday morning spot – workmanlike but unexceptional. We weren't too worried. After all, Sunday was supposed to be a day of rest.

That did not apply, however, in Wrigley Head . . . wherever or whatever that was.

Maybe it was a secure unit for the mentally unstable, and maybe Sunday was earmarked as a fun day out for the inmates. All I can add to these suppositions is that, after our modest dance spot, there was a sudden commotion akin to a pitch invasion carried out by what looked like a bunch of bedraggled survivors from the Battle of Culloden. Closer inspection revealed that they were actually dressed as a Northwest morris side, but as wild as the heather moors. Apparently they came from Wrigley Head.

Sartorially, this crew was reminiscent of the exaggerated flair of the Directoire period of crazy Parisian fashions from the late 18th Century – *Les Incroyables*. They wore the sashes common to many Northwest sides, but theirs contained enough material to make a pair of curtains, with a maroon one over one shoulder and a pale ochre one over the other. Their bright blue velvet knee breeches were topped with a huge tartan cummerbund, but were not tight around the knee, thus their white socks had no means of upper support and were in various stages of descent from knee to ankle.

Their dancing was like their kit – a bit on the wild side, a little at odds with tunes that included *The British Grenadiers*, a tune more usually heard during that exercise in precision, Trooping the Colour. They did a dance introduced as 'never completed successfully in practice, and never attempted before a live audience'. They launched themselves into this with the energy of enraged bull elephants, leaping through the moves and choruses whilst being cajoled, harangued and generally intimidated by their whistle-blowing leader. He seemed to be everywhere at once, like a sheepdog on roller-skates, attempting to talk each of the twelve dancers through their next move. The band played, the dancers danced and twelve pairs of clog irons shook up a dust storm from the ground. Working on the 'short sharp shock' principle, these frenzied dervishes electrified the air for what seemed like no more than a few minutes and then they were gone, the dust settling behind them.

We had never seen anything like it. Inured by years of watching so-so morris, we had become blasé about our own ability to stand head and shoulders above the rest. But this Wrigley Head stuff was so good, so totally insane, it had us spellbound. It was so refreshing to be on the outside of something like that instead of having to create it from within. Morris on mescalin – there's a lot to be said for it.

Thanks to Wrigley Head, a superb weekend had ended on a high. Since our arrival, the people had been friendly, the pubs lively and the Mossley girls very patient. None of us had been lynched as a result of the 69 cards, no infighting had occurred and Kathy's home had suffered no damage. All in all, a perfect weekend away.

Chapter 16

Swahili For Beginners

• • • • •

"One man went to mow,
Went to mow a meadow.
One man and his dog,
Went to mow a meadow..."

I really don't know why I went to the Exeter ring meeting. I was in poor condition, following a little mishap on a building site that had resulted in getting cement dust in my eye, which was now playing host to a malevolent sty. Logic would have suggested that staying at home and taking it easy might have been the best option for me, but logic was never allowed to interfere when it came to supporting Silurian.

So there we were. Another minibus, another motorway. These superhighways are as tedious today as they were cheerless then, even though there were fewer vehicles using them. There was a time when roads used to offer the traveller the prospect of adventure, new horizons, a surprise around every corner. But all that is long gone, replaced by a convenient but mind-numbingly dreary arterial road system that sends drivers to sleep.

In an attempt to lighten the tedium, I considered breaking into *One Man Went To Mow*, something my younger brother and I used to sing on long car journeys. Having spent the first twelve years of my life in Uganda, I had of course learned this little ditty in Swahili, and this version readily found its way into my head again. I thought about teaching it to the other lads, but new recruit and fiddle player, John Smith (who was the only John Smith we knew, so he was always called by his full name, because it was such a novelty), was the only one remotely interested, so I quickly gave up on the idea, lapsing back into silence.

The tedium was getting to me. Ugly little thoughts, normally locked up in the back of my brain, had managed to escape confinement. Popping through the veil of inactivity in my head, they were swaggering around daring me to challenge them. All of the troubles that represent life in modern times are sufficient to tip even happy people into gloom and despondency. But I had a propensity for melancholia, so I stood no chance once the black dog was on the prowl.

I rolled a cigarette.

Is there life after Old Holborn? The Government Health Warning on the packet assured me there wasn't, but I lit the cigarette anyway. Can't be that bad, surely? After all, this was pure tobacco, not like the stuff in those factory-made cancer sticks, laced with a toxic chemical cocktail. And I was using Rizla Wheetstraw papers. Wheat straw – the natural killer.

I turned back to the depressing view, gazing sullenly through the window.

"What's the matter with you, you miserable old bugger?"

Willy's voice strode into my reverie, and dark thoughts scuttled away like hermit crabs.

"Just thinking," I assured him.

"Just thinking!" replied Willy, unimpressed. "You haven't said a word for about two hours. Anyway, look, we're nearly there, so get a grip. Remember, we've got to stick together! And we don't want no miserable gits."

Shaken out of introspection, I became reacquainted with my immediate surroundings. As if in some recurring dream, there were a dozen of us cramped up in the minibus with all the gear and instruments. One thing that was different from last time, however, was my vision. My right eye was causing me a lot of bother. The sty seemed to be about the size of a plum and the eye was weepy with mucus. Still, I told myself, we were only about fifteen minutes from our destination, so I would soon be on the anaesthetic. Maybe all would be well by morning.

It wasn't.

The anaesthetic put me to sleep, and the accommodation was comfortable enough to allow that sleep to continue uninterrupted until breakfast time. But when I woke up, things looked very different – I had lost the benefits of stereoscopic vision. The right eye was sealed up, and the left eye is what I call my 'bad eye'. Its malfunction was due to having permanently strained it whilst in my school shooting team. Allegedly something to do with peering through a gunsight at backlit targets on an indoor range. Reduced to left-eye vision was like looking at the world through the bottom of a pint mug smeared with butter.

On top of that, this one-sided impaired vision had an alarming effect on my balance and judgement of distance. The breakfast hall was some distance from our accommodation and downhill all the way. I wobbled, staggered and generally meandered down the road, pausing only to apologise to a lamppost with which I had nearly collided. Sympathy from the lads of course was non-existent. They quickly concluded, when I walked into the door on the way to the toilet, that I was still suffering from the excesses of the previous evening, communicating that conclusion to me with the brief, but descriptive, observation, "You're pissed!"

Feeling that breakfast might be a bit of a challenge, as it involved the use of sharp utensils, I headed for the bathroom and a mirror, narrowly avoiding a collision with both. With the help of some warm water and an oxy-acetylene torch, I broke open the weld across my eyelid. The bloodshot weepy orb that appeared beneath the crusted lashes looked like something from a cheap Halloween mask, but at least it could still focus. With both eyes open, I nipped back into the breakfast hall and promptly devoured a full breakfast with an alacrity fuelled by the fear that my ability to see clearly might be short-lived.

It was.

By the time we boarded the coaches for the Saturday tour, the wind had whipped up a bit and was aggravating the sty. The situation worsened through the day until finally, at some seaside venue in the afternoon, the combination of wind, sea spray and airborne fine sand drove me frantically searching the chemists' shops in town for an eye patch. In the third shop, I was offered a proper Long John Silver black patch. With the aid of the assistant, I fitted it immediately and groped and stumbled my way back to the dance spot.

A high-spirited cheer went up at my reappearance, plus the usual daft comments about peg legs and parrots, but the consensus was that my raffish image was set off a treat by this latest addition to my kit. Considering we looked like a bunch of brigands anyway, I wondered whether we would benefit from the acquisition of more pirate gear – cutlasses and hook hands for example. For my part though, I was content with the eye patch. It was as much as I could cope with, as it rendered me practically blind. Attempting the Dilwyn Stick Dance was a poor decision, and I was lucky to escape with no broken fingers. So was the man dancing opposite, whoever he was.

For obvious reasons, memories of the day are hazy, and I can't recall much before our return to Exeter for the evening festivities. By then, a number of negative forces seemed to be at work. My personal situation had deteriorated, and my eye had turned into a festering red blob glowing in the blackness of my face. It was so painful, I found it difficult to concentrate on anything but my own situation. That was not the only problem, however. Silurian's unity had been rattled by some unknown influence, and internecine squabbling was breaking out during the meal.

None of us could make any decisions about what we should

be doing that evening. Some wanted to skip the feast even before it started. Others thought it unmannerly to do so, and much divisive bickering was breaking out. At one point, Willy decided he'd had enough argument, and wandered off in search of liquid refreshment. Noticing a bottle of well-aged Chateau Lascombes sitting on the top table in front of the Squire of the Ring, he decided wine would make a pleasant change from beer, so he simply grabbed the bottle and began swigging from it.

Willy's behaviour was symptomatic of the unhealthy belligerence manifesting in our ranks, which in turn precipitated nervous glances and anxious whispers soughing through the hall like an unquiet spirit. The Silurian entity was always mercurial and close to the edge, and there were those in the ring who expected such miscreants to crash and burn, simply because they disapproved of us. But we were still a ring side and up until then had done nothing to warrant dismissal. It was clear that many of those in the room believed Silurian were about to go completely over the top, which would precipitate the full bell, book and candle excommunication. They were disappointed when we settled down to a low simmer and no further disruptions occurred.

At this point I stood up, causing another ripple of apprehension to unsettle the assembled company.

"It's the one with the eye patch! What're they up to now?"

I wasn't up to much of anything, for all my outlandish appearance. I really didn't feel too special and I had made a positive decision to forego the feast, the beer, the singing and even the trip to the pub later. I was happy to trade all this for bed. At least my eye might have a better chance if I was asleep. So, inadvertently conjuring up an image of Blind Pugh as a part-time coalminer, I navigated my way out of the dinner hall and up the road to the sleeping quarters.

I lay there on my sleeping bag, not really tired but completely worn out, mumbling to myself like a delirious malaria case, mostly in broken Swahili.

"Mimi mgonjwa – I'm sick," I thought, "Or is it *ni* mgonjwa?" I wasn't too sure about some of the grammar. "Mimi mgonjwa ndani ya kichwa – my head hurts!" I knew that was right, as I had said it to my African nanny often enough. "Nimechoka zaidi, choka kabisa – I'm completely done in!"

I went back to *One Man Went To Mow*, feeling as if the evening was turning into another long journey. Trouble was, I had learned the Swahili version parrot-fashion many years previously and, trying to piece it together was causing me endless problems with the complicated grammar.

John Smith, on the other hand, had no hang-ups at all when it came to the finer points of Swahili grammar, as I was to find out in due course. He simply saw his meagre grasp of this exotic tongue as an opportunity for a killer chat-up line. Allegedly, whilst I was in self-confinement back at base, Silurian had been invited to a private party, and John Smith had wasted no time in assessing the availability of single females.

Before long, he had some unsuspecting girl pinned to the wall and, noticing her attention was wandering in the direction of the exits, he thought she would be an ideal subject upon whom to demonstrate his linguistic ability.

"Did you know," he said, pausing for effect and giving her a gentle prod on the shoulder to guarantee her undivided attention, "did you know I can sing '*One Man Went To Mow*' in Swahili?"

He beamed and gave her his 'you're-so-lucky-to-have-found-me' wink.

"Oh yeah?" she replied, with a touch more defiance than John Smith was expecting in a situation where he had complete mastery, "Go on then . . ."

"Umm . . . moja moto, moja moto . . . er . . ." he faltered, "Kwenda . . . umm, something . . . shamba . . ."

He was on shaky ground, but he wasn't going to let that stop him. After all, she hadn't got a clue whether he was right or not.

So he ran through the first line again, complete with mistakes, but with considerably more panache and to the right tune.

He glanced at her blue eyes, expecting the half-closed 'take-me-I'm-yours' swoony look. Instead there was a sharp glint that temporarily unnerved him.

"I think you meant *mtu*?" she suggested.

"Eh?"

"You said *moto*, but I think you meant *mtu* – 'person' or 'man'," she said, "*Moto* means 'fire'. Perhaps you were going to sing 'Mwanga Moto Yangu'. *Light My Fire*?"

Then, in impeccable Swahili, she ran through the first three men and their dogs. Finding it difficult to conceal a little smirk of triumph, she slipped off to replenish her drink, leaving John Smith lost for words, foreign or otherwise, and wondering whether he would have been better off telling her the Red Riding Hood joke.

Maybe this was the root cause of his disgruntled attitude when Silurian, still disunited, returned to the dormitory in the early hours. Whatever the reason, I was woken by what appeared to be a serious altercation, with John Smith in the thick of it. There was much commotion and sounds of packing, interjected with expletives, concluding with a slamming door.

"Hey, John Smith's gone home!" someone said.

"Good. At least I can have his bed then," said Chris Mulvey, adding, "Some kind of place this is, when some of us have to sleep on the floor!"

It was true though. John Smith had indeed walked off, in the middle of the night and in pouring rain, with his rucksack and fiddle.

I was still more concerned with my eye than with all this hostility and midnight raving, so I went back to sleep. I woke the next morning with no thoughts of young John until I saw him, albeit mistily, at breakfast.

"Morning, John Smith," I greeted him, partly to verify that I'd got the right man.

"Mornin'."

Silurian, together again, crowded around him for his version of the night's mysteries. His reply didn't give us much to go on.

"Well, I got to the bus stop and checked the timetable for buses to Worcester, but there didn't seem to be any from Exeter, so I kipped in the bus shelter. And now I've come for breakfast."

An outburst of laughter followed this revelation, instantly healing yesterday's wounds and magically reuniting us, though it unsettled some of the other men in the room. Seeing us all sitting together in the full kit and laughing conspiratorially, they probably thought we were planning some new reprehensible prank. But no. After breakfast, we just gave them the benefit of a few impromptu tunes to set the tone for Sunday, which began with avoiding the church service as usual.

Disappointingly, the pubs weren't open until midday, so we looked for somewhere else to pass the time. There was a Wimpy burger shop in town so we ambled down there for a coffee. We tried giving the sparse audience the benefit of some live music, but we reckoned without King Kong, the manageress, who was having none of it. She chucked us out amid howls of protest from the other customers, who preferred to be entertained by a bunch of crazies than put up with the lifeless canned music. So they followed us out onto the street where we continued to play, and we rewarded their support with a couple of our favourite dances.

They loved it and so did we. By opening time we were in high spirits as we took over a lovely little pub just opposite the cathedral, where the main display was taking place just in front of the majestic west frontage. When it came to our turn for the show dance, we were still feeling very excitable and we gave it our best shot again. It was a very large space and we aimed to fill it. Memories of Thaxted came rushing back as we widened the set to push the crowds from the edges of the arena. We winged past them with our rounds and fast, high-flying heys. Drawing the crowd in emotionally, we wanted them to understand that morris dancing could be flamboyant even with the simplest of dances, and exhilarating for us as well as the onlookers. It was also cathartic after the previous evening's meltdown. Above all, it showed the real face of Silurian to those disapproving critics at the feast. When it was time to deliver, we did it in style.

Admittedly, we could be unruly, over-exuberant and abusive. Without a doubt we were anarchic, with a healthy disregard for the morris establishment and the authority that drove it. How could it not be so? Having had the Welsh Border morris tradition dismissed as not worthy of further consideration, we were hardly likely to toe the Cotswold party line and be all good chums together. The 'us and them' stand-off was volatile and one spark could ignite an explosive reaction. But our ultimate objective was to create a performance that elevated the morris dance to a higher level. On a good day, it would be almost spiritual and, on those days, we really felt as if we were getting close to something elemental. Like the first freemasons, however, in their search for the higher understanding within themselves, we were dealing with something elusive. It was this that made the whole experience worthwhile, even the viewing of endless boring motorway panoramas as we drove home . . . well, for those of us who could see, that is.

Personal Reflection: 3

Talking Greatcoat Blues

• • • • •

"I think you'll make a drummer,
So please step this way, young man..."

It was a bitterly cold January morning as I stood frozen to the pavement, amusing myself with trying to build up my own personal cloud formation by panting warmed bursts of breath into the icy air. A couple of minutes of this and I felt faint, giddy and vaguely nauseous, so I stopped, just short of passing out. Pulling the huge collar of my coat around my ears, I buried my hands in its cavernous pockets and waited. It was six-thirty in the morning and I was waiting for Keith Close and a minibus full of Silurians.

There are bad gigs and there are odd gigs, but this one fell firmly into the latter bracket. We were going 'dahn the smoke' to teach Welsh Border Morris to the Royal Ballet. Needless to say, the more I thought about this and about the fact that it necessitated my standing out there in the pre-dawn half-light wearing a black face and a huge coat, the more unreal the world seemed. I began to think that I must have died at the last gig after all, and that I was now in some kind of suspended animation in a weird morris limbo land, cold and featureless.

"If that's the case," I said to myself, "I'm glad I've brought the coat. I might need it." I moved my shoulders inside it, comforted that this garment, though cumbersome, was more useful than the trendy leather bomber jacket I had been seen in on occasions.

"At least this keeps the cold out," I muttered, making a note that talking to oneself is bad for one's sanity.

I loved that old coat. And I still love it today. Actually, it had been brand new when I bought it – Royal Navy pattern, but with Civil Defence buttons, made in 1951 but evidently never issued. The reason for its purchase was to keep me warm in winter, my job as a land surveyor requiring me to work outdoors. I was twenty-four years old when I acquired it. The coat was twenty. On the frosted roadside that day, it had reached the venerable age of thirty-six but still looked like a teenager. Regulation navy blue, it came complete with blanket lining and a profusion of big black buttons. Inside was a small rectangle of material that bore the legend 'Greatcoat – Men's – 5'8" to 5'10" '. Wrong size, I would say, because I was 5'10" and a bit, but once inside the coat, it took a while to find me. It fitted where it touched – somewhere between the collar and the shoulders. The big black buttons, embossed with the letters CD and a crown, didn't do much for me, so I added a touch of chic by replacing them with plaited leather buttons. Distinctly Harris Tweed and staid, but dangerously dark blue.

But even upgrading it thus to its rightful haute couture status cut no ice with my hard-to-please spouse, Dizzy, whose finely honed sense of design told her instantly this was a job for the Fashion Police. To her credit though, she extended the hand of amnesty by allowing me time to review my dress sense before the offence was officially reported. I wore this huge coat several times over the ensuing weeks before I finally gave in, but they were miserable weeks. The swagger had gone, and I felt like a tone-deaf infiltrator in the fashion choir.

It had not always been like that.

There was a time when, making my way through Worcester's ancient backstreets to the Greyhound Inn on a windy, wintry night, the black pavement glossy with rain, I wore it with a black trilby. I felt this hat and coat combo was the last word in fashionable rainwear. The non-existence of anyone else similarly attired was of no consequence to me. What did I really care in that age of wear-what-you-dare individualism? Surrounded as we all were by everyone else's fashion statements, where everything you thought was trendy wasn't, and vice versa, I felt unassailable in my greatcoat. I was safe in the belief that, in terms of street cred, I was so far out I was coming back in the other side.

Thus it was with some panache that I would head for the pub, the vast collar up around my ears and the brim of the trilby down over my eyes. With hands buried in deep pockets and a neatly rolled cigarette stuck to my bottom lip, I was doing the Bogey Walk. Friar Street was Casablanca in the rain and I was destined for Rick's Bar. I felt confident. But perhaps that was because I knew nobody could find me inside my blue fortress.

Despite the adverse observations of my charming consort, I reckoned I cut a dash. In reality, I probably looked like a Harlem hood or a hitman for the Mafia. Or maybe I just looked like someone who couldn't afford a proper coat. Ultimately, of course, it made no difference. The oracle had spoken, and the inescapable truth was that I had to upgrade my image. With some reluctance, I admitted defeat and headed for the High Street kasbahs in search of something zappy.

I found her in Burtons, in the shoe department. She had eyes that could melt steel at twenty paces. Thumbing through the choice of jackets in the adjacent clothes department, I was hypnotised by those eyes and overcome by an urge to show her I was nothing like the dull old-before-his-time thirty-something, to whom she was trying to sell a pair of trendy shoes. Catch me going to seed like him? No chance! Though my temples were greying, I was still well on the case. Okay, so I made a serious mistake with the greatcoat, but underneath that coat lurked a manifestation of colour-coordinated subtlety worthy of a special mention in Vogue. What with the grey shirt, blue baggy trousers and black suede shoes, all cunningly set off with a bottle-green roll neck jumper and orange Liberty print tie, I was the epitome of streetwise self-expression. Or maybe just another victim of self-delusion.

Whichever it was, I felt comfortable and assured. The young oldie in the shoe department probably felt comfortable too, but in a safe and predictable way. I was never going to get like that. With this thought in mind, I gravitated towards the leather section. I had fancied something in leather ever since my little brother got himself kitted out in a studded and zipped motorcycle jacket. But, by the time I thought I could afford one, such things had moved from risqué to trendy to commonplace. From its cult status as the symbol of rebelliousness, the leather jacket had ambled into the arena of middle-class respectability along with that other rebel icon, blue denim jeans, the whole ensemble worn by everyone from rock bands to royalty. I wasn't happy with the thought of getting drawn into this kind of mass hysteria.

With brows puckering into a thoughtful frown, I wrestled with the dilemma. Would the wearing of the leather jacket confer upon me anarchic sex appeal, or just pure anonymity? At least the greatcoat demonstrated individuality, though in the sex appeal heats it didn't even make it off the starting blocks. Also, we were talking serious money. One wrong move and that was well over a hundred quid down the pan.

The girl in the shoe department shot me a glance, which just missed my head and burned a hole in the wall behind the sales counter. I wondered how she would react to me encased in black leather. I wondered how *I* would react to me. Then there was Dizzy, in the shop with me now, keeping the kids from each other's throats. She was the one who had precipitated this whole quandary.

In a sudden flash of bravado, unequalled since Blondin first crossed Niagara Falls on a tightrope, I tried the jacket on. The hint of an approving smile from Dizzy. So far, so good. I tried a couple of poses in front of the mirror, and a voice inside my head said,

"This is not for you – way too smooth. Forget the whole idea and stick to the greatcoat."

"Don't be so boring," said a second voice. "Just go for it – nothing to lose!"

"Except a hundred an' odd quid!"

I could feel panic coming on. I looked around the store in desperation. Somebody help me with this decision! I looked at me in the mirror; I looked at the girl with the eyes of fire; I looked at Dizzy. No reaction. Like chatting to the three wise monkeys.

Nonchalantly moving through the coat racks to a mirror closer to the shoe department, I ran through a couple more poses while watching the reflection of The Eyes. Turning my back on the mirror for a rear view shot, I could see Dizzy with the two kids on their leashes. She was looking me over with a quizzical, "Hmmm . . ."

Just then, the mirror shattered as The Eyes shot me what I fondly convinced myself was an admiring glance. The spinning coin in my head came down on the side of the second voice. Guiltily, I went to the sales desk, paid my money and left the shop with a carrier bag containing the trendy leather.

"Prat!" said the first voice.

I had to agree, standing on the frozen pavement in that cold January air. The greatcoat was a winner. No way would that silly little leather thing keep me this warm for this long.

As the light of morning gradually asserted itself on the receding darkness, I reckoned I must have looked slightly demonic rooted there immobile and blacked out against the sky. Certainly motorists were beginning to veer away from me as they passed. Luckily the minibus appeared before any major catastrophe occurred. It glided to a gentle stop with the door right opposite me. Such service!

"Need a lift?" asked the cheery little gnome behind the wheel. Why Keith Close should change from a deputy head teacher to a gnome as soon as he blacked his face was a mystery to me. But, then again, the blacking did strange things to all of us – it made my own face look like a black melon. Pondering on this, I climbed aboard.

"Don't forget your drum!"

The Drum! I looked over my shoulder. There it sat on the pavement, its brass body gleaming in the dawn. How could I forget it so easily? Something to do with not being able to play it, I suspect. A lack of bonding. But it looked every inch a Silurian drum and I had paid good money for it. Reluctantly, I retrieved it and hid it on the bus.

As a drummer, it has to be said, I made a pretty good triangle player. I was certainly no natural drummer. However, one of those step changes had occurred in the side when Dion stopped coming out on away weekends, and the music was the worse for it. Meanwhile, I was the rash and possibly foolish owner of this drum, and it was with me on that trip to London. If all else failed, I could render it unplayable by slitting the skin.

I'd spotted it at Bromyard Folk Festival in 1987, in one of the many peddlers' tents pegged out on the main campsite. Its red painted wooden rim encasing the brass body gave it a very alluring look. Like a baby kitten in a pet shop window, it appealed to me. It seemed to be calling to me. "Yo – Silurian fellow! Over here! Please don't leave me in this tent with all these nasty bodhrans and djembes and stuff!" I'm a sucker for these impassioned outbursts. Plus I was able to lay my hands on the wherewithal to release this unhappy object from captivity. It turned out, on closer inspection, that the drum was an old Boys Brigade model made in 1947, an auspicious year for drums, Chateau Latour and idiots. So it came home with me.

Whether I could play it was a question I had not considered at the point of sale.

I bashed away at it for weeks, but it was like walking on melted tar. Visions of life as a child in Uganda would flash through my brain. All those African drummers I had seen weaving an intricate mesh of percussion with their ceremonial tribal drums. All those nights when I had gone to sleep to the sound of drums down the road in Nakawa village. From the seven-foot tall Watusi dancers performing for the young Queen Elizabeth to our houseboy tapping out hypnotic rhythms with two sticks on a hollow log, I had seen the lot. Yet here I was, with my own personal private drum, and I seemed unable to build any kind of rapport with it. The rhythm I was producing gave the impression that one of my hands was probably tied to the other foot.

Practice nights were hopeless. I was so nervous, and the drum sounded so loud in the room, that holding a steady beat seemed to be about as easy as packing an electric eel into a suitcase. Willy was very tolerant, but the occasional withering look over his glasses left me in no doubt as to his true feelings.

"The only way to sort this out," I thought to myself, "is to take the drum next time we're out and play it in front of a proper audience."

Its first outing was on the Boxing Day tour that year. I thought this would be akin to easing my way in, as it was familiar territory. No chance. Outside the Malvern Hills Hotel, I was so anxious, the drum seemed to be growing bigger and bigger as the time to play it drew near.

"Come on then, you 'orrible lot!" yelled Burco, appearing from the gloom of the pub, "Let's go and do a bit!"

I gave the drum a frantic glance. *Uuurgh*! Eight feet across! I couldn't possibly play a thing that size . . . Look at the sticks – they're like telegraph poles!

The other lads were filing out of the pub. Bernie, Mick, Smudge . . . Trying not to make any sudden moves and draw attention to myself, I furtively looked around for a bolt hole. My palms were damp. Why was it so hot all of a sudden? Perhaps if I just sneaked in behind the rest of the lads, I could slip through the door and hide in the loo, or –

"Hiya Dion!"

"AARRGH!"

My head whipped round so fast, I very nearly sustained a whiplash injury. There was Mick talking to Dion, who seemed to have appeared from nowhere and was now a couple of feet away from me, looking suitably fearsome in full Silurian regalia. My eyes stared, my jaw fell, my heart sank. Dion, of all people – a drummer of inestimable virtuosity. And he was standing right there! I thought he had stopped coming out with us for health reasons, yet here he was. Had he got better? Why hadn't he told us? Why hadn't he been at the first spot in Ledbury?

"Long time no see," Mick was saying.

'Long time!?' I thought. 'I should say it's a long time! Long enough for me to buy this poxy drum. What am I gonna do?' I always assumed resurrections took three days. But I hadn't seen Dion for months. Why was he doing this to me?

"Hello, Rob!" Dion suddenly said, turning to talk to me. "Nice drum," he added benignly.

"Oh. Yes . . ." I replied, eyeing the monstrous instrument warily, "you can play it if you like."

"Nah, it's all right, thanks – you play it. I've brought the banjo."

Bugger! Trapped!

There was nothing for it but to brazen it out, so I attached the drum to its mooring on my belt, noticing it had shrunk almost back to normal size, and joined the band as inconspicuously as possible. Predictably, the drumming was rubbish. Willy gave me The Look, and Dion gave me some helpful hints. But having to play in front of Dion, the best snare drummer in the known world, just turned me into a quaking uncoordinated mess. I was glad when the day was over.

Just a month later, there I was, still with the drum, and heading for London and the Royal Ballet. No doubt the picture of Silurian running riot at the Royal Ballet is an alarming one, but we were there by invitation and really, when required, we could be very sensible. We were, after all, just normal individuals under our costumes. Well, okay, maybe not quite *normal*, but we were not stupid. So we behaved according to what circumstances demanded. And, in the case of the Royal Ballet, circumstances demanded a certain level of decorum in order to become teachers for the morning.

Some of their male dancers had become interested in dance forms other than ballet, and had formed a team called Bow Street Rapper, principally a rapper-sword side but with a bit of Cotswold thrown in. We had seen them perform at the Exeter ring meeting and they were brilliant – faultless precision rapper moves as well as the best Cotswold dancing we had seen in a long time. They were equally impressed with us and wanted to know all about Border dances. Thus we lost no time in arranging a mutually convenient date for our visit to the Royal School of Ballet in Richmond Park.

As we drove through the park, I was disturbed by the amount of devastation caused by the infamous hurricane which rampaged through the southern counties of England back in October 1987. I had seen the media coverage at the time, especially the TV footage, but that industry's callous profit-motivated mentality, and the consequential 'good news is no news' attitude, does no more than blunt the emotions without getting to the real pain of any disaster. We see two-dimensional images and we hear sounds, but we can't smell, taste or touch it. Thus, when we meet reality, we are totally unprepared.

It hit me hard in Richmond Park that day. My emotions were deeply shaken by the shock of seeing such huge numbers of fallen trees, broken and dying throughout this serene parkland. The majestic ancient oaks, kings of the forest, ripped out by the roots and smashed to the ground alongside scores of their lowlier subjects, were still lying where they fell. I was filled with profound sadness travelling through this haunted desolate wasteland.

Our arrival at the school was a relief, for me at least. Spending the morning teaching Border to these ballet stars was guaranteed to focus our minds on something other than death in the park. I don't need to dwell on the finer points of our morning's instructional though. As expected, ballet dancers are quick learners – and very athletic. By the time these boys had learned a couple of our dances, we began to question our own skills, but in the end decided that Border probably needs a rough edge, and that too much refinement dilutes the magic.

In the afternoon, we went out with Bow Street Rapper to visit a couple of their favourite pubs and entertain the locals with two very different styles of traditional dancing. At one point, Bow Street did a Cotswold dance called 'Leapfrog' which, as the name suggests, involves dancers leaping over each other. We had seen this dance performed, and had even attempted it ourselves when we still wore Cotswold kit, but never had we seen it accomplished with such elegance, precision and style. Ballet and morris dancing is a potent combination.

As for me, I don't think my drumming skills developed much that day, but my attitude to life certainly did. The personal grievance caused by my poor playing was put into sharp perspective by the sight of the wreckage in the park. By the time Keith dropped me off that night, I was feeling positively bouncy. All was now right with the world as I walked the short distance back to my house, lost inside my greatcoat and with the drum dangling from my left hand.

"At least I had a chance to wear the old coat," I said to the darkness, "and the drumming can only improve."

Chapter 17
Allegro Con Moto

• • • • •

"When owls call the breathless moon
In the blue veil of the night,
The shadows of the trees appear
Amidst the lantern light..."

I phoned Burco.

"'Ullo?" he said.

"What do *you* want?" I asked.

"Whaddya mean, what do *I* want? You phoned me, you daft bugger!"

"How many times have I told you not to ring me on this number?" I put the phone down. My thoughts turned to tea. Unplugging the kettle, I went over to the tap and topped it up. The phone rang.

"'Ullo?" I said.

"What do *you* want?" asked Burco on the other end.

"I want to know if you would like a lift to practice tonight."

"Oh! Yes please. Ta very much."

"Right. I'll see you about the usual time, then? Bye!"

A couple of hours later, seated around our favourite table in the Horse and Jockey, the subject of local tours had come up, prompted by Andy pointing out that we didn't do any.

"We don't need to – we're world famous!" beamed Burco, chest swelling and simian grin breaking out.

"Well, that's it exactly," said Andy. "We're always off for the weekend and so the locals don't ever get to see us."

"The locals never want to bloody see us," Willy chipped in.

"And nobody ever wants to organise a local tour anyway," said Keith Close, our newly appointed bagman, in that exasperated and lugubrious tone that ultimately affects every bagman. A bagman's lot is indeed not a happy one.

Smudge, inexplicably on the defensive, jumped in. "Oi organise local tours!"

Mick said, "Yes, but only in Ross, Dave."

"And generally centred on the White Lion," Bernie pointed out. "You can hardly call walking from the lounge bar to the public bar of the White Lion a 'tour', can you?" Little eddies of laughter rippled around the table.

"How about a walking tour of Colwall?" suggested Mulvey, leaning back against the plush padded bench seat, unwrapping a small cigar and wafting its length under his nose. His wife had told him a while back that he was getting through too many cigarettes so he must give up smoking. He had challenged that by suggesting an occasional cigar wouldn't do any harm. But his consumption had gone up. So he was now smoking nearly as many cigars as he had smoked cigarettes. Same numbers – five times the price.

"What's the matter with you, Mulvey?" demanded Willy. "You been out in the sun again? *Walking tour of Colwall* – do me a favour!?"

"No-no – it'll be all right," Mulvey countered, in his 'that's-the-price-of-the-job-and-no-haggling' voice. "We can do it for Paddy's Night. I'll bring the shamrock, look, an' we can go from the Park Hotel to the Crown, an' then back here to the Horse and Jockstrap to finish up. Whaddya reckon?"

He looked from face to face and, finding no obvious dissent, added, "Perhaps Des will do us some of his Voodoo Chicken again!"

That did it. The clincher. Desmond's Voodoo Chicken. Nothing to do with the dark arts of Haiti, it was actually a Caribbean dish, Des being from that part of the world. The real name of the dish didn't do it justice, so we had come up with something more appropriate to convey the spell it wove around all who consumed it. As for Desmond himself, he was a real bonus. The only black landlord we had ever encountered and he was running *our pub*! At the time, before the zealous yet misguided champions of Political Correctness had created an issue around black-faced morris dancers where none existed before, Desmond and his bunch of blacked-up patrons were best of friends. He understood the concept of disguise and the whole subject was simply a non-issue. Oh happy days!

So, the date was set. March 17th, St Patrick's night, and a bitterly cold night it turned out to be. On nights like that we were almost certainly guaranteed no audience. When people had braved the elements to occupy a cosy corner of the pub by the blazing log fire, it took more than we could offer to entice them back into the cold. Outside the Park Hotel, we did the first couple of dances watched by no one except three kids jostling for space in an upstairs window across the street. Local tours? Waste of time.

As the third dance began, I had decided that being a drummer in arctic conditions had serious drawbacks. Hopping from foot to frozen foot, I was wondering whether being unable to feel neither my fingers nor the drumsticks might improve my playing.

"Interesting drum roll you've developed there, Rob," said Willy, cutting across my thoughts.

"Uncontrollable shivering, Willy," I pointed out, my chattering teeth and frozen mouth making me sound like an amateur ventriloquist's dummy. This would have been the right time to don the greatcoat again, along with scarf and gloves, but none of these was part of the official kit. I made a mental note to bring up 'winter kit' as an item at the next AGM.

By the time we got to the second spot, the Crown, just a couple of hundred yards from the Park, the shamrock in our buttonholes had wilted with severe frostbite, and some of us looked to be going the same way.

Bathed in the pale glow of the street lights, we looked quite intimidating in our black get-up, standing around in the cold, blowing tiny fogs of steam with every breath and trying to summon up the energy to dance. There was something sinister yet bewitching about the scene which reminded me of another evening tour about four years previously, when the magical element that Silurian had created really struck me deeply.

It was one of those mystical nights in the undulating Herefordshire borderlands when the full moon looms up over the horizon so close you feel you can touch it. A night when the road shines silver-grey and the trees seem to be cut from black velvet. When the fields are awash with light but shadows fall densely. All is still but not still, and you can imagine the nymphs and dryads out and about. It is a time of spells and hexes and a boon to hunters of the night.

The trees on the high ground behind the remote and isolated pub were bleak against the blue-grey sheen of the grass. Yesterday's gales had died, and the crisp stillness of a perfect autumn evening turned a walk to this cosy retreat into an exceptional pleasure. In yellow squares of light the interior was well defined – the people with their drinks, laughing, smoking; the landlord at his pumps, the rows of bottles behind him. All was cheery and mellow, and one could almost feel the warmth of the log fire. From the outside, the building itself was barely discernible, tucked into the dark shadowy lee of the hill, but the dull whiteness of its half-timbered frame just showed up in the gloom.

Anyone passing by on that still night, when sounds waft easily on the motionless air, might have been diverted by the sound of a melodeon drifting along the lower slopes of the hill, through the moonlit gorse and bracken. Pausing to trace the source of the music, our wanderer might have seen in the shadows other shadows moving. Closer scrutiny would have revealed a number of dancers, shades in motion, circling and weaving, brandishing yard-long sticks.

In the twilight glow of the rising moon, the musician would have looked eerie. Little more than an effigy of a guardsman in an ill-defined homemade busby, his red coat was the deep colour of blood in this monochromic light. His bearded face was blackened and he would have appeared completely featureless apart from his round gold-rimmed glasses, picking up the occasional spangle of cold moonlight. Legs apart, toes pointing in, slightly hunched and moving with the music, he was releasing from his instrument a hypnotic string of notes to which the dancers stepped and wheeled. He was the puppet master, their Pied Piper. The music held them all in its spell, unwinding the dance as it unwound itself.

Moving with the notes, the dancers wove the pattern the music presented, spicing the sequence with powerful clashing of sticks, puncturing the fabric of the air with shocks of sound which hit the evening stillness like pebbles in a pond, rippling away to the edges of the night. Black-faced and black-clothed, the dancers betrayed their shadowy movements with glimpses of white shirt, eyes and teeth, the latter flashing in smiled demonstration that enjoyment was very much part of the scene.

And so they danced, with tinkling bells around their knees, weaving the music. Dance and music, musician and dancers, all were one. Without the dance, the music was no more than a melody; without the music, the dance was just a sequence of steps. In symbiosis, a higher level was reached. Though essentially alone under the light of the moon, the dancers performed with vigorous energy, caught up in the music's spell. In the shadow of the hostelry a handful of watchers stood, drawn here and reeled in by the music. They too became part of the tableau as its hypnotic rhythm enfolded them and the music became part of the fabric of the night. I was there that night, and I knew then for certain that this was the spirit of the Morris.

St Patrick's night, 1988, and Silurian were dancing in the dark again. There was much to be said for the eeriness of it all, in the unreal glow of the street lights. Somehow it wasn't the same as that wild and mysterious night in the borderlands, but we still gave it our best. Reluctance preceded action, however, as we stood around for a while before the first dance, sipping chilled ale from cold grey tankards. The need to warm up spurred us into movement, and we executed the first number with commendable zeal. Predictably, no one stirred from the pub to watch us, so Burco marched in and press-ganged a small audience from the public bar. They shuffled out and formed up in a self-conscious line close to the front door.

We danced, and the applause from our supposedly impassive audience sounded genuine. They even cheered for more. We decided the Dilwyn Stick Dance would be the one, as it was quite lively, with long crossovers and hostile stick clashing, not to mention a little ditty in the middle in praise of Uncle Billy and his ten-foot willy. The pavement outside the pub being too narrow, we elected to use the whole of the street for the crossovers. Our conscripted audience was impressed and, playing to this small gallery, we danced with some enthusiasm on that bitterly cold night.

On the second set of crossovers, the two lines of four black-coated dancers swiftly traversed the road. Marking time for two beats on the far side of the road, that line of four was just about to cross back when the onlookers noticed the car.

An Austin Allegro was approaching the dancers from behind. It seemed to be slowing down, but suddenly we all knew it wasn't going to.

For the next few seconds, we became part of one of those sickening slow-motion sequences beloved of contemporary film makers as the minutest details of the scene unfolded before us in an unstoppable chain of inevitability. Everyone appeared to have noticed the unwelcome intrusion of the Allegro, and we all saw it beginning to drive through the middle of the set as the crossover started.

All except Vas, that is.

The first three dancers on the far side of the road checked themselves as the car approached, but Vas, fully engrossed in the music, started to cross back. As we helplessly looked on, he stepped right in front of the car.

It had taken just a few seconds, but an age had gone by from the time the car had appeared to the shocking screech of skidding tyres, as the Allegro hit Vas from behind, jolting us out of our mesmeric trance. Vas, thrown over the bonnet by the impact, crashed into the windscreen before somersaulting the front bumper as the car stopped, throwing him face first into the road. He rolled a few times and ended up on his back.

For an instant, nothing happened.

Somebody said, "Oh, Christ!"

Then everyone seemed to be moving at once, most of them aimlessly. A couple of people checked on the driver, shaken but unhurt, fretfully explaining that he thought the dancers had stopped to let him through. Chris Mulvey ran into the pub to phone for an ambulance, whilst three of us attended to Vas. He was still lying on his back, breathing fitfully. His blackened bearded face glowed horribly in the neon light and, more gruesomely, his eye sockets were filling up with blood from his smashed nose. As I was taking in this repugnant sight, one pool began to overflow, the blood running down the side of his face into his ear.

By the time the ambulance arrived, Vas's breathing was alarmingly erratic. What with that and his uncontrollable shivering, some of us wondered, as the ambulance sped away, whether we would ever see him again. We all felt hopeless, awkward, ill at ease. Not knowing what we could do or say to improve the situation, we soon drifted from the scene and back to our homes to await news of our compatriot.

As it turned out, the damage was nowhere near as bad as it looked, once the nurses had fought their way through the blacking to clean up the wounds. A couple of days later, the medical opinion was that, apart from a permanently modified nose, Vas would soon be back to normal. And indeed he was. The next time he came to the Horse and Jockey on practice night, the banter was humming along at a good pace, generated by the sense of relief that he had survived the accident.

"Great move that, Vaz," Bernie complimented him, "Perhaps you could teach the rest of us tonight?"

"*Vass*," muttered Vas.

"It still needs a bit of work, I reckon," added Mulvey in a cautionary tone. "For instance, that somersault was a bit sloppy!"

"Plus it was an Austin," Mick pointed out. "If you were going to go to all that trouble, you could have picked a Morris!"

"An' you lost yer 'at!" chipped in Smudge, in mumbled astonishment.

"Well, I've got to admit," said Vas gravely, "I am still working on the bonnet flip, and it does need ironing out, but I do think the nose dive was perfect!"

"Which is more than can be said for your actual nose," observed Willy.

"Oh, and by the way, Chris," Vas added, "thanks again for the lucky shamrock – I'd have been in real trouble without that!"

Exactly twelve months later, we did the St Patrick's walking tour of Colwall again. If you fall off your bike, best to get back on again. This time round, however, when we got to the Crown, we danced in the car park. As an extra precaution, Vas was presented with a motorcycle helmet and a fluorescent safety harness, courtesy of Super Steve. The event was also commemorated with a special anniversary card, designed and illustrated by our very own resident cartoonist, Andy Griffin.

It worked. We danced without mishap. The ghost was exorcised. And, best of all, we completed the tour, ending up at the Horse and Jockey, where Desmond's Voodoo Chicken was lying in wait for us.

Chapter 18
Legless Again

• • • • •

"Your baby has gorn down the plug'ole,
Your baby has gorn down the plug!
The poor little fing was so skinny and thin,
It should have been bathed in a jug...!"

"Something wrong with life," I thought morosely, staring glumly through the coach window. "Another morris tour, another row." Brightening suddenly, I thought, "Hey, that sounds like that song . . . how does it go? . . . Tum-ti-tum-tum, ti-*tum*-ti-*tum* . . ."

No, I couldn't remember the song. I couldn't even remember the second line of the tune. I slumped back into gloom.

My being a morris dancer was causing problems at home. Morris and marriage had entered my life at the same time fifteen years previously. And now I'd had another row with Dizzy. She was disgruntled with the amount of time it took up, or so she said. I guessed there were other reasons, though. She had seen the strange mesmeric effect Silurian had on women, and I felt it may have been turning her eyes from brown to green. What she probably hadn't understood was the addictive effect of being part of a side that caused such positive reactions from the audience, and indeed from the women amongst them. A cocktail of adrenalin and endorphins is a heady mix.

To compound the problem, we were running on high octane male energy ignited by overt female admiration with undeniable sexual overtones. Some saw us as warriors, others as mystical gatekeepers at the entrance to other worlds. Some simply saw great entertainment and memorable performances. And we just lapped it all up. We were high on the drug and, like all addicts, we found ways of justifying our behaviour. It was true that some of us neglected domestic duties and responsibilities some of the time, but it was the get-up that did it. To transform oneself from an ordinary world-weary, stressed-out social automaton into a component of an entity that operated at a different level from mere mortals was irresistible, and we would risk a spouse's wrath to escape into that strange realm.

I grappled with these notions as the coach rumbled on. "I bet there's a book in this," I thought.

Passing a signpost saying, 'Evesham', I remembered what I was doing on this coach in the first place. It was 1988 and Faithful City's 21st Birthday Tour . . . another chance to 'have the crack' with them for the first time since the Lassington Oak evening. We had been writing a little song for them, on and off, since then, and the birthday tour was an opportunity to focus on getting it finished.

There were two other sides on the coach with us, and we were quite happy when one of them opted to kick off the show at the first dance spot, as it gave us the time to organise ourselves. A couple of Cotswold numbers were performed, during which time a few people looked on out of curiosity. Then it was our turn. Quite a few people stopped doing what they had been doing and gathered to watch. Seemingly appearing from nowhere, the crowd grew during our second number, to which we added a quick getting off dance. A huge cheer from what was by then a substantial audience followed us out of the impromptu arena and, verily I say unto thee, we were uplifted. We felt a celebratory drink was in order, so we headed off in search of an inn. Unbeknown to us, most of the crowd also headed off, to continue with whatever people did in Evesham on a Saturday.

Our only concern at that time was to fill our tankards before the coach left. We had no inkling that we might have left a problem in our wake until Andy and I heard one of the Cotswold guys complaining to the Faithful City tour guide, "That Silurian lot just buggered off to the pub, and took the audience with them – they should have stayed to watch the rest of us!"

"We didn't take anybody with us," I said to Andy, "We left the audience *with them* – can't help it if they can't keep a ready-made crowd, can we?"

"No, quite right," agreed Andy. "Anyway, looks like the knives are out again."

"Only a question of time," I said. "Our reputation goes before us, and there are those who think we are nothing more than beer-swilling hooligans."

"Oh, well – might as well be hung for a sheep," replied Andy, eyes twinkling and teeth gleaming through a broad black grin. "Fancy another pint for the coach?"

"Yeah, why not."

Back on the coach, Silurian were settling down on the back seat like rooks in the high branches. A casual observer might easily have understood why the Cotswold contingent would feel unsettled in the presence of these black-clothed outcasts. As far as we were concerned, however, we were on a day tour in full regalia and we were going to do what came naturally. So out came the instruments and we began to play. We were seventeen in number and had ten instruments between us. Through Willy's encouragement, there was an understanding amongst us that, during a performance, anyone not dancing should be adding to the music, and thus had the band grown. On that day, in addition to Willy's melodeon and Super Steve's accordion, we had two fiddles, a saxophone and some assorted percussion, including a set of bones. I was still trying to improve my drumming but, as a fall-back precaution, I also had my triangle with me.

We played all the way to the next venue, and indeed between each venue for the rest of the day.

By half-six in the evening, the day's touring over, we were relaxing in the compact and historic Cardinal's Hat, the oldest pub in Worcester, mulling over the day and debating the pros and cons of spending the rest of the evening at the Birthday Feast in the Guildhall. A few of the other morrismen were there too, but they were keeping their distance, eyeing us warily from the far side of the room. We kept ourselves to ourselves, something that was second nature to us by then through the lack of common ground with the formal morris establishment. In any case, we were engrossed in our own lively discussion and reliving of the day's events, as well as putting the finishing touches to our song for Faithful City.

At one point, Smudge got up and squeezed his way past a table on his way to the toilet. As he did so, the tail of his coat caught a glass, which fell to the floor and smashed. Gathering up the remains and taking them to the bar, Smudge explained to the landlord, "Sorry, Oi just broke one o' yore glasses." He was assured this was not a problem. The way the evening takings were increasing probably had the landlord reflecting on how many new glasses he would be able to buy without straining the budget.

This incident faded instantly from the minds of all concerned. Feeding off rumour and resentment, however, it was reborn in mutant form a while later. We had decided after some deliberation that, out of politeness and deference to our hosts, we would attend the feast, and we were heading for the Guildhall when we were accosted by two of Faithful City's more confrontational members.

"What's the matter with you lot!?" they demanded.

"Whaddya mean?"

"You're bloody legless again – that's what!"

"No more legless than you are. What exactly is your problem?"

"We've heard all about it," the talkative one continued,

addressing himself mainly to Willy, possibly because Willy's red tunic was the only part of us he could see in the murky darkness around the Guildhall entrance. "You've been putting yourselves about a bit all day, and now you're creating a bloody public nuisance and smashing up the pubs in Friar Street!"

"Smashin' up the pubs!?" retorted Willy in disbelief. "On yer bike! Who's bin giving you that crap?"

"We've heard all about it," repeated our inquisitor. "If you're going in there for the feast, you just better behave yourselves."

"Or else," he added, after a pause.

Much of this venomous attack seemed to be directed personally at Willy, who certainly took it that way. He trudged up the steps to the first floor, hands thrust in pockets, melodeon dangling over his shoulder and bell clanging quietly below the rear of his jacket. He was muttering to himself about what he was going to do to that 'loudmouthed prat'.

"Perhaps we should just sing 'em our new song," suggested Mulvey hopefully. "There's bound to be a singaround in the feast, so we could do it then, look. Eh? What about that for an idea?"

The song was certainly finished and it was certainly too good to waste. This occasion would be a momentous opportunity for its first public performance, but . . . We knew where to draw the line. We seemed to be in enough trouble for one day, even though it had mostly been fomented through a potent cocktail of jealousy, suspicion and resentment. Reluctantly, we felt it best to keep it under wraps that night, and three months went by before the song was officially sung in public, at our next big weekend outing of 1988. Then it was performed before a neutral and receptive audience somewhere in Cornwall as guests of Trigg Morris from Bodmin, hosting a ring meeting.

It was with Trigg that I had enjoyed my first taste of morris dancing back in 1973, when I was working around the Camborne area. I had kept in touch with them sporadically since then, and I was looking forward to meeting up again, particularly as a member of Silurian. We were going to put on a great show. We had our best dancers and a strong band, plus Wilf was still Bagman of the Ring, in his undertaker's rig and disturbingly cadaverous appearance.

"Pity about the drummer, though," I thought, sitting in the minibus on our way to Cornwall. I was filled with panic and fear that I was going to let the side down in front of my old mates. I had to admit it – my drumming was not up to Silurian standard. Travelling with us to Bodmin was Graham, a friend of ours from Vancouver Morrismen (yes, morris dancing had found its way to our old colonies), and I was confiding my anxieties to him in the back of our minibus. Overhearing my mutterings as we sped down the M5, Willy turned to me and said, "D'you want some advice?"

"All helpful hints gratefully received," I assured him.

"Well, to put it simply – don't play the drum."

My heart plummeted and my confidence shrivelled like a deflating balloon. My worst fears confirmed! All that encouragement from Willy, and now here he was, shooting from the hip.

"I had a feeling you were going to say something like that," I said dejectedly. "What about the triangle?"

"Give the triangle to someone else," replied Willy impatiently.

Oh no! That was me finished in the band . . .

"Give the triangle to Graham," Willy added. "It will give him something to do."

My dreams of glory vanished with this wake-up call. As a dancer, I had succeeded with Silurian, but it was obvious that now I was no longer going to be part of Willy's Magic Band. Sliding helplessly into a pit of dark despair, I hardly noticed that Willy was still talking.

"Hey! Are you listenin' – or wot?"

"Eh?"

"I was *just saying* – don't play the drum. *Let it play you.* Just go with the music, let it flow. You've nearly got it, so just relax. The music will guide you. The music will show you how to play."

Suddenly, the minibus was filled with sunshine, and heavenly choirs filled the sky. The clouds parted and there was Willy, seated at the right hand of God. The world had burst into flower, full of colour and light. Realising there was hope for me yet, I was happy to continue my chat with Graham and discuss the finer points of advanced triangle playing.

Willy's suggestions were put into practice the next day, with a notable improvement in quality, acknowledged by the maestro himself with a quick nod and a smiling glance over his gold rims.

Later that afternoon, the usual ring meeting massed morris display was scheduled. The weather, however, was appalling. Plan B saw us safely relocated in the old church hall, with the rain thrashing at the windows. Acoustically, that was a brilliant move. Although we usually felt cramped dancing indoors, we could make the music fill that building, and we let it rip. Willy and Super Steve were balancing each other perfectly, whilst Martin Russell (yet another Silurian man with a physics PhD) played his tenor sax as if his life depended on it. And right in there amongst it was this terrific snare drum rhythm. I looked down and, to my amazement, noticed it was coming from my drum. *My* drum! I felt inspired. *Let the drum play you . . .*

With the acoustics helping our sound to reverberate around the room, the dancing was once again on another plane. I had come to understand that Willy's advice to me regarding the drum applied to the whole of what was imprecisely referred to as our performance. Though it appeared to the audience to be a 'performance', to us it was more than that. It felt that as soon as Willy opened his instrument to release the notes, what followed was an inevitability, a process that took on a life of its own, a sequence that drew us in, held us for its duration and gently released us at the end. I am sure this was something Jonesy never felt with his focus on footwork, lines and endless practice. When we were firing on all cylinders, it was possible to be part of the dance whilst remaining outside of it, something akin to an out-of-body experience. We were simply in the moment. Pure Zen. That's why we never really needed to talk about it. We simply accepted the fact that Willy was the gatekeeper and the first note from the melodeon was the key to another world. Dancing in that rain-lashed school hall was a memorable end to a great day's touring through the beauty and mystery of the Cornish landscape.

On the programme of events for the weekend, it said, 'Saturday Night – Feast'. We ignored this, mentally writing it off as the usual homage to Cecil Sharp with the added burden of mediocre food and long speeches. But we should have had more faith in my old mates from Trigg. Their approach to the Saturday feast was very different. They were thinking more in terms of superb food and short speeches. Decades before the phrase 'local food' had become the populist concept it is today, these boys down in Cornwall ensured that we were presented with the best food the locality could offer. There was even a choice on the menu, something rare indeed in a situation where two hundred beer-focused morrismen were being catered for. The Trigg feast was exceptional in every sense – the food, the presentation and the service. Everything was right with the world.

With one exception. Victory Morris from Portsmouth.

It's not that there was anything essentially wrong with them, but one or two of their number had consumed more alcohol than their safe limit and had strayed into the murky shadowlands of unacceptable behaviour. 'Boisterous' might best describe their attitude as they entered the dining hall, but it was downhill from there. The room had been set out with rows of refectory-style tables, one table per side. In what turned out to be an unfortunate juxtaposition, Victory were on the table adjacent to Silurian.

We hadn't yet forgotten the unjustified ear-bending we had received on the Faithful City day, so we were wary. Understanding what provokes such hostile reaction to us, we also knew that news travelled quickly on the morris grapevine. Right at the start of the weekend, we could see signs of negativity amongst the other morrismen. Clearly some thought us to be uncontrollable wild men with a total disregard for civilised society. Unfortunately, when testosterone begins to flow, the perceived presence of wild men tends to generate the need to challenge these beings. Thus, taking all this into account, and in consideration to our selfless hosts, we were keeping a low profile in the dining hall and our conduct was commendable. Victory's conduct, however, was not.

Quite possibly they felt they could challenge Silurian, either through provocation or by proving they were every bit as wild as our reputation suggested we were. Maybe they thought that having a table next to us gave them leave to go berserk. Whatever the reason, whilst we were sitting there chatting quietly amongst ourselves about the brilliant food, a bread roll came flying out of the animated melee around Victory's table. It narrowly clipped Bernie's bowler on its way to the table behind him, from which an annoyed "Oi!" flew back on an instant rebound. The look that accompanied this shout made it obvious that we were considered the perpetrators of this affront, and any attempt at denial would have been useless.

Without warning, a second edible missile winged its way over our table. It was Willy's turn to shout "Oi!" At the same time, Vas turned to Victory's table and delivered a short message on the theme of 'cease and desist'.

Splat!

A smoked mackerel skin cartwheeled through the air and slapped onto Bernie's plate. With a sudden and loud scraping of chair legs and the jangling crash of falling cutlery, Bernie hurled himself across our table at the Victory man that had lobbed this third projectile. Grabbing a fistful of shirt and hair, Bernie jerked the miscreant right out of his chair and dragged him to within six inches of a face boiling with fury under the blacking.

"Now listen, you fuckwit!" Bernie hissed at him, eyes blazing under his bristling brows. "You try that again and I'll personally give you a bloody good smacking! So just sit down, shut up and *bloody well behave yourself*!!"

Spontaneous applause broke out as this fellow was propelled back into his seat at such a speed he promptly toppled backwards and hit the floor.

"Well done, Bern," said Stuart quietly, giving voice to the murmur of approval from the rest of us, now sitting nonchalantly around our table as if nothing had happened.

Actually, we were all amazed. Firstly, we were astounded by the distance Bern had covered in reaching his quarry - over our table and Victory's in about a second and a half. Secondly, Bern was one of the more level-headed, quieter members of the side. An important executive in the accounts department of an international company, his organised nature was not prone to such volatile outbursts. His sense of justice and fairness, however, left him in no doubt as to what to do on this occasion. And it worked. Victory settled down after this outburst, quite probably paraphrasing William Congreve's famous quote as 'Hell hath no fury like a Silurian scorned'. They might also have considered it unwise to further provoke a side that was renowned for smashing sticks whilst dancing.

Reliving this incident for the audience in the pub later on that night, we were obliged to explain ourselves in terms of our much-maligned reputation. We recounted the events of the Faithful City weekend and our ongoing 'feud' with them, mentioning in passing the song we had written about it, which of course we were promptly asked to perform. For the benefit of those of an academic inclination, the words to the song can be found in Appendix 1, together with some useful notes.

Sunday morning came, and the Trigg boys had planned a special surprise for Silurian.

"Knowing you pagans don't do church services, and not wanting you to get bored, we've arranged for you to do some entertaining at the Old People's Home," said their organiser with a smirk, "while us good Christians go to church."

Following the directions given us, we trudged through a drizzly Bodmin, up the hill to the Home. We knocked on the door.

It opened, and a bespectacled grey-haired head popped out. It was wearing a small blue nurse's hat and an expression of genuine consternation.

"Yes?" it said.

"We're the morrismen," said Willy, adding comfortingly, "come to entertain you."

"Just a minute," said the head, closing the door and disappearing, leaving us huddled outside in the rain.

While we waited for further instructions, I tried to see it from the blue-hatted head's point of view. It's ten o'clock on a peaceful Sunday morning and the doorbell rings. So you open the door to see what appears to be a cremated Grenadier standing in the rain, with a posse of manic black-faced butlers bobbing about in tailcoats and bowlers, nodding and grinning in the background. They all look seriously unhinged, but tell you they are morrismen. And they are threatening to entertain you. In an Old People's Home. What would you do? Frankly, if I was in that position, I would say, "Just a minute," close the door – and phone the police.

So I, for one, was quite surprised when the door opened again and the head, now attached to a body in a blue matron's outfit, said, "Come in, come in. Don't stand out there getting wet."

Ushering us into a spacious hallway that offered the usual combination of antiseptic smells, cream paint, slippery terracotta tiles and dying cheese plants, the matron said, "We're just getting things ready for you. Would you care for a biscuit and a drink?" Spotting the tankards hanging off various belts, she added, "I'm afraid we don't have anything terribly alcoholic here – but a little sherry perhaps?"

Vas could see that inviting us to shelter from the rain had not entirely alleviated this good lady's sense of foreboding, so he answered for the side in that calm, reassuringly authoritative voice of his, "Thank you very much. That's very kind of you. A sherry would be very nice. Thank you."

Seemingly calmed by the fact that at least one of us could speak in a language known to her, she left to organise the refreshments. Soon a younger nurse appeared, in one of those pale yellow outfits that always makes you feel considerably more ill than you really are. She was carrying a tray laden with Rich Tea biscuits and tumblers full of cooking sherry.

"Stone me!" said Willy under his breath, as the liquid refreshment came his way.

Time passed. We stood around in the shiny cream hall, sipping sherry and munching biscuits, an unprecedented experience for us. Before long, our bespectacled matron reappeared, saying, "Would you like to come through now?"

With a gentle sweep of her hand, she indicated the direction to a large pale-carpeted room, furnished with a grand piano in the large bay window and a dozen or so easy chairs along the walls. With their imitation leather, in Waiting Room Red, and hard wooden arms, they looked anything but easy, a fact confirmed by the various awkward and lop-sided poses adopted by their frail occupants. A couple of the residents were present in wheelchairs, which looked much more comfortable.

This plainly furnished room was surprisingly sunny, considering the grey day outside, and exuded a peaceful atmosphere. The silver-haired old ladies slumped in their uneasy chairs seemed to blend into the general paleness of the place. All was calm and very quiet, except for the rattle of teacup against saucer in the unsteady grasp of one old lady smiling benignly to herself over by the piano.

We filed in, with unaccustomed discomposure. Congregating by the bay window, we looked starkly out of place. Not so much Daniel in the lion's den – more Mephistopheles in the temple. Not daring to dance for fear of fatalities amongst the audience, we decided to play a couple of tunes and give them a few songs instead.

The whole scene was surreal, like something out of a Martin Scorsese movie – the quiet low-key scene just before something really bad happens. Super Steve at the grand piano, framed in the light of the bay window, doing that old music hall number, *My Baby's Gone Down The Plug'ole*, to an audience in various stages of dementia. Though we were not used to audience participation with this number, some of those in the room began clapping along with the song, some of them almost in time with the beat. The shaky teacup holder by the piano was nodding and smiling in a complete world of her own, which may or may not have included the pianist a couple of feet from her. In the half of the bay window not occupied by the piano stood Willy in his scarlet tunic, with the rest of us wedged in behind him. We joined in the choruses as required, but otherwise we did little more than sip sherry from those enormous tumblers.

Later, as we wobbled back through the drizzle into Bodmin, we realised we'd met our match with this heady beverage.

"I wouldn't wanna be on that stuff all day," mused Stuart.

"Where's that bloke from Faithful City?" wondered Willy, "cos we could really show him now what 'legless' means!"

"Yeah, we're 'armless enough, though," Andy commented, hoping somebody would spot the play on words. Instead, Willy said, "Except Burco – he's insane!"

Unnoticed by most of us, Willy was guiding us into something . . . a line from the song *The Band Played Waltzing Matilda* by Eric Bogle. But he wanted us to get there under our own initiative.

"Hey," someone said, "that's got the makings of a good motto – legless, armless, insane . . ."

"It needs something else."

For a while, as we continued on our way, all that was audible was the deep jingle of Silurian bells and the creak and clank of my tankard swaying on the triangle hooked through my belt.

"Hard to think when you're blind drunk," observed Andy.

"*That's it*!" said Willy, no doubt pleased with our efforts. "So you've got: legless, harmless, blind and insane. Rolls off the tongue quite well . . ."

Yes, I expect that's what Eric Bogle thought when he wrote it. But we didn't know that. As far as we were concerned, we were still in the process of creating a motto.

As we walked, we concluded it was a brilliant idea, but the motto needed to be in Latin. As I had once achieved 105% in a Latin exam (earning a 5% bonus for getting it all right), I was given the translation job. Andy, by unanimous vote, was commissioned to produce a suitable coat of arms. Satisfied with this decision, we put ourselves in the right mood for the forthcoming activities by marching the rest of the way into town, where crowds were beginning to gather. Willy and Super Steve were leading the band to the tune of *The British Grenadiers*, with the rest of the band behind them.

Our band grew by one when we came on to dance, because Graham, our Canadian fellow traveller, reappeared from wherever he had been for most of the weekend, to become our stand-in triangle player.

After all the sides present had completed their individual dance spots, we were all free to do as we pleased. As it was still raining, we opted for a cosy corner in a local tavern and fired up a musical jam session until closing time.

Travelling homewards, our discussions in the bus brought us to the conclusion that, despite the weather, it had been a memorable weekend, particularly Sunday morning.

"And I learned to play a new instrument," said Graham brightly.

"Ah," said Willy, "So did Rob."

Chapter 19
How Much For The Women?

• • • • •

"So they gathered the crippled, the wounded, the maimed,
And they shipped us back home to Australia.
The legless, the armless, the blind, the insane,
Those proud wounded heroes of Suvla..."

"So where's this ceilidh then, Dave?"

In the Horse and Jockey, Angie looked like the token female. Having been married to Smudge for some time now and having come to know his ways, she was suspicious.

"Dave! *Where's this ceilidh then*?" she repeated, winding the volume up a few decibels.

"Eh?"

"Well, I can't see a band or anything. So what's happening?"

"*I* don't know, *do* I?"

"*You* said . . ."

"Never mind that – *Chris* said . . ."

"Said what?"

"That there was goin' t'be a ceilidh. An' an extension." Smudge paused and glared at Angie. "And free beer," he added decisively, knowing that no one was going to argue with facts like that.

Angie, all dressed up and looking lost and somewhat out of place amongst sixteen or so Silurian men at the wrong end of a day's tour, slid into exasperation.

"Well, he's just in the back room. You know – where the *ceilidh*'s supposed to be? Why don't you *ask* him, Dave?"

"Oh, orl roight then!"

Smudge stomped off, looking for Mulvey.

He wasn't in the back room. In fact, the back room was devoid of people altogether, a situation which Smudge registered as mystifying bordering on alarming. He backed out of the empty room and headed for the bar, where he found Mulvey ordering a pint.

"So where's this ceilidh then, Chris?" asked Smudge, repeating Angie's question verbatim to be sure he was asking the right thing.

"Eh? Wot ceilidh?"

"You said summat about a ceilidh."

"When?"

"*You* know. At practice last Monday. 'Ceilidh', you said – and an extenshun. And free beer!"

"Eh? I never said – "

Suddenly it clicked, and Mulvey started laughing.

"Wo'chew laughin' at?" demanded Smudge indignantly. "Come on, tell me!" His indignation was backing down in the presence of a growing suspicion that he had somehow been ambushed.

Seeing Mulvey gurgling and groaning, staggering around trying not to spill his pint, several of us went over to see if he needed assistance. Just in time to hear him say, "I'm sorry, Smudge! But I'd been talking about somethin' else – I was just tellin' Willy about my own extension. You know? On the end of my house?"

"What're you on about?" Smudge was still convinced he was the victim of another wind-up.

Punctuating his speech with further titters, snorts and guffaws, Mulvey explained to Smudge that he'd been telling Willy, that night at practice, about some chap he'd met at a ceilidh, who was going to do some work on the extension at Chez Mulvey, in exchange for which Mulvey was thinking of giving him some free beer.

"Oh."

Smudge was crestfallen.

His imperfect hearing had let him down again. The way he tackled life was to move through it as best he could, picking up odd words from half a dozen conversations, like some omni-directional mike, and then attempting to organise it all into some semblance of coherence in his own head. But it rarely worked. On this occasion, he had misheard Mulvey and also picked up something from Keith the bagman about our next outing, which indeed was the one that had just finished. So of course he had put two and two together and come up with an unknown number. His only problem now was to explain to Angie why it had been necessary for her to drive in her finery from Worcester to Colwall just to say hello to us. Even offering to buy her something from Des's exotic menu was not going to make up for it.

As ever though, once Smudge had seen the whole situation from an observational point of view, he took it in good spirit. He hardly seemed ruffled as he watched Angie driving off rather too hastily in the direction of home.

I have thrown in this little anecdote at this point, not because it is a vital link to the next part of the saga, nor indeed a link to anything else. It is merely there to illustrate the value of Smudge to the side. Without Smudge, Silurian might still have been a fortress of Border morris, but without the comic relief. As well as being innately and unwittingly comedic, he also had other talents. He was a brilliant screen printer, a very useful asset to the side in those exciting days before the digital takeover of the planet.

Following the Trigg weekend, I had come up with our Latin motto, and Andy had built it into an astoundingly convincing coat of arms. The artwork had gone to Smudge and he had printed it, in a discreet four inch by three inch size, onto a batch of black sweatshirts. In the pre-design preparatory stages, Wilf had pulled a few faces when I'd handed him a bit of paper and asked him to check the Latin for grammatical correctness, but that was mainly because I had ditched the idea of 'harmless' in favour of 'armless' or, more literally, 'without arms', which sounded better in Latin.

"I'm not sure about this," he had stated. "'Without arms' is a bit odd, isn't it?"

"But the Latin for 'harmless' is *innocens*," I had pointed out, "And I feel people would get the wrong impression of us, if you see what I mean. Innocent we are not!"

Wilf could see the logic in this, but the academic scholarly side of his nature was not happy, struggling with its own better judgement. Finally though, he did pass it fit for purpose, and I handed it to Andy, saying, "There you go. See what you can do with that."

"You'd better put the English translation underneath," he suggested, "So I don't get the sequence muddled up."

"Fair enough."

So, beneath EBRIUS SINE BRACHIA CAECUS INSANUSQUE, I wrote, "legless, 'armless, blind and insane."

By next practice night, there it was – our brand new coat of arms. We thought it was nothing short of brilliant, though I doubt the College of Heralds would have agreed. Smudge took care of the printing, producing it in white on black, and we agreed it looked really classy, especially in the breast pocket position.

"Better than going around with 'Blah-Blah Morrismen' in letters six inches high right across your chest," commented Mulvey.

"Yes," agreed Vas. "This is discreet – nice and subtle."

Not many weeks after this, the validity of Vas's comment was confirmed when a stranger in a bar asked him, "Whose coat of arms is that?"

"St Andrews College," said a poker-faced Vas.

"Oh, yes . . . yes! Of *course* . . ." replied the stranger, nodding to himself in that 'silly-me-fancy-not-recognising-it' way that people adopt when they've been caught with their social guard down.

If he had scrutinised it more closely, he may have wondered what three pairs of dark glasses and a strait jacket were doing on the heraldic shield of St Andrews College. But he didn't.

And then there was the question of the wolves, of course.

All sorts of animals appear on heraldic motifs – lions and unicorns for instance. And maybe the odd dragon, gryphon or wyvern. Plus there are boars, stags and the rest. Wolves, however, remain scarce. Even if they did appear, one would expect to see them in one of the traditional heraldic poses, such as rampant, passant or regardant. Not defecating in the corner or urinating on the shield.

"Why have you got wolves on your coat of arms," people asked. They were serious. They thought this emblem was real.

"Well," they were told, generally by Andy, "the one on the dexter side, in heraldic parlance, is having a poo, and his mate on the sinister side is complementing the balance by having a wee."

Inevitably, they asked, "Yes, but *why* is he having a poo?"

"Ah," we would say, "it's all to do with the Red Riding Hood joke. Part of our folklore, you know."

Of course, they didn't know, but they really wanted to, so we had to tell them the joke, one of the thousands in John Willy's repertoire.

Red Riding Hood is skipping through the woods on her way to Grandma's house, when suddenly she meets the Big Bad Wolf.

"Oooo, Mr Wolf," she says, "what *big eyes* you've got!"

"Fuck off," says the wolf tetchily, "I'm having a shit!"

And there you have it – the Englishman's obsession with toilet humour clearly demonstrated. When Willy first told us this joke, we instantly posted it at Number One in the All-time Greatest Jokes chart. For a long time after that, we couldn't look at anything canine without collapsing into hysteria, leaving many an Alsatian with an unaccustomed sense of trepidation and anxiety. The joke had become so dear to our hearts that its inclusion in our coat of arms was incontestable.

Also worthy of note are the pear-shaped faecal droppings beneath our wolf. These are the three black pears on the Worcester

'Faithful' City coat of arms. Need I say more? A nod's as good as a wink to a blind horse. Or, as they say at Mensa meetings, 'an inflection of the cranium is as adequate as the spasmodic movement of the eyelid to an equine quadruped devoid of its visual capacity'.

Once our coat of arms had been publicly unveiled adorning our new sweatshirts, all sorts of undesirables were queuing up for them. However, we had taken the precaution of having only enough printed for the members of the side, so everyone else went without.

Mike Rust, who had left us some time ago to join the Ironmen up in Ironbridge, pleaded for one.

"Why?" he was asked. "Why should we let you have one?"

"Well, I'm ex-Silurian," said Mike.

"Precisely. *Ex*-Silurian. As in '*no longer with us*'."

"Right, okay," he said, "I'll let it go, but I need you to do something else for me."

"Oh yeah?"

"I'm organising a Black Meet and I want you to come."

"Bugger off, Rusty – you know that is a really bad idea! It's as bad as a ring meeting. You'll be turning Cotswold next!"

"No, honestly, it could be really good," he insisted.

The reality was he had been banging this particular drum ever since he discovered there was more than one Border side out there. We knew that he would not stop rabbiting about it until we signed up. So we agreed, just to keep him quiet. But he still wasn't going to get one of our sweatshirts.

And so the day came, one Sunday in spring at a pub in Ludlow. Mike Rust and the Ironmen had organised it, and managed to entice not only Silurian but also Dave Jones and his new boys, Old Wonder, to come along. Completing the line-up were the Leominster men and the legendary Shropshire Bedlams.

Although Silurian had been the first side to dance blacked up in public, since 1969, the appearances had been restricted to

Boxing Day tours. The Bedlams were the first side to go out as a full-time Border side. With their rag jackets, black faces (and hands, interestingly) plus hats bristling with pheasant feathers, they certainly looked the part. They were inspirational, and a real shot in the arm for morris in general. Founded and led by the innovative John Kirkpatrick, one of the godfathers of the 1970s folk revival, they carried the torch for Welsh Border and, it has to be said, helped to galvanise Dave Jones in his own efforts to collect enough material to launch Silurian as a Border side.

Dave's approach was more orthodox than John's, though their objectives were similar. John was reproducing the flavour of Border morris but, feeling there was insufficient material to compile a set of dances strong enough to hold the audience, he was happy to add some invented dances in the Border style. Dave, on the other hand, painstakingly researched his material, producing dances that were considered genuine, and therefore 'user-friendly', by the ring. So the Bedlams were seen as mavericks whilst Silurian, under the tutelage of Dave Jones, collected praise and respect from Those Who Know About These Things. It was only after Dave left us that Silurian became the real mavericks.

Pressure from Mike Rust had brought us to Ludlow for this congregation of Border sides, and it was a chance to see the Bedlams on home territory, so we were looking forward to that. Their dances were wild, full of whoops and shouts. At the end of the dance, they would suddenly scream off into the crowd and disappear, which was extremely effective. But after a while, the dances seemed a little unvaried, which gave the impression of going on just a bit too long. By contrast, our dances seemed to be over in no time. Bromsberrow Heath, for instance, took less than two minutes. Personally, I felt that the audience preferred this kind of short sharp shock, even though that put me in danger of sounding biased.

However, it is not unusual for something to happen which reinforces an opinion, confirms a suspicion or proves that a hunch is right, and so it was on that occasion. When all the sides had done their thing, strutted their stuff and, for all I know, engaged in other lesser-known transatlantic perversions, I was outside the pub sipping ale from my tankard, and Sue Harris, John Kirkpatrick's partner, came up and started chatting about the dancing.

"I don't know," she said, "the Bedlams try so hard to look like wild men, but you lot – all you have to do is just stand around and you look dangerous. And that's even before you start dancing!"

"Thanks, Sue," I said, "that's the nicest thing anyone has said to me all day!"

Her views would be echoed by others before the year was out. One person in particular would go to the trouble of writing down her thoughts in a letter to me explaining what it was about Silurian that was so enigmatic. More on that later.

After the dancing in Ludlow, Chris Mulvey and Dave Jones were in the pub, and they too were discussing the dancing and analysing the day. After a while, Dave turned to Chris and said, by way of a summing up, "Well, as far as I can see, there is really only one side here today, and that's Silurian."

Well, thank you Jonesy. That was a big statement coming from someone who had split from us somewhat acrimoniously not long before.

Despite our reservations about Mike Rust's Border get-together, that event turned out to be a relative high spot that year. Perhaps, more accurately, it was a case of the other events on the calendar turning out to be less exciting than counting pebbles on a beach. Perhaps we should have known something was up when we got thrown out of a pub in Abergavenny for playing *Men of Harlech*. If that was a portent of doom, we didn't spot it, and it was without any fear or apprehension that we headed off in May to perform at the 1989 Potteries Folk Festival in Stoke-on-Trent.

When we arrived, however, the town seemed to be closed.

Initially, we thought we must have picked the wrong weekend, but some conscientious searching revealed an official person prepared to check us in. He ticked something on a sheet of paper and showed us where the scout hut was – our accommodation for the weekend. Dumping our stuff, we wandered into town looking for the festival. We checked all the pubs for the usual signs, such as finger-in-the-ear singers or knots of musicians but, as Charles Wolfe might have observed, 'not a drum was heard, not a funeral note'. Perhaps the festival had died and we had long since missed the funeral. All we saw in the town's pubs was thickets of burly locals picketing every bar with an obvious loathing for outsiders.

Finally, just before closing time, in the last pub we tried, we were told there was a folk club 'oop sters'. Sure enough, at the top of the dingy stairs was a perfect example of *Homo rusticana* on sentry duty outside a darkly varnished door, be-sandalled toes twitching to the tune muffling its way through the keyhole. When the music stopped, he let us in – just in time to sit through about eighty-six verses of some 'woe-betide-me-for-I-am-undone' Scottish dirge. It was sung by a large female wearing a barrage balloon with sleeves, in a shade of grey only slightly less mournful than the sombre ode and the room in which we found ourselves.

Before we entered, there had been only about seven people in there, so we instantly tripled the numbers. The magnificent seven looked like part of some nightmarish still-life, the absence of movement making them blend into the furniture. They all looked asleep. Indeed they may have been asleep up there for years. Certainly, they must have been much younger when they came in.

Clearly, we had stumbled on what could have been a singaround or something of that ilk, because the girl in the zeppelin, having finally finished her musical marathon, nodded to us as if to say, "Perhaps one of you lads would care to sing a song?"

Chris Mulvey, never one to resist a challenge, broke into one of his more rousing Irish numbers, with the rest of us joining in on the choruses. All the zombies woke up, clawing cobwebs from their faces to reveal staring eyes and shocked expressions. Their ears rippled in the blast of the full Silurian chorus. The room had woken up, but the bar had shut down. We quizzed the generously-proportioned balladeer as to any options left open to us at this late hour, and were told there was a late-night ceilidh at the Town Hall. Like heat-seeking missiles, we were soon standing at its doors.

"You can't come in without tickets!"

A professional bouncer – this place was full of surprises!

"We don't need tickets. We're performers," Mulvey informed the bouncer, with some emphasis on the word 'performers'.

"You can't come in without tickets!"

"We haven't got any tickets," Mulvey said evenly. "But we *have* got these performers' badges. See? Look – it says here, 'PERFORMER'. Okay?"

"You can't come in without tickets!"

We had dealt with some troublesome people in our time, but never a six-foot parrot.

"Well – sodya then!"

We turned our backs on our last opportunity that night to get a drink, leaving us with no choice but to return to the scout hut. Still needing an outlet for all that stored-up adrenalin, however, we welcomed Willy's whispered idea of hiding Burco's tuba. It had been done before, of course, but it was always good for a laugh. Once inside the scout hut, we looked for a suitable location.

"Up there," said Willy decisively, his eye on one of the roof truss beams.

With us that weekend was one of our more recent recruits, Roger Page, a window-cleaner by trade, and tall enough to save a fortune on ladders. By standing on Roger's shoulders, Willy was just able to reach high enough to tie the tuba to the beam.

"There, that should do it!" said Willy, jumping down.

"Donk!" said the tuba, bouncing off Willy's head.

"*Fucksake*!" said Willy, as a halo of stars and small twittering birds appeared around his head.

"Kraaang!" said the tuba, hitting the floor.

"*Uurrff*!" said Willy, hitting the tuba, as he staggered backwards and tripped over it.

The rest of us didn't say anything. Speech is impossible when impeded by uncontrollable laughter.

Next morning, we were all dressed up and, ever optimistic, buzzing in expectation of the real festival kicking off. Willy was quiet, nursing a headache, a bruised hip and stiff neck.

"Serves you bloody right!" admonished Burco, nursing his dented tuba *.

Outside the Town Hall, no bouncer was in sight, but there were dozens of Northwest dancers gathering, including our friends, the Mossley ladies, still with their chaperones. Satisfied at last that we had the right weekend, we spent the day doing what we usually do at such events, travelling around by coach and dancing in various venues. Around Stoke-on-Trent, this turned out to be well below par.

By the evening, that old sinking feeling was back. Either the festival had ended at five o'clock, or the whole world had gone to somebody else's party.

"Well, it can't be all over," Roger pointed out, "because we're booked to dance at the ceilidh."

"I 'spect that's where they all are, then," said Andy, eyes glazing over in anticipation of all those gorgeous girls he was going to dance with.

"Huh! Huh! Huh!" grunted Smudge, as if reading Andy's mind and finding something salacious in there.

Compared with Friday's folk club, the ceilidh was heaving. I counted at least eighteen people. Admittedly, five of them were in

*Not long after the Stoke weekend, we had another public outing. Burco appeared with a shiny new brass sousaphone. Willy gave him one of his looks and said, "So, what's with the golden toilet?"

"Well, the tuba's got a dent in it," replied Burco.

the band, but it's astounding how much bustle a dozen or so people can generate if they really try. Lurking in the background, we waited for our spot. We were keen to put on a good show, despite the lack of audience. With so few people in the room, however, the acoustics were appalling, the sounds reverberating and echoing around the space like a multi-tracked recording out of sync.

Whilst Willy played the tune for White Ladies Aston, Andy was doing the calls for Pershore Stick. But these couldn't be heard, lost as they were in the upper reaches of the hall. Those at the far end of the set guessed they were doing the Dilwyn dance. Bernie was about the only one who thought the dance actually was White Ladies, but noticing he was virtually isolated in this deduction, he suddenly stopped dancing, threw his stick and an expletive across the room, and walked off.

Within seconds, the dance collapsed as more dancers followed Bernie's lead.

The audience loved it. They thought it was all part of the act, part of the madness of Silurian, and they clapped enthusiastically for more. It was a surprising amount of noise for such a small gathering. We appreciated their enthusiasm and came back on to complete our spot. Staying for the rest of the ceilidh, however, was far less inviting than the prospect of a curry, so we quietly slipped away in search of the local tandoori palace.

Smudge, disappointed by the lack of nubile young women at the ceilidh, was on the lookout from the moment we left.

He was in luck.

Coming up the stairs as he descended was an androgynous young blonde girl and her rather more curvy companion. Suddenly, like some black praying mantis, Smudge pounced. The elfin blonde was trapped. Struggling to free herself from Smudge's oppressive hugs, she was all arms and legs and pleading eyes. Anyone who has seen the Looney Tunes cartoon character, Pepe le Pew, will be able to picture this. For those of you unfamiliar with these brilliant characters, Pepe was a skunk who didn't realise his aroma was, shall we say, troublesome. He was also romantically attracted to black and white cats. So the cartoons always centred on his latest 'conquest'. Inevitably, each episode would feature yet another hapless two-toned cat finding herself the unwitting and unwilling object of desire from Pepe, this oversexed skunk with a pseudo-French accent. And there, on the Town Hall staircase, was our very own skunk capturing another irresistible but resistant female.

Each of us had his own way of spreading the luck of the morris amongst the females, some more subtle than others, and all of us more restrained than Smudge. Mick reckoned he had come up with a completely foolproof way of enticing females to get close enough for him to black them up. He had acquired from a sympathetic groupie a badge bearing, around its perimeter, the words 'HUG THERAPIST', written in capitals to emphasise the point. He attached it to the front of his hat. On its first outing, he tried out its effectiveness by standing in front of the latest woman of his dreams, beaming a broad grin through his sooty face and pointing at the badge.

"You what?" asked the woman, in an unexpectedly antagonistic tone.

Mick simply tried out the grin again and pointed to the badge once more.

"*What*? *Hug the rapist*?" said the woman, now moving towards aggression. "You must be bloody joking!"

You win some; you lose some.

Meanwhile, finally managing to drag Smudge off his writhing victim, we questioned him as to whether he was still hungry enough for a curry. Thinking there may well be more females in the curry house, Smudge answered in the affirmative. Burco and I, however, were not really up for it, so we opted to wait outside until the others had eaten.

We needed something to occupy us, however. The restaurant was on a corner site at a crossroads with traffic lights. Motorists stopping at the lights were unaware of our presence, as we blended easily into the shadows.

"They can't see us," Burco pointed out, mischief on his mind.

"No, they can't," I conceded.

"But they will in a moment."

"Yes, they will."

"When the next car stops, then?"

"Okay."

A taxi was the next car, with a couple of presentable young ladies on the back seat. We detached ourselves from the wall, leapt into the road and bounded over to the car, our coat tails flying.

"How much for the women!?" demanded Burco, jerking open the driver's door and thrusting his face round the door pillar to inspect the girls more closely.

"Yeah, how much for this one?" I echoed from the passenger side.

The driver, momentarily robbed of the power of speech, looked on the verge of something terminal. This was obviously a new experience for him and he appeared noticeably agitated. We wondered what his problem was. After all, we were merely making polite enquiries as a preamble to trading with him, and we considered his rubber-burning take-off on the green light to be uncalled for. Not to mention demonstrating an unwarranted disregard for the comfort of his passengers. Silly man. We had been prepared to negotiate. We'd have offered a fair price, and he would have made more than whatever the women were going to pay him for the taxi fare.

"There's no pleasin' some people," observed Burco.

As we waited for the others to get through their chicken tikka and naan breads, we kept up our mild terrorism sporadically, ambushing unsuspecting passenger-carrying motorists whenever we felt boredom setting in. It made an interesting change from blacking up women, but it was a wonder that we could keep it up without a visit from Stoke's police force, unless of course it too had stayed at home with the rest of the city's population. I can't speak for the motorists we questioned, but Burco and I certainly found the exercise entertaining, and we tried it out again many times during the course of that year, whenever we were feeling bored, fidgety or simply in need of light relief. And, in Stoke, it was the most fun we had throughout the whole weekend.

In fact, there was nothing else in the calendar that was going to top this until August, when we were scheduled to make what had become an annual pilgrimage to the Saddleworth Rushcart Festival.

Chapter 20
Breakfast At Hilary's

• • • • •

"And did the Countenance Divine
Shine forth upon our clouded hills?
And was Jerusalem builded here,
Among those dark satanic mills?"

Our very first outing to Saddleworth was 1983, when Dave Jones was still with the side. He advised us to turn down the invitation for the following year because of the danger of overkill. But we ignored him. 1989 saw our sixth consecutive visit to Saddleworth. We never tired of it, and the festival-goers did not tire of us.

That first year, I drove my own car rather than cramming into the minibus, because I was dropping the family off with friends in Prestwich, on the north side of Manchester. Having done that, I drove east. I successfully negotiated Oldham's busy road system and was cruising comfortably into open countryside, keeping my eyes open for a sign saying, "Welcome to Saddleworth: Please drive slowly through the village, etc." No such sign appeared. Instinct told me I was in danger of driving aimlessly around the satellites of Greater Manchester, so I pulled into the kerb to accost a passing pedestrian.

"Excuse me," I said, to someone who looked as if he may have lived there for decades, "could you tell me where Saddleworth is, please?"

"Aye lad," said the old boy, "you're lewkin' at it."

"Oh! Am I? Er . . . where?"

"Ower uther side o' t'trees," he replied, gesticulating in the general direction of the heather-clad hill in front of me.

My mystified expression identified me as just another clueless southerner. With an exasperated, "Jus' keep gowin'!" my local tourism ambassador trudged off.

Two further encounters with similar results were needed before I realised that Saddleworth *was* the heather-clad hill in front of me. This was pointed out to me by a woman of ample proportions, whose soft-spoken northern lilt was well out of context with a body that looked as if it would be quite at home wrestling crocodiles. "No, no luv," she had said soothingly, "Saddleworth *is the moor*!"

Saddleworth, the Moor of Lancashire. I bounced this phrase around my brain a few times, trying to make it sound dramatic. I tried to visualise Desdemona falling for someone called Saddleworth, but it just had no snap to it. No wonder Shakespeare opted for some guy with an Italian-sounding name from Venice. Suspecting a wind-up, I focused my attention more closely on this woman, thinking it might just be Les Dawson doing one of his impressions.

"If you want t'rushcaart," she was continuing, "you're lewkin' for Uppermill. Only place rownd 'ere as I know of where they 'ave t'rushcaart."

Disappointed that it wasn't Les Dawson, I thanked her and drove on. Sure enough, I soon came upon Uppermill. Life there seemed to be centred on or, more accurately, crammed into, the Commercial Hotel. There was evidence to suggest that at least some of these people were there for a festival, so I parked the car and entered the hotel bar. I found Mick and Smudge inside, so I assumed I was in the right place, unless they too were lost. By the time the bar closed of course, we were all lost – lost in that dreamland of folly and make-believe where nothing is as it seems, where everything is very far away, where voices are disengaged from the bodies they once inhabited and the bar is tilted at an angle of 42 degrees.

Next morning, everything made sense. There were morris dancers everywhere, mostly in Northwest costume and, lurking in the back yard of the Commercial, an old farm cart with a fourteen-foot mountain of rushes built onto it. The big banner on the front of this creation declared that this was indeed the Saddleworth Rushcart and the year was 1983. I had a bad feeling about the whole idea when I watched this overloaded farm vehicle manoeuvred into the main street, revealing a huge wooden-runged rope ladder attached to the front shafts, with a similar arrangement at the back. Evidently – and here we see another example of that renowned northern sense of humour – half the morrismen present were expected to get in behind the bars of this huge ladder to pull the cart along, with the remainder of the men at the back acting as a brake. A challenge, it seemed to me, especially with most of the participants wearing steel-shod clogs.

I looked around frantically for a means of escape, but I was too late. The lads were on to me.

"Come on," admonished Mike Rust. "Don't think you're sneakin' off somewhere! You're not getting' away with it. If we're pullin' it – *you're* pullin' it! So get yerself in 'ere!"

"It's me legs," I said, clutching at the only straw that floated by.

"Whassa matter with 'em?"

"I've got to save them for dancing."

"Dancin'!? Hmph, that's a laugh – you're always tryin' to escape into the band with that bloody triangle of yours!"

"It's an essential part of the Border sound!" I protested.

"Bollocks! Don't gimme that!"

"Well, how come you've got one then?" It was true. Rusty did have a triangle that he used as a passport to the band.

There was no answer to that, apart from, "Look, just get yourself in 'ere with the rest of us!"

No sympathy there, then. And so I became part of the haulage team. It could have been worse though. I could have been the one sitting on the top of the rush mountain, fighting off branches, birds' nests and sudden desperate urges to urinate.

Off we went, the musicians all marching ahead of us. We toured the 'five towns'. Diggle, Dobcross, Delph, Greenfield and back to Uppermill. It seemed like four hundred miles and my legs felt as if they had been worn down to short stumps by the time we finished late afternoon. However, as part of the festival, the pubs were open all day – a treat back in 1983, when strict licencing hours generally applied. The weather and the local girls were gorgeous and, bizarrely, people kept throwing money at us. In the case of one of our number, Carl Broughton, the girls threw flowers. Uber-sexy 'Pretty Boy' Carl, with his dark curls and serious good looks, was about the only member of the side whose already handsome features were enhanced by the blacking, especially with a red rose between his teeth. The Saddleworth girls swooned before him.

With adulation and money being thrown at us, we thought we were in paradise – apart from having to lug that cart wherever we went. A while later, we found out that the locals were not used to black-faced morris dancers. They thought we were collectors, and that was why they threw money at us. And there was us thinking it was unrestrained hero worship.

We need not have been disappointed, however. The real hero worship came from the local girls, whose face-to-face contacts with us left them duskier but defiant. We usually targeted the prettier ones first, working on the theory that gauging their resistance to having their perfection marred would be a useful litmus test for any potential opposition to our advances.

All the indications were that resistance in this wild part of Lancashire was nothing more than a thin veneer over an uninhibited desire to be blacked up. The first victims of the day would squeal and squirm in feigned defiance, a tactic that Smudge, with his encyclopaedic knowledge of female behaviour, described as a 'stop-it-I-like-it-job'. Once the encounter was over, however, they would swagger around, smiling haughtily through their black smears and looking down on the plainer girls as if to say, "*You*'ve got *NO* chance!" Not to be outdone, these others would step into the line of fire, so to speak, like kamikaze sacrificial offerings, to be symbolically ravished by these wild demons from the borderlands of Wales.

The symbolism was overt and undeniable, the sexual connotations inherent in our behaviour and the responses of our victims. We knew we had put the sex back into morris, and the girls loved it. But there are always exceptions that prove every rule and, during that first visit to the festival, the exception was a waitress.

On the Saturday night, all the guests of the Saddleworth Morrismen were treated to a banquet the likes of which I had never seen before or since at any kind of morris event. There were legs of ham, whole poached wild salmon, salads, cold platters, pies, pickles and sauces. There were white tablecloths, plates, knives, forks . . .

And there were waitresses.

Always a problem, waitresses – when Smudge is about. Of course, he'd spotted them straightaway, as we were filing into the hall, and there he was lying in wait for them at our table. With razor-sharp perception, he had noticed that, while their hands were occupied with three or four hot plates at a time, they were powerless to resist his advances. He was practically drooling with anticipation.

"Huh! Huh! Huh!"

There were times when I thought that Smudge must have been the inspiration behind the Loony Tunes cartoons. Having done a convincing impression of Pepe Le Pew in Stoke, at this banquet he had taken on an appearance starkly reminiscent of Wile E Coyote, smug in the knowledge that he had at last concocted a totally foolproof plan to annihilate his long-term quarry, the superfast Roadrunner.

"Hiya!" said Smudge nonchalantly, as the waitress for our

table placed a dinner plate in front of him.

"Entchew got noice lips," he continued, giving her what he thought was a seductive glance, but which the rest of us could see was simply a hungry leer.

The girl eyed him warily.

"An' noice legs!"

"Oi! – get *OFF*!"

Managing to extricate herself from Smudge's mobile exploration units, our waitress retreated to the kitchen, her eyes firing tracer bullets at Smudge's head.

"Huh! Huh! Stoppit oi loikit job!"

One observation that could be made about Smudge – he was blessed with an optimism that knew no bounds. Plus an unshakeable belief that women found him irresistible. Convinced that this girl had been saving herself just for him, he turned on the charm again when she reappeared later with a tray to collect the dishes.

"Cor! Enchew gorra noice bum!"

"Hey! I *told* you – *GEROFF*!!"

"Aw, go on – give us a ki – "

Tang! Tang!

The tray came down on Smudge's head with a force that did not suggest affection. Smudge sank lower in his chair, his hat over his eyes.

Tang! Tang! *Tang*! *Tang*! *Tang*!

The waitress, with admirable presence of mind, had retaliated with the first weapon that came to hand. Having flattened Smudge's head, she was now striding back to the kitchen with a flush in her cheek and a bent tin tray in her hand.

Smudge, meanwhile, had ended up crumpled in his chair, chin at table level. With eyes peeking out from under the rim of his bowler, now firmly jammed over his ears, he was struggling to get the hat off without joining the Van Gogh fan club.

"Oi think she fancies me!" he beamed, finally emerging from

his hat with ears glowing pink.

Apart from isolated incidents of a similar nature over the years, which inexplicably always seemed to involve Smudge, we enjoyed a satisfying rapport with northern girls. The outlaw image bestowed an aura of dignified defiance upon us and we had something of a swagger in our step. There was a touch of the 'villain with a heart' about us. It sometimes felt as if we could do no wrong, or that we could get away with anything. Take, for instance, the Strange Case of Mick and the Docker.

It was a Saturday night. We had spent all day pulling the cart and were in need of a pint. The Commercial was heaving, so we had gone for a drink to the Granby Arms, a more modest establishment just down the road. As we entered, with Mick leading the way, he saw the girl of his dreams sitting at the bar. Homing in on this vision of pulchritude, he dazzled her with his scintillating repartee and enchanted her with his 'come-with-me-to-the-kasbah' routine. Putting his arm around her, he escorted her to the other end of the pub, remaining oblivious, throughout this display of single-minded determination, to the prominent fact that this young lady was in the company of a twenty-stone tattooed man-mountain with no neck. Back in the days before tattoos became the must-have accessory, they tended to be displayed mainly on all-in wrestlers, ex-army veterans, contract killers and dockworkers. The guy at the bar may well have had all of these occupations listed on his CV.

Realising Mick was not long for this world, the rest of us removed our hats, clasped them to our chests and tried to think of a suitable prayer – difficult for a bunch of pagans.

To our amazement, however, the illustrated man did nothing. He just stared after his erstwhile companion, drained his glass, pushed it across the bar in the direction of the barmaid and said, "Same again, please."

Even when his girlfriend finally returned, her face sullied with a copious amount of Mick's blacking, he still seemed unconcerned and remained calm. But I am convinced that if Mick had tried to pull a stunt like that dressed in his ordinary clothes he would have died a sudden and nasty death.

The Rushcart weekend was filled with many such incidents, and produced a wealth of stories over the years. Too many to record. But if you were to offer to buy a drink for any Silurian man who was there in the 1980s, you'll get to hear quite a few more than I have chronicled here. There was something fundamentally compelling about this particular festival, and we found it impossible to turn down the annual invitation.

One of the high spots was breakfast. This was obtained at the local grocer-cum-sweetshop in Uppermill, and was served around a table right there in the middle of the shop, between the sacks of potatoes and the jars of mint humbugs. It was a proper job, as they say in Cornwall, consisting of a huge fry-up, with tea, toast, marmalade, the lot. The shopkeeper and his daughter did the serving, in between the local customers popping in for their newspapers and pints of milk. Anticipation of the joys of breakfast in this shop ran high and, for some of us – well, those who were not allowed this kind of breakfast at home – it may have become the only reason for going to Saddleworth. It certainly took on a ritualistic element which blended easily with the mystery of the moorlands.

And then, in 1989, intending to book ourselves in for the Saturday morning, we got as far as the door and found that the shop had closed down. *Oh woe*!

Trying not to panic, we asked a few of the Saddleworth lads whether there was anywhere else. Replies ranged from, "Aye, thur's a transport caff in Oldham," to, "Thur's t'chippy on t'corner, but he's closed in t'mornings."

Thanking them for their help, we stood around gloomily on the edge of an abyss of despair. No breakfast! No toast, even! Life, for me at least, defined as it was in terms of toast, was beginning to lose all meaning. Hope was fading fast when there appeared in our midst what was presumably a guardian angel. It was effectively disguised as a Saddleworth morrisman and answered to the name of Ron. And, lo, thus spake the angel, and we were lifted up, yeah, even unto the heavens.

"My missus, Hilary – she'll give you some grub."

Back from the edge of doom, we crowded round Ron eager for more details.

Does she do toast? I wondered.

Fully briefed with all the necessary information from Ron, we were all set for Breakfast at Hilary's. A dozen of us, in full kit, marched single file down to Ron and Hilary's abode, ideally situated in a little side street two hundred yards from our sleeping quarters.

In estate agent terms, the place was 'compact and bijou'. In our terms, it was 'firkin small'. A bit like Kath's place in Mossley. Set in the middle of a terrace built in grey millstone grit, soot-blackened over the years, it was another traditional two-up, two-down, but with the added luxury of having a separate bathroom and toilet 'suite' – I use the word loosely – in what was probably once the coal cellar under the kitchen, and was still doubling as extra storage space. The bath and toilet were actually in one corner of this utility space, behind a wooden partition. This allowed just enough room, once the door was shut behind you, to fall off the toilet and into the bath.

Arriving at this residence, we knocked on the faded blue front door, fully expecting this to turn out to be a scam – another little wind-up by those rascally Saddleworth boys. But no, the face that appeared at the door was indeed Hilary's. Though she appeared to be a little breathless as she scrutinised us, blinking though her owlish glasses, she was obviously expecting us.

"Come in, come in! I've jus' put t'kettle on an' I'm doin' t'bacon. But you'll have t' take it in turns, cos I've only four seats in t'dining room!"

Dining room? We never expected that.

It turned out to be a small table in the corner of the kitchen, forced into this position by another smaller table piled high with a home computer and its varied paraphernalia, as well as books, records, a football sock and an empty packet of liquorice allsorts. This left just enough room to squeeze past the cupboards opposite to get to the cooker and the stairs to the bedrooms.

Hilary looked like the original inspiration behind the expression, 'slaving over a hot stove'. At the business end of the kitchen, it was all hustle and bustle, clouds of steam, spitting fat and hissing gas burners. In the midst of it all was our dauntless hostess, chopping mushrooms, slicing tomatoes, opening cans of beans, juggling hot plates, checking on the toast – and all without the aid of a safety net. Or indeed a worktop.

Breakfast was, as Hilary had suggested, a four-man relay, with each sitting washing up the plates and cutlery for the next lot. The washing up was done in a stone sink housed in a cupboard on the far side of the room. This gave Ron and Hilary the advantage of being able to shut the door on it when they couldn't face it.

Those not in the 'dining room' were sprawled across the front room. With space there also restricted, there was some overflow onto the pavement outside the front door. In the midst of all this mayhem and Silurian bodies, Ron and Hilary and their two kids simply carried on as if all this was just an everyday occurrence.

We were seriously grateful for this unconditional hospitality. It set us up for the weekend. With a breakfast like that, we were completely unfazed by the idea of pulling the cart around all day Saturday and then up to the church on the Sunday. After the spreading of the rushes, the remainder of the weekend's festivities centred on the two pubs. As well as dance displays, there were also various competitive events, such as a wrestling match between the morris sides present.

By 1989, our own performances at this festival were restricted to dance displays and musical jam sessions. Although we had been involved in certain other events over the years, we liked to quit while we were ahead. For instance, one time when our token Welshman, Dai Thomas, came with us, we entered him for the wrestling match. We didn't ask his permission. The first he knew of it was when he was pushed into the ring. With the fire of Wales burning in his breast and the survival instinct of the Celts in his favour, he fought his way through each round against opponents who were taller, heavier and, above all, younger than himself to emerge as runner-up – even then he lost by only a whisker. Thanks to Dai's efforts, Silurian picked up about a million brownie points that year, and we left for home with a bigger reputation than the one we arrived with. On subsequent visits, we simply rested on our laurels. However, we were very happy to dance, sing and play. Saddleworth was the place where our band had been christened the Silurian Wall of Sound because, on one occasion, we had put on the four-man Brimfield dance accompanied by sixteen in the band. We were dear to their hearts and the feeling was mutual.

One year, there were no events or competitions, because monsoon conditions had driven everyone into the two pubs. Silurian were in the Cross Keys, in charge of a huge music session, running through our favourite dance tunes and quirky songbook, raising the roof with old favourites like *Jerusalem*. Much ale was being consumed and a liberal quantity of blacking was appearing on the faces of various young ladies. Due to a combination of rain and perspiration, it was sliding easily off our own faces. Grinning through a mask of smeared blacking that made her look like a Royal Marine on exercise, one of the girls confronted Burco, our very own Countenance Divine.

"Where's your blacking then?" she asked.

"Eh?"

"I just wanna know if I can borrow your tin of blacking."

"Yeah . . . okay," answered Burco, looking for the catch but finding nothing, "I don't see why not."

"Ta!" she said. "Back in a minute!"

Clutching Burco's tin and his smelly little black sponge, she disappeared into the crowd. She returned a while later looking flushed and exhilarated.

"There you are," she said, giving Burco back his tin. She was grinning. Burco looked mystified. Sensing his non-comprehension, she explained, "I've bin blackin' up the fellas!"

Sure enough, looking around we saw evidence of her handiwork. One thing leads to another of course, and one tin of blacking leads to another. By the time the pub closed, the whole place looked like a coalminer's working convention, with everybody in the pub including the bar staff, displaying smudgy black faces. And all because it was raining that day.

It was in Saddleworth that we came to understand a bit more about why any women would allow themselves to undergo the somewhat unwholesome ritual of having their faces smudged with our blacking. The females in that part of Lancashire seemed strikingly receptive to the idea, to the point where they became pro-active in their eagerness to get involved. An unofficial fan club appeared to be forming, which grew in strength from year to year.

Amongst the stalwart members of this club were the two we had met on the stairs of the Stoke-on-Trent town hall during the Potteries festival. Saddleworth was one of their favourite festivals, and they were delighted that we were there. In due course, I wrote to one of them to ask some questions about the effect Silurian had on women. Without hesitation, she wrote back, on behalf of the two of them. What she said summed us up in one word – sexy.

She commented on our kit, describing us as 'smartly dressed' and wearing the kit 'with a certain pride', the black faces adding 'a touch of mystery and a desire to discover more'. Our phallic dances came across as demonstrating virility, with all the implications that brings. Regarding the overall feel of our performances, I quote directly from her letter: "*You dance for the audience and enjoy what you're doing and this is conveyed to the audience and to other teams.*

This appears to be specific to you, as other teams we've watched seem to dance for their own enjoyment and not for the audience, e.g. the Bedlams are very 'showy' which is appreciated but they have no 'intercourse' with their audience. Their style of dancing seems to be quite selfish." Maybe that is what Sue Harris was picking up on at the Black Meet.

As for having their faces blacked up by us, these two saw this as a kind of initiation into the secret inner world of Silurian, and it prompted envious reactions from other females. To quote from the letter again: "*We felt our position was being coveted by others.*" Knowing what I know now, I find it exciting to speculate on the idea that, just under the surface, we humans are much as we have always been. Our basic needs, fears, desires and aspirations have hardly changed over the centuries, and we are really not very far away from our ancestral selves, celebrating the cycle of birth, growth, death and rebirth. Fire festivals involved the whole community, and everyone had to be symbolically touched by the fire, smearing their faces black with the charred wood, synonymous with fertility. Perhaps the girl who borrowed Burco's tin to black up the men in the pub, and all those girls who wanted to be 'touched by the magic' of Silurian, were unconsciously behaving as our ancestors might have done.

Undoubtedly, and at the risk of sounding fanciful, I suggest there was another kind of energy that took over at these times. It connected those Silurian warriors with nubile females as a necessary part of the celebration – female and male energies linked. Not that anyone at the time was consciously thinking like that, but we could all 'feel the force'. Regarding our effect on women, it appears from that letter that it was all positive, despite the situations in which Smudge found himself. Above all, it seems that we came across as friendly and great fun to be with. Even getting drunk allegedly made us 'sillier' not 'rude or offensive'. Such comments were a comforting endorsement of how we believed ourselves to be – comforting because it is all too easy to lose sight of personal integrity when put on a pedestal by supportive audiences. We believed our integrity, as well as our positive interaction with our audience, was intact, and this written testimony proved to us that we were still on the right side of the line.

Personal Reflection: 4

The Big Four-Oh

• • • • •

"Happy Birthday to you,
Happy Birthday to you,
Happy Birthday dear sacrificial victim,
Happy Birthday to yooooo!"

The one thing one can say with certainty about growing older is that we do. By the day, by the minute. I am already older than when I wrote that. And now that you are reading it, I am older still, assuming I am still alive. Funny old thing, age. A bit like porridge – an inevitable item on the breakfast menu that absolutely no one wants. Yet we all celebrate it every year. Another year older? Oh, great! *Didn't you do well*!?

It must be a relic from the past, when ageing another year was some kind of serious achievement, when being born was basically stepping into the ring with that well-known tag team, Pestilence and Famine, knowing that if one of them didn't get you, the other one would. These days of course we don't need to worry about all that. Disease is now propped up by a war chest of pharmaceutical drugs, and famine has been replaced by obesity. Famine and Pestilence have been given one-way tickets to the 'developing world', while we in the civilised world produce more food than we can possibly eat just so we can throw most of it away. Has the world gone mad? Of course it has. In a myriad ways.

Take birthdays, for example. Total lunacy.

Up to the age of twenty-one, a birthday is a meal ticket (to tables laden with completely unsuitable imitation foodstuffs) and an acquisition bonanza. Birthday campaigns are run with a two-month lead-in period, during which time hints the size of logs are dropped for family and friends to trip over, in the hope they will turn up on the big day with pantechnicons full of goodies. After twenty-one, this gets more problematic, because the first thing that happens is you think, "God, I'm twenty-one – I'm one foot in the grave! I *never* want to have another birthday . . ." You still want loads of goodies, but you can't get them without fessing up to your age. We invent all sorts of ways to keep them guessing, but somehow they always know. We dread each succeeding milestone, especially as we get close to the Big Four-Oh.

This is the one, isn't it? The killer. Life begins at forty. What a load of tosh. We all know, from the age of thirty-five, that there is *no* life after forty, only some kind of vague after-life, so commemorating that particular landmark is not what we want to do. But we also know that someone, somewhere, is plotting and planning One Of Those Parties. You know the sort of thing. The party you're supposed to know nothing about, but the one that's obviously going to happen. Why? Because this is the one that nobody is talking about. Not a squeak. For the last thirty-nine birthdays everybody has been giving it the old back-slapping routine – or head patting up to the age of ten – then all of a sudden it all goes quiet.

It's like you've suddenly caught some unmentionable disease. On or around your fortieth birthday, you're going to be attending to your everyday business, and you'll be doing something perfectly innocent, like opening your own front door when, without warning, your world is going to explode before your eyes. That comfortable room you've known for years is going to transmute into a seething swarm of manic cackling faces, shouting, laughing and singing at you. The Fortieth Birthday Party is a major cause of premature ageing, and it ought to carry a Government health warning. People have been known to go from thirty-nine to fifty-three and three quarters in the space of a few months just by worrying about The Party.

As my fortieth approached, I was indeed growing visibly older, riddled with anxiety and panic. However, I checked my diary and, in a brief moment of rejuvenation, realised that Silurian were playing away that weekend. Oh, bliss! Thank you, God! We had been invited to perform at Fylde Folk Festival, near Blackpool . . . aye, whur t'rock cooms from. What better way to avoid the dreaded Party?

Arriving on the Friday night, I was in relaxed mood and looking forward to a fun weekend. Starting as I meant to go on, I applied myself to tasting the different ales on offer, an exercise to which I gave my full attention and which concluded when the pubs closed, leaving me and the lads to meander off in the direction of our accommodation for the weekend – predictably, the local scout hut.

Next morning, with most of the side in varying stages of cerebral paralysis, we climbed into the kit and blacked our faces, dramatically improving our appearance. Staggering out of the hut, blinking in the strong light, we faced the prospect of a coach tour to such delightful dance venues as Blackpool Shopping Centre, an uninviting prospect for me, considering my frail condition. Only myself to blame of course, but I was beginning to fantasise about The Party with a disturbing degree of nostalgia. Anything would be better than any shopping centre anywhere.

My brain had shrunk in the night, detaching itself from its moorings. It was now on the move inside my skull with a hitherto unnoticed will of its own. Every time I turned my head, my brain would stay where it was, thus colliding with the inside of my skull, resulting in several distressing side effects, such as double vision, cold sweats and wobbly knees. As the coach bumped along the road on its ancient suspension, my brain felt like a sultana, but it was still emitting occasional sparks, like a dying fire. One of these carried the message, 'today is your fortieth birthday'.

This came as a revelation. Silly me. As the morning progressed, I had been thinking, 'today is the end of the world'. I wished I had kept more control on the number of pints I had put away the previous evening, and I spent the rest of the morning thinking I would never live to see forty-one.

At lunchtime, we were taken to a pub, but I couldn't look a pint of beer in the face and I knew that any attempt to consume food would be nothing short of idiocy. Whilst the others were wolfing down enormous sandwiches bulging with cheese and ham, washed down with pints of the local ale, I had become one of the walking dead, complete with staring eyes, jerky robotic movements and a face of stone.

"Here, try this." Mulvey's kindly voice sounded soothing as he held out a small glass for me.

"What is it?" I asked, eyeing it with mistrust.

"Medicine," replied Mulvey emphatically. "It works for me, so give it a go."

I took a sip.

"It tastes like gin and tonic," I conjectured.

"At least your taste buds are still working!"

I took another sip. The sun started to edge through the cloud bank in my head. "That's not bad. Not bad at all," I said.

"Well, Happy Birthday, mate!"

People talk about the hair of the dog, but I had never heard anyone mention the galvanising effect of half a tumbler of sparkling effervescence. The contents of the glass were soon drained and I was up at the bar ordering another one. My brain rehydrated and, within the hour, I was a born-again morrisman. I was back with the all-conquering Silures for the rest of the day, but pacing myself of course.

By the evening, all thoughts of the Party that I had escaped were long gone. Being a folk festival, a ceilidh was the entertainment for

Saturday night, and we had been booked to do a spot. The first dance went well. As the applause died down, our squire announced to the crowd, "Before the next dance, there is something we must do." Suddenly, the lights were dimmed and the lads surrounded me. The next five minutes were a blur. Forty candles were inserted in my hat band and set ablaze with someone's trusty Zippo lighter. The lads sang 'Happy Birthday', joined by the assembled masses, and then danced around me while I stood there like a fiery pagan totem. I might have avoided the Party, but I hadn't escaped unscathed. However, where surprise parties score pretty dismally on the usual scale of one to ten, this little celebration – pure Silurian – rated about twenty-three.

To attempt a description of this in normal prose would not do it justice, so I have taken the decision to quote from a letter I wrote to my parents, residing at that time in the Good Ol' U S of A. It was part of a thank-you letter for their contribution to this anniversary but, with a nod to my mother's deeply religious world view, I wrote it as the 17th Epistle to the Floridians.

"And lo, it came to pass that at the going down of the sun, a multitude had gathered at the appointed place, called by the people the Old Pavilion Dance Hall, to bear witness to these black-faced strangers from the South and yeah it was a goodly throng. And I say unto thee these men of mystery did whirl and dance, and put themselves about in such a manner, yeah, even unto the rising of the moon, that the multitude was seized with a great fear and asked, one to another, 'Who are these men?' 'Whence came they?' 'What manner of beverage do they consume?'

"And lo, these men did enter unto the temple itself, the place called Old Pavilion, and the multitude did surge forth also and gathered about to witness the dance of the demons again, and stood again struck with awe and wonderment.

"And it came to pass that he who called himself leader of these men did speak unto the multitude gathered about and said, 'Verily I say unto thee, that on this night shall be done a deed the likes of which has not been seen in heaven or earth and will not be seen again after this time'. And, yeah, the multitude was sore afraid and their eyes were cast down. The leader of these devil dancers did give the sign and yeah they did set upon one of their number, one who had reached that day two score years, and whose time had come, and they did circle him round and about, and they did adorn his headgear with many small sticks of white and verily, I say unto thee, they did put fire to these sticks and showed him then to the multitude, who were sore amazed and possessed and sang 'Happy Birthday' all in one voice.

"And henceforth this man was called Firehead and much revelry attended him in the temple that night and the women of the throng were bedazzled as with a strange spell and many of them attended him also, and yeah, he was ascended into heaven and took up his place on cloud nine and was at peace, and she who was called Sheila was cast out by another with jealousy in her heart into the outer darkness, with much weeping and wailing and gnashing of teeth, but I say unto thee . . . that is another story . . ."

Chapter 21
Barking Mad

• • • • •

"Show me the way to go home,
I'm tired and I want to go to bed.
I had a little drink about an hour ago,
And it's gone straight to my head..."

Some people are born bagman, some people achieve bagmanship and some people have bagmanship thrust upon them, to paraphrase the Bard. And we had our very own Malvolio upon whom to thrust the role of bagman.

However, when you know the whole world is thinking, 'these boys are a couple of sandwiches short of a picnic', it is prudent to err on the side of caution. You would not want to confirm what the world is thinking by elevating to high office the wildest loony in the bunch, whose brain is considered by most outside observers to be permanently out to lunch. And I'm not talking about Smudge.

Sitting in our favourite corner of Colwall's Horse and Jockey, we deliberated for a long time on our options and choice of candidates, with liberal quantities of Ansells oiling the cogs. All the usual problems were resurrected and discussed again at length, and all the standard questions asked, such as, "Why doesn't this pub sell Bathams or Old Hooky?" As candidates were considered and then rejected, the list grew ominously short.

Chris Mulvey was there, wearing the face of authority normally reserved for clients when pricing a plastering job. Sitting next to him was John Willy, who had in the past done some part-time casual labouring work for Mulvey. Being well acquainted with this customary display of narrow-eyed shrewdness, he was ignoring it.

"Course – fact of the matter is . . ." said Mulvey, leaning forward and stabbing the table with his forefinger, "Fact is – no bugger wants to do it!"

He leaned back and took a swig of beer, satisfied with his ability to size up the problem so quickly and concisely.

"What about Keith?" Willy ventured.

"He's done it once," noted Burco, "and he doesn't want to do it again." His eye wandered around the room, which was nothing remarkable, it being independently mobile.

"Mick!"

"Wot!?" answered Mick, jumping out of his conversation with Smudge and donning a defensive expression, in anticipation of something confrontational. He hadn't spotted the short straw Mulvey was about to hand him. Mulvey beamed at him, using one of his 'offer-of-a-lifetime' facial expressions.

"You've bin in the side long enough – it's time you did something useful. *You* have a go at it, eh?"

"Forget it," said Mick, smarting under the implication that his little bass drum wasn't contributing anything useful to the side, "I'm happy just being one of the lads."

"But you're practically one of the founder members! And you've never been bagman or squire or *anything*!"

"So what?" said Mick, defiant now, "I am *not* going to do it!"

"Oh."

Mulvey's authoritative note had drawn a blank. Used to rejections from potential clients, however, he wasn't going to flog this particular dead horse. It was bad enough dealing with them at work. He had come out for a quiet pint, after all. So he turned his attention to his beer and unwrapped another panatella.

"Why don't you have another go, Rob?" suggested Burco,

turning towards me to give me the full benefit of his chimp-like grin.

"Well, I wouldn't mind," I replied warily, carefully considering my position, "but, like Keith, I've done it once, so maybe someone who hasn't done it before? Why don't you do it?"

"Eh? Whaddya think I am?"

"An accountant," said Willy.

"And a bloody good one," agreed Burco. "But that doesn't mean I want to be a *bagman*."

"See?" said Mulvey, to emphasise he had been right all along. "No bugger wants to do it . . ."

"Well, *you* do it then Mulvey," suggested someone.

"Me!? Sod off – I haven't got any spare time! I think Burco should do it."

For a few seconds, conversation was suspended as each one of us kicked around the imminent possibility of Burco as bagman.

"Okay."

Eyes turned to the source of this quiet affirmative, suspecting another Burco Wind Up.

"Okay," he repeated.

The grin was still there, and the eyes were doing their usual dance, but the voice was serious, and he *had* repeated the word.

"I'll give it a go," he added, warming to the idea, "I was fed up with being Complaints Officer anyway – no one ever complained about anything! But, if I was bagman, I could tell 'em all to sod off when they ring up about their rubbish fetes and such!" The grin widened. "Yeeeah! I'll give it a go!"

And so it came to pass that Burco was duly elected as bagman. The Jekyll and Hyde nature of this brass-playing lunatic became instantly apparent the moment he turned his attention to bagbiz. Switching into sensible mode, he became Colin Robinson, star financial guru. He was full of quirky money-making ideas to replace all the above-mentioned fetes. Take the New Year's Eve Ceilidh, for instance.

Not long after his appointment, our sensible bagman, Mr Robinson, presented us with the startlingly obvious fact that, on a good day, Silurian could muster a fourteen-piece band, the core of which had at least ten years' experience in playing for ceilidhs.

"So why don't we do our own ceilidh?" asked the new bagman, "an' we can charge loadsa money for it, cos it'll be New Year's Eve!"

"Great idea!"

"Right – those in favour! Show of hands . . . Unanimous. Right – carried! Thank you. *Shaddap*! Thank you. Next item . . ."

Come New Year's Eve, we all turned up at the Horse and Jockey in our kit and looking suitably menacing in the darkness. The back room was quickly milling with people, numbers swelled by quite a few sixth-form boys and girls from the local private schools, fizzing with teenage hormones and well up for having a good time. A Silurian band was just what they needed to enhance their effervescent mood, infusing the older participants with the zest of youth.

The band members were feeling pretty positive too, this being a new venture in the Silurian saga, and the tone was soon set for a wild evening. Everyone danced as if they were auditioning for the Dervishes. Those Silures not in the band were on the dance floor, preferentially choosing their partners from amongst the female sixth formers, whirling them through the jigs, waltzes and polkas. At half time there was a short display of Border morris as a justification for being in kit – and to show what real morris dancing looks like.

At the far end of the room, the band looked terrific. Being on a stage had allowed for certain useful changes. Vas was there with his cello, and Super Steve had swapped his accordion for a keyboard. He had draped the keyboard with tinsel and adorned his bowler with green and red flashing lights. The lights in the room winked and danced in his specs and his teeth defined his manic grin, seemingly carved out of his matt black face. He looked like an eerie voodoo version of the Phantom of the Opera.

With an unexpected flash of forethought, Burco had organised a free taxi service for those of us who couldn't make other arrangements to get home. He had press-ganged his niece into ferrying inebriated black-faced revellers from Colwall to Malvern in the small hours after the gig. She must have owed Burco a favour, or else he hadn't explained it to her properly. I suspect the latter. Either way, the poor girl, having taken us all to the pub earlier, was faced with the tricky business of returning us all safely to our respective homes.

Burco had removed at a stroke the Damoclean threat posed by Her Majesty's joy-killing custodians, whose presence was always more obvious on any occasion of national merriment. At times like New Year's Eve, officers of the law were acutely aware that everybody except them was out there having a rare old time. Understandably, said officers were best avoided. Thanks to the brilliance of our new bagman, we didn't have to worry about getting nicked, so we were all boogying on down with not a care in the world, drinking next month's wages, and all well out of the reach of that terrifyingly long arm.

With the countdown to midnight, the New Year was welcomed in riotously, with everyone singing Auld Lang Syne and sweating into each other's palms. Having successfully transcended the inanity of that perplexing bit of tradition, the dancing was taken up again with unbounded enthusiasm for the remaining hour or so.

"New Year? Start as you mean to go on!" Andy yelled at me over the noise of the band, as he whirled past with some girl. From my viewpoint on the stage, watching the speed Andy was moving, it struck me that his example should not be followed by some in the room. There were several out on the dancefloor who, if they attempted to move at that pace, would not live to see the dawn. However, it was not my place to make these thoughts known, so I just kept bashing away at the drum.

Two o'clock in the morning saw the last of the dance junkies drifting off, leaving the Silurian boys awaiting Burco's shuttle service and surveying the disaster area that had once been a dance floor. Coloured streamers, polystyrene foam, fag ends, balloons and the odd broken glass littered the floor. Overflowing ashtrays cluttered the tables, whilst empty bottles and glasses lurked malevolently under the chairs among the forgotten items of personal property – scarves, coats, car keys, a handbag or two. Up on the equally littered stage, the band members were packing up, and one by one they swirled out of the cancerous fug which had enveloped them for most of the night. Wobbling through the debris and pools of beer on their way to the toilet, some called in to the bar to see if it was still open for business. Sadly, the towels were up, so the last of the instruments and equipment was packed away, and we sat around waiting for our turn in the shuttle.

Eventually, Burco and I were the only two left, so we started walking, thus giving the landlord the opportunity to lock up. We were still in kit of course, with tailcoats on, and blacked up. It was a dark night and we must have been very difficult to see as we strolled up through Colwall. But what we lost in visibility, we made up for in audibility, what with the bells clinking and jangling round our knees, and the ribald exchanges between us as we remembered the highlights of the evening. At one point, we were progressing along the pavement arm in arm, singing the posh version of *Show Me The Way To Go Home.*

"*Indicate the way to my abode . . .*"

"*I'm fatigued and I wish to retire!*"

"*I consumed a little beverage sixty minutes ago . . .*"

"*And it's gone straight to my crani-ani-um!*"

Suddenly, the air was filled with aggressive yapping.

We were just passing the gravel drive of one of those really twee suburban bungalows, and this really twee suburban terrier of dubious pedigree was standing there, barking and yapping with such venom that his little front paws kept lifting off the gravel as he hurled canine abuse around the gatepost.

I stopped and barked back. Nonplussed, his next bark died in mid flow as he backed off a couple of paces, his innate fear of six-foot alien hell-hounds made of bells temporarily weakening his resolve.

Burco was still walking, so I set off again. But as soon as I moved, the barking recommenced in earnest.

Yap! Yap! Yap! *Bark*! *Bark*! Yap!

I thought I'd better give this idiot dog a fair chance, so I got down on all fours behind the cypress hedge by the gate and barked back a couple of times. He came scuttling down the gravel with renewed bravado. Although he had lost sight of me, he must have worked out from the direction and height of this new bark, that he was more likely to be meeting something his own size. As he reached the open gate, he heard Burco's bells. Taking this as a sign of submission, he shot through the gate and belted after the sound, barking like a dog that knows it has the upper hand.

At this point, I was just about to resume my stroll when a new, and heavier crunch on the gravel betrayed the presence of what was obviously the terrier's minder, whistling and calling for his diminutive guard dog to return to base. A reasonable request, considering time was moving towards three o'clock in the morning, his beast had gone AWOL and the sound of his barking was carrying dramatically on the still night air. He stopped in the gateway just in front of me, hands on hips.

"Where's that bloody dog?" he muttered to himself.

On hearing this, my overwhelming sense of social responsibility overcame my desire to remain hidden by the hedge. I was still on all fours and thus remained invisible to this sleepy fellow in his dressing gown and boots, though he was only three paces from me. I felt he needed my help, so I got up, like a silent graveyard spectre.

"I think he's gone that way," I said, pointing up the street, my voice piercing the darkness like the ghost of Christmas past.

"*Gaaarrrh*!!"

I swear this guy must have jumped about three feet backwards before bolting back to the house, either to grab a gun, to take a sedative or to phone the police.

"Well," I thought, "at least I managed to tell him where his dog went." Having accomplished my first good deed of the New Year, I quickened my step to catch up with Burco, just in time to join him in the phone box, from which he proceeded to phone everyone to wish them a Happy New Year, on the pretext that really he was making sure they'd made it home and got to sleep alright.

"Bloody hell," he said after the fourth call, "people got no sense of humour these days. An' me going to the trouble of checkin' up on 'em. Wassa matter with'em all?"

What indeed? As Burco's witness, I would have to add that one person in particular was unjustifiably curt, bordering on hysterical as he demanded of us, in a pitch that was potentially damaging to his voice and heart, whether we knew what time it was. Then, without waiting for a reply, he invited us in two words to take a short job involving sex and travel, then slammed the phone down.

"Huh! There's no pleasing some people!" Burco said.

"I know," I sympathised. "You're just trying to look after them, if only they knew. Anyway, don't worry about it – you did a brilliant job organising that ceilidh!"

"Oh, ta."

"Dunno why we never got you to be Bagman before now – we could have been having even more fun all these years."

"Yeah, well. Things can only get better."

Our lift arrived. Burco's niece behind the wheel was looking surprisingly relaxed, but that was probably because she knew we were the last two on her list. We piled into the back seat and she turned the car around to head back to Malvern.

"I wonder what happened to the dog," I said.

Chapter 22

The Horsemen of the Apocalypse

• • • • •

"Alouette, lovely Alouette,
Alouette, you're the girl for me.
How I love your plates of meat
(How I love your plates of meat)
Plates of meat (plates of meat)
Oh-oh, Alouette, you're the girl for me..."

The dust kicked up in little clouds under the thump of my huge site boots as I trudged along, weighed down with a theodolite, tripod, 14-pound sledgehammer and half a dozen wooden pegs.

"What am I doing here?"

No reply. There never is when you are talking to yourself, except from the other voice inside your head, of course.

For me, this was a brief return to civil engineering prompted by an urgent need to improve domestic cash flow. Ten years prior to this job, I had quit the industry in repulsion at its merciless desecration of our landscape.

Coming to a halt to avoid being pulverised by a couple of gigantic roaring Volvo dump trucks bouncing towards me nose to tail, I scanned the devastation around me. It was only Day Two on this job. The day before, I had entered a green field full of clover, king cups and birds' foot trefoil, with the remains of ancient blackthorn hedges riddled with secret tunnels and dens for small boys. A tranquil spot, full of birdsong and humming bees, which belied its suburban location.

There had hardly been time to take all this in before the machines started up, belching noise and noxious black clouds into the air – clanking tracked excavators crushing the colour out of the field and ripping away its green cloak. Soon those lumbering bull-nosed dump trucks with six-foot tyres were roaring across the mutilated ground, turning it to dust. Topsoil stripping, they called this. The field turned quickly from green to brown and then to grey clay as the precious topsoil was ripped away – the damage we can do in just a few short hours is astounding. The excavator's bucket, teeth burnished by constant use to a dazzling silver finish, gouged the life out of the earth. A cubic metre with every bite. A few days later, trenches were dug and filled with concrete for the brick footings to begin their inexorable rise above ground. Six months later, houses occupied the ground and it was no longer possible to visualise this lost corner of England.

Watching it gave me that sick sad feeling I remembered from the previous time, on road building projects in Cornwall. It reminded me why I gave up what was an extremely lucrative career. And there I was again, facilitating the slaughter of life – Man the Destroyer. I didn't want this job, but black-cloaked penury rattled his dungeon keys in my face and frightened me into submission.

In these dark times, morris kept me vibrant, helped me to understand what was precious in life and what was a sham. To some, morris dancing would always be no more than a strange English eccentricity, an odd pastime that somehow had managed to survive the onset of civilisation. For me though, morris filled me with energy, transported me to places I could not reach except in the company of my dancing compatriots. It was my drug of choice, my pick-me-up and my spiritual passport to otherwise inaccessible levels of awareness. And there was another day trip coming up, this time at the invitation of Westminster Morris, and I was looking forward to getting away again.

Before that, however, Dizzy and I were going out for a meal with Smudge and Angie.

We had been planning a steak supper for months, the four of us, and finally the time had come. We were on our way to the White Pheasant in Tenbury Wells, because Smudge had heard that this place was like Steak Nirvana.

Once we had made ourselves comfortable at our table and concentrated our attention on the menu, it took Smudge only a second or two to spot the '24oz Special Rump'.

"Ooo! This looks aw'right!" Turning to the waitress, he asked, "'Ow big is it?"

"Well . . ." she began, shooting Smudge a glance of mild astonishment which said, 'this idiot has obviously never seen a pound and a half of meat'. It was clear that a number of appropriate answers were forming in her head but, remembering that the customer is king, she decided to take it one step at a time.

"It's . . .um . . . twenty four ounces," she confirmed.

"Yeah, I know that," said Smudge, "but 'ow big is it?"

"Well . . ." she said again, pausing before answering, "It's not *that* big."

"That's it then!" replied Smudge. "Tha's gorra be roight!"

"And how would you like it done, sir?"

The waitress was eyeing him warily, secretly regretting she'd changed her night off to Thursday. I was just pleased for her that Smudge was not in his Silurian kit. While he was pondering, her brain was whirring through some plausible options she could run past her manager if this turned out to be a hoax.

"Well," said Smudge, coming to a sudden decision, "Oi don' want none of that blood an' stuff . . . an' I don't want it overcooked!"

Angie gave a little squirm of embarrassment and tried to blend into the wallpaper.

"Medium, then," said the waitress, taking a shrewd guess.

"Er . . . yeah. Medium then."

Turning to the rest of us with visible relief and pencil poised, she asked Angie, "And for you, madam?"

"Oh!" said Angie, realising with a jolt that the wallpaper stunt hadn't worked. "I . . . er . . ."

"*And* . . ."

An urgent monosyllable from Smudge prevented further discourse on Angie's needs and caused a ripple of panic to traverse the waitress's features.

"An' I don' want any of that salad stuff – with lettuce leaves and cucumber," Smudge informed her. "Especially cucumber – it does things to me!"

"I'll make a note of it. Is that all then, sir?"

Luckily it was.

Taking the remainder of the orders, our waitress then hurried off. On her return, she placed Smudge's plate in front of him with an ill-concealed expression of gleeful malice. Not so much a steak, more a carpet square of meat. It hung over the edges of a very large plate, leaving no space for anything else.

Smudge toiled late into the night dissecting and consuming this monstrous slab of beef. By the time the rest of us were on our second round of After Eights and coffee, the steak had long since gone cold and re-entered a state of rigor mortis. "Eyes bigger than his tummy," my Granny would have said. Our failed carnivore finally gave up the struggle, leaving at least half the portion, which ended up accompanying us home in a plastic bag.

It reappeared at seven o'clock the next morning, on a Silurian minibus bound for London for our day of dance with the Westminster men. To a chorus of howls, protests and derisive banter, Smudge proudly held his trophy aloft and proclaimed it would be recycled as lunch. However, this aspiration quickly evaporated under the influence of Andy's homebrew, five gallons of which had been brought aboard to sustain us through the interminable two-hour journey. The consensus was that seven o'clock in the morning was as good a time as any to put us in the right mood. Rounding things off nicely, a bottle of Jack Daniels was also passed around by way of a chaser.

This tasty bonus came with the compliments of one of our more recent recruits, escorted to our practice venue one night by Burco.

"This is Dave Parkin," Burco had said, introducing his companion, "but he's a pillock, so you can call him Dave Pillock."

Burco felt able to make such a judgement because he knew Dave Parkin from school, and from the justly famous Malvern Chase Brass Band which had its origins in the Chase High School. We were surprised when Dave didn't give Burco a quick jab on the nose for calling him a pillock, but he didn't, and the name stuck.

He was a bit of a chameleon, was young Parkin. Certainly he was unhinged enough to fit in with Silurian, but he had at least two other personalities. Ostensibly, he was a cornet player, and had been recruited by Burco to swell the band, both in numbers and in sound. Once the cornet was back in its case though, and Parkin was out of his Silurian garb, he morphed into Bikerman, zooming about on his chopper through the streets of Malvern, with his dark blond locks flowing out from beneath his helmet and the fringes of his leather jacket flapping in the wind. Sometimes, at night and mainly on the weekends, Parkin the Roady appeared, as he was indeed a road manager for a heavy metal band from Evesham, Wrathchild.

Despite having to deal with multiple personalities, he was a cheerful soul, and very generous with the Jack Daniels. Most of it followed Andy's homebrew to refresh the parts of Silurian that tea and coffee had no effect on, and so life had taken on a very rosy hue by the time we reached Westminster. There was much chortling and general amusement as we attempted to disembark without mishap.

Needless to say, Smudge immediately failed this simple test as he tripped on the solitary step from the bus, colliding with Mick on his way to the ground.

"Whoopsh! Sorry! Sorry, Mick – didn't shee te'shtep!"

"Bloody hell, Dave! Nine o'clock in the morning, and you're as pissed as a parrot!"

"Huh! Huh! Huh!"

Mick, having declined the offers of refreshment on the bus on the grounds that it was 'too early for that sort of thing', was now painfully aware of the fact that, apart from Keith, who had once again volunteered to drive, he was the only one who was stone cold sober. He was as bristly as a porcupine, and the last thing he wanted was Smudge acting up. Showing a commendable ability to make the right decision, Mick steered clear of Smudge and found someone sensible to talk to. As soon as the pubs opened, however, he wasted no time in catching up with the rest of us.

In addition to Silurian, a number of other sides had been invited to this day of dance, and they were all gathered in a pub near Westminster Abbey. Each side took it in turn to do a dance spot outside the pub, watched by virtually no one other than the other morrismen. I looked around in disbelief. Eight million people in London, yet I had seen a bigger audience on a howling winter's night on Bringsty Common. Dancing outside the Abbey was more rewarding, however, as tourism still had a beating heart here. A sizeable crowd stopped to watch these English eccentrics prancing about. Silurian were girl-spotting of course, and managed to hold the attention of two lovely mädchen from Stuttgart. A bizarre conversation took place as Dave Parkin attempted to communicate with them in very poor, halting German, whilst they spoke to him in perfect fluent English.

Suddenly, one of the Westminster guys shouted, "Lunch!"

In no time at all, these two girls were left to enjoy their tourism on their own whilst we vanished from the scene, reappearing moments later in the Barley Mow. As we munched our way through some much-needed and very tasty comestibles from the buffet counter, Vas kept insisting that he knew a better pub than this one. Looking around, we couldn't see much wrong with the one we were in – good food, choice of beers, Woods 100-proof Navy Rum, comfortable seats. It was good enough for us.

But it wasn't *real* enough for Vas. He was into old salt-of-the-earth spit 'n' sawdust places. Plush seating and imitation brasserie tables made him angry. We could see his point, but we had no problem with the Barley Mow. Perhaps we just had lower standards. However, Vas was spending his working days in Westminster at that time, with a new job as part of a team of scientific advisers to the Government. He knew the area well and this other pub had become his new local, so we went with his recommendation.

It turned out to be as good as Vas had suggested. It had Young's beer, an Irish landlord (with smiling nubile daughter) a sexy barmaid and a receptive audience – and no fruit machines or yuppies. Quickly getting the audience on our side with Mulvey's Irish medley, we got down to the serious business of the day by going through our little toe-to-head number with some unsuspecting girl standing on a chair. We used to do this to *Touched Her On The Toe*, but now we had a much better version, picked up from the Exeter men at their ring meeting. More appropriate for a London audience, albeit an Irish one, this was sung in Cockney rhyming slang to the tune of *Alouette*.

Detaining the unsuspecting barmaid, we stood her on a table for all to see and then set about singing the praises of her physical attributes, touching the parts in question for the benefit of those unable to translate the rhyming slang. We sang about her 'Barnet Fair', her two 'mince pies' and even her 'plates of meat', but we were really in it for her 'thre'penny bits' and her 'bottle and glass'. Enough said.

Later that afternoon, we found ourselves in Trafalgar Square. We were greeted by a sight that reminded us it was also the FA Cup Final day. The lions around Nelson's Column were adorned with groups of skinheads, punky junkies and other professional hooligans, presumably waiting for a fight to the death over the result of the Final, expected about an hour from then. A relatively small window for a massed morris display, but one the Westminster lads were keen to exploit. Soon there were nearly as many morrismen as skinheads. The latter began to fidget restlessly on their perches amongst the bronze statuary.

Fearing a takeover by a horde of jingling wimps, a few of the braver skins jumped down from the nearest lion and took up a kind of mock defensive stance on the periphery of what was rapidly becoming morris territory. Little grunts of derision and half-hearted abuse were thrown in our direction, and there was much hopping from foot to foot. Such behaviour looked very familiar and I was searching my memory banks to establish where I'd seen it before. And then it came to me. It was on one of David Attenborough's programmes, in which he had been exploring baboon behaviour, and this scene in Trafalgar Square looked exactly like a baboon troop defending its territory against an intrusive male. As a species, we are still far closer than we think to our primate cousins.

The self-appointed spokesman for the skins decided to make a name for himself as he approached me and Tony Price, our new side-drummer. Checking out the tattoos on his forehead, I thought the star tattooed beneath the legend, 'MADE IN ENGLAND' was a very neat touch, and the eight silver rings along the rim of his left ear complemented his nose stud perfectly. He was a picture of sartorial anarchy, and his clothes were as much a uniform as those worn by the morrismen around him.

"Oi!" he said, getting the formalities out of the way.

I felt like saying, "Yes, my good fellow, and what can I do for you?" But realising that I probably looked as silly as he did, I settled for, "Yeah, wot?"

"Why're you dressed like that?" he demanded aggressively. Anyone would think he was on patrol with the Fashion Police.

"Why are *you* dressed like *that*?" I retorted.

"I *like* dressin' like this!" he barked, astounded at my impertinence.

"Well, I like dressing like *this*!"

Faced with the fact that there were quite a lot of people more or less dressed like me, and that many of them were brandishing three-foot sticks, he was temporarily lost for words. Taking no further part in our conversation, he regrouped with his mates. There was much huddling, low voices and finger pointing, then he was back up on the lion to tell the others. From where I stood, I could just hear the message going around, "They *like* dressing like that." Subdued, but not cowed, they sat on their lion and, from this vantage point, kept Silurian in their sights, paying little attention to the other dancers.

For the benefit of the skins as well as the Cotswold contingent, Mulvey, in his new role as Squire, decided we should do Upton Hanky, just to show how spectacular a hanky dance could look. We had an enormous space to fill and we would be able to make it fly. Detaching myself from my drum, I joined the set, with no thought of the potential hazard of footwear with slippery leather soles. When the dance was really motoring, my feet suddenly went from under me but, according to those in the band, I never broke rhythm as I sort of flipped and cartwheeled in position, landing on the correct foot and continuing the dance as if nothing had happened. I didn't even know what was occurring until the dance was over and I was being told about it.

A huge cheer went up as we finished on the rounds, but the biggest cheer was from the skinheads and punks up amongst the lions – and we hadn't even done a stick-smashing number for them yet!

After the massed display, we followed our guides back to base camp, Westminster Conference Centre, on the promise of food. Much ale had been consumed since Silurian had left Malvern at six o'clock that morning, and solid food was required. Internecine squabbling was breaking out, always a sign with us that the food/drink balance was out of kilter. Mick was very belligerent and threatening to resign, not for the first time. Dave Parkin was threatening to kill him, or indeed anyone else for that matter, and Smudge too might well have become very abusive by then had it not been for the fact that he was asleep on his feet. Willy, the incorrigible Fool, was brewing his own special kind of mischief as usual. Passing the gates to Downing Street, and beckoning to Burco and Parkin to join him with sousaphone and cornet, he stood there in his mock guardsman's uniform and played *The Red Flag* for Mrs Thatcher.

By the evening, all was well. Silurian, reconciled again, were present to a man, which surprised everyone in the room, even us. There were more surprises to come, generally involving the meal, seemingly over before it really had a chance to gain any traction.

It began well enough. Bread rolls and butter and a bowl of meaty broth – a good start to any meal. The trouble came with the apple crumble, the next item on the menu.

The soup bowls had been cleared and more crockery was heading our way. A plate of apple crumble was placed before Smudge.

"Wha's *this*?" he demanded.

Politely, he was informed it was apple crumble.

"Yeah, I can *see* that," replied Smudge impatiently, "but I ent 'ad me main course yet!"

Politely again, he was informed that everyone had had their mutton stew and potatoes, because the kitchen staff had checked the numbers of plates and they had all been returned.

"Mutton stew!?"

Smudge's eyes did a quick traverse around the table, searching for the person that had set him up this time.

"Mutton stew!?" he repeated, "I had a bowl of soup with a spud floatin' in it!"

With unwavering politeness, the waiter assured him that, whatever Smudge's observation may have conveyed, nevertheless that was the main course and this was dessert.

"Well, stroll on!" Smudge finished lamely.

"Don't worry, Smudge," Mulvey said. "You've still got half a joint of beef in your bag somewhere!"

"Never mind about that," Smudge replied, "I haven't had me main course!"

Smudge was miffed, as were most of us. We were also still hungry. Once the tables had been cleared, we felt we could leave without offending our hosts. With Vas as our guide, we left the building in search of further sustenance before bedtime.

Awake at 7.30 the next morning, I realised in a panic that breakfast was not part of the deal. This gig was officially a 'day of dance', and the day had ended yesterday.

No toast! Sunday morning – and no toast!

I began to fantasise about soft boiled eggs and armies of toast soldiers marching across a white tablecloth . . .

Someone was shaking my arm.

"Hey – are you coming?"

It was young Parkin.

"Are you coming to breakfast?" he asked me again.

"Breakfast? But there isn't any breakfast!"

"Oh, yes there is . . .but we've gorra drive there."

It transpired that Keith had been given directions to a café which was open on Sunday mornings. Despite morris activities having ended the day before, we hadn't arrived home yet, so we were still 'on tour', and therefore still in kit. Making sure our blacking was in order, we climbed into the minibus and made for the café. Predictably enough, it turned out to be a definitive Greasy Spoon, with red formica table tops and the heavy smell of overused fat hanging in the air. The far corner was occupied by a 'gentleman of the road' and indeed the place would have been incomplete without him.

Each table sported the usual condiment set: a salt cellar bunged up with damp salt, a pepper pot that was deceptively empty and a suspicious-looking red plastic tomato with a huge and ancient clot of dried ketchup obstructing the passage of whatever was inside.

The proprietor, trying to act normally whilst serving a posse of what looked like zombies in bowlers with faces charred in some extraordinary way, was perspiring heavily in the heat and steam on his side of the counter. His shirt sleeves were rolled up and his balding head was glowing. He looked typical of the genre, with one notable extra detail. He had a dotted line and 'CUT HERE' tattooed around his neck, and an abundant collection of tattooed graffiti on his arms, including several references to Millwall Boot Boys. We kept this fellow busy for some time while we ate our way through his stocks for the following week, finally rolling out of the place and into the minibus quite a bit later than expected.

"Everybody fit?" asked Keith from behind the wheel, obviously keen to get moving.

A chorus of monosyllabic affirmatives greeted this enquiry, spiced up with the odd expletive, a fart and some feeble early morning attempts at humour.

"Nobody needs the toilet or anything?" continued our driver, going through the usual checklist to avoid unnecessary stops.

"Right – everybody happy? I'm going then."

The engine trembled into life and off we went. Passing Speakers' Corner, we toyed with the idea of speaking, but no one was up for it and there was nobody to speak to, so we kept going.

Smudge, however, decided he did want to speak. But only to Keith.

"'Ere, Keith. If you see a loo anywhere, can you st –"

"*SMUDGE*! You bloody simple-minded dipstick! What did I just say when we left?"

"Eh?"

"I asked if anyone needed the toilet!"

"Yeah, I know. But Oi didn' need one then!"

"Prat."

Keith drove on. Silence resumed. We looked out of the window at bits of London floating past our eyes.

"Come to think of it – *I* could do with a piss," said Willy absent-mindedly to himself.

"An' me," came another muffled voice from the back of the bus.

"Bloody *Hell*!" said Keith.

Despite this outburst, Keith had an admirable level of patience, no doubt bestowed upon him through having to deal with kids as part of his day job, so he did stop as soon as he saw some public toilets. They happened to be in Bayswater Road, a bit of a tourist honey pot, so we prolonged the break by strolling around for a while, admiring the prints and paintings on display. We had to suffer the usual clutch of puzzled faces from inquisitive passers-by, who wanted to know why we were dressed like that and, predictably, why we had black faces. We supplied them with the usual stock answers.

"I've been dead three weeks."

"Dunno – just woke up this morning, and there it was!"

"Black face! Oh no! This can't be happening to me – quick, get me a mirror!"

Some were even told two versions of the truth: "It's a disguise, so you don't know who I am," and "I didn't wash it off last night!"

All the while, cameras were clicking, as the tourists switched their attention from the paintings to us, knowing that the folks back home would not believe their description of this strange manifestation without photographic evidence. We were approached by a German who said, "Exkuse plis? Vot are you looking like zat?" For a German, his English was poor.

Tony looked at him and replied darkly, "We are the thirteen Horsemen of the Apocalypse. The world will end at midnight."

"Oh, ja? Gut! I take your picture zen!"

He took several and then hurried off, presumably to sell this major scoop to the world's press before midnight.

Squire Mulvey, meanwhile, was getting restless. All dressed up and nowhere to go, he felt an irrepressible urge to justify his appearance in terms other than 'pedestrian'.

"How about a dance, then?" he asked casually.

"How about you go an' boil yer 'ead!"

"Oh, I just thought –"

"Well, stop it. Too early in the morning for thinking!"

Having dealt with this traditional preamble, we then did a couple of dances. Though the reception was good, we decided that two was enough for a Sunday morning, and it was about coffee time. Espying a very pleasant little pavement café, we took over a few of the outside tables, ordered some drinks and just sat and watched the world go by for a while. Much of the world wasn't going by. It was stopping at the traffic lights just opposite the café, in some cases, only just. With their attention diverted by a knot of thirteen black-faced morris dancers under the café's awning, they were missing the amber light and screeching to a halt just before colliding with the crossflow traffic.

At one point a chauffeur-driven Mercedes stood on its brakes as the lights changed to red, causing the toffee-nosed female passenger in the back to wake with a start, closely followed by a Westie terrier, whose face and front paws appeared on the window ledge. A bark died in its throat as it did a quick double-take, staring at us in mute disbelief. Clearly unenthusiastic about the prospect of having to defend its territory against such overwhelming alien odds, this button-nosed bottle brush seemed suddenly to remember that it had something better to do, and it quickly vanished into the floor well.

We sensed that we had become a traffic hazard as well as a threat to the local canine population, so we finished our coffees and made our way back to the bus.

Just a mile from the top of Birdlip Hill on the A417, there is a lovely old stone-built pub called the Golden Heart, nestling in a dip called Nettleton Bottom. Keith was confident that we would be in good time to make this a brief lunchtime stop, as long as we didn't have to factor in any toilet breaks on the way. Even Smudge recognised this to be a good plan, and we arrived in time for a relaxing pint and some tasty sandwiches.

However, when you are the Thirteen Horsemen of the Apocalypse, it is impossible to enter a pub without being noticed. The locals, impressed by our appearance, cajoled us into providing them with some entertainment, so we played some tunes and sang some songs for them. Ultimately though, dancers have to dance, and our audience was keen to see that happen. We piled outside and began dancing in the car park.

The effect on passing motorists was much the same as it had been in London, as their heads turned to get a closer look, with two major differences – the A417 is a faster road than the Bayswater Road, and Nettleton Bottom is in a dip below a blind summit. Suddenly, one motorist decided to pull into the car park, slowing very quickly, although he was indicating to turn right. The next motorist that came over the brow of the hill saw him too late. With locked brakes and smoking tyres, this car crunched heavily into the back of the stationery one.

Though an air of panic was wafting through the onlookers, the landlady was almost nonchalant as a couple of badly shaken passengers were escorted into the pub for a sit-down.

"Happens all the time," she casually said to us as she refilled a few of our tankards.

Keith of course had not been drinking, so he offered to take those involved in the accident to a phone box, there being no public phone in the pub. For the benefit of 21st Century readers, this is the answer to that frequently asked question, "Whatever did we do before mobile phones?"

The other thing you couldn't do before the age of mobile phones was phone your driver and say, "Where are you then?" We just had to wait patiently for our man to return. By the time we saw his face again, it was nearly five o'clock. Keith was wearing a thunderous brow and muttering about people taking advantage of his good nature. His look said, "Don't even think about saying anything!"

So we didn't. It was to be some days before we discovered that the two accident victims had leaned heavily upon Keith to be their personal taxi service for a good part of the afternoon, driving them to the shops, to pick up kids and finally to their homes.

Meek as lambs, we piled on the bus as soon as Keith returned. We realised that Keith, already lumbered with driving us home, really didn't need to be driving around little known parts of Gloucestershire as well, so we did our best to be well behaved for the remainder of the journey. Mostly, we were preoccupied with our own thoughts, but it was impossible for us to remain totally docile, and spontaneous flashes of Silurian lunacy did break out from time to time. At one point, Burco opened a window, stuck himself half through it and shouted to passers-by for assistance.

"Help! Help! Get me out of here – I'm being deducted!"

"You mean *abducted*, foolish boy!" came a voice from the depths of the bus.

"No I *don't*," insisted Burco, "I mean *deducted* – I'm an accountant!"

Little moments like these passed the time quickly, and soon enough Keith was pulling up outside Chris Mulvey's house to drop off the Worcester contingent. As they disembarked, Vas summed up the weekend for us.

"One car crash, two fights, one resignation and four pounds twenty-three left between us – pretty average weekend really!"

"Yeah, except that Smudge has still got a pound of steak in his bag!"

Chapter 23
Send In The Clones

• • • • •

"Where are the clones?
There ought to be clones.
Quick, send in the clones..."

"Right then," said Keith, our tireless bagman, "Who's in favour of going to Thaxted again?"

The question had come up every AGM since our first visit. And each time we quickly voted against the idea. We were superstitious about spoiling the magic of the first experience. We felt it had been a one-off, and most of us were happy to leave it at that, but the idea of going again was not without support.

"Well," Burco said, "we've been to Saddleworth more than once, and that's been okay . . ."

"True," agreed Bernie.

"Show of hands, then," suggested Keith briskly, spotting the opportunity for a decision.

Hands were raised and counted, the vote was carried and the 1990 Thaxted ring meeting was added to our list of outings for that year.

We were still the only Border side in the ring, outnumbered by Cotswold sides but, in our opinion, never outclassed. The Saturday tour bus was full of Cotswold men, but we paid them no attention. They were almost an alien species to us, and we mostly just kept to ourselves, leaving them to fill the front seats of the bus whilst we dominated the back section like a knot of mischievous schoolboys.

At the first venue, The Red Lion at Great Sampford, we set our own pace for the day by ripping through Bromsberrow Heath in record time. Willy loved winding up the music, but the dancers always rose to the challenge of keeping pace whilst retaining the shape of the figures. Our little set was soon over, and a thirst-quencher was required. Though barely ten o'clock in the morning, the pub was open. Never slow to take advantage of an opportunity, Silurian managed to relieve the publican of around forty pints by the time we boarded the coach again twenty minutes later.

It was about then that we noticed the video camera.

Evidently, one of the tour sides, from the village of Belchamp St Paul, seventeen miles north-east of Thaxted, was making a recording of the day's activities. It seemed that their camera was mostly pointing at us, even on the bus. However, with a strong side of sixteen, we were confident we could show them what morris dancing should look like.

Getting off the bus at the second venue, The Red Lion at Steeple Bumpstead, it quickly became apparent that the only space for dancing was in a side street onto which the pub fronted. Cars were using this thoroughfare, so Silurian traffic control was brought into play by installing our Wall of Sound right across the entrance to it. This impenetrable barrier of twelve musicians stopped the cars and protected those engaged in a four-man Brimfield. All the while, the camera rolled. The Belchamp boys clearly appreciated our efforts. On boarding the coach again, they talked to us about Border morris all the way to the next stop, The Globe at Clare, so called because the whole world was there.

Surmising correctly that, with such a crush of people, the chances of dying of thirst were greater than the possibility of slaking it, we headed straight for The Cock Inn just along the street. The landlord was an angry-looking fellow, probably because even his usual customers were now ensconced in The Globe along with the rest of mankind, in anticipation of better entertainment than that provided by the fruit machines in his own pub. His face fell into the crevasse of a deep scowl once he realised we had simply come in to top up our tankards before heading off again. Taking advantage of the milling throngs of receptive people outside The Globe, we danced Dilwyn for them, with Belchamp's camera reeling it all in. Satisfied with the warm reception, we left that outdoor arena in favour of a corner of the pub to kick off a music session in the bar. Having captivated the audience again, we deserted them for the second time as we concentrated our efforts on the pub's lunchtime menu – cottage pie and chips.

Following this welcome lunch spot, the tour continued through the picture-postcard villages of stockbroker Essex, with the next stop being The Fox at Finchingfield, complete with its all-too-perfect village green and duck pond. Once inside the pub, it became instantly clear from the appearance of the three foxy barmaids why this place wasn't called The Red Lion. The barmaids were like the Three Graces fallen from that high office after eating the forbidden fruit. On seeing them, Silurian switched into hunting mode, but we knew this was red-line territory and the barmaids were untouchable. In any case, these snooty foxes had looks that could turn you to stone. Leaving well alone, we ventured outside for other damsels to distress. One of our victims turned out to be a reporter for Channel 4 on location. Her invitation into the exclusive Silurian honorary members' club, and her subsequent loss of cool when her face was daubed with our traditional tribal markings, was being eagerly filmed by her camera crew, whilst her producer and other overpaid hangers-on were all mincing about, snorting and giggling in their pale trendy suits and horn-rimmed sunglasses.

Meanwhile, of course, Belchamp's own camera was still rolling.

Towards late afternoon, the coach stopped outside The Bell at Great Bardfield. If there was any dancing done here, it passed me by unnoticed. I had reached the stage where a traditional Silurian freshener was required. I found the bar, wedged my knee against it to stop it bobbing about and placed an order for a gin and tonic with the identical twins behind the bar. Quickly getting on the outside of this potent elixir, I sank onto a bar stool, closed my eyes and listened to my brain snapping back into position, galvanised by this effervescent little restorative. Opening my eyes, I was disappointed to see that one of the twins had disappeared, but put this down to the effect of the gin, as I had it on good authority that it could be blamed for a whole range of disappointments.

By the time we had left The Bell to return to Thaxted, most of Silurian had put away a surprising number of alcoholic drinks in the seven or so hours that had passed since we sipped the first pint in Great Sampford. We still had one more performance to get through, however – dancing at the massed display in Thaxted itself. Personally, this didn't bother me, having consumed another two Vera Londons (Rhyming slang: Vera Lynn – gin; London Philharmonic – tonic), plus a pint of best bitter to wash them down. I hadn't a care in the world as I left, thanking the identical triplets behind the bar for their hospitality.

As may have become apparent thus far in the tale, Silurian were of the opinion that they could drink all day and still dance the socks off anyone. It could be argued that this was simply male bravado. More cruelly, it might be supposed to be nothing more than a rumour put out by the Silurian men themselves, and if not a rumour, then wishful thinking. Or indeed, quite simply a pack of lies. The true facts, however, were about to be decided that evening in Thaxted.

Belchamp's cameraman was still recording the proceedings when we came on to dance at about half six in the evening. That was of no interest to us though – we weren't dancing for him. We were dancing for the audience or, more accurately, with the audience. And, from their generous applause, we felt we had probably done a good job. Some weeks later, Belchamp sent us a copy of their video, which we watched in The Horse and Jockey one Monday night.

On viewing it, we knew for certain that, even after a long day of touring the pubs, our dancing was still second to none.

After this clear confirmation of our abilities, we felt elated, and it was very refreshing to see our dancing from an audience's perspective. We could see what it was they were engaging with, and we had a real sense of the energy exchange between us and them. Though grateful to Belchamp for this opportunity to see ourselves objectively, we didn't appreciate at the time that these Essex lads might have had an ulterior motive in producing the film. Having sent us a free copy of the video, they then asked us if we would like to come over and give them a Welsh Border instructional. Happy to disseminate what Dave Jones had so painstakingly researched, we were quite willing to accept this invitation.

Subsequently, in November 1990, we were on our way to Essex again to spend a whole Saturday giving the Belchamp lads intensive instruction in Border dancing, getting through Much Wenlock, Pershore Stick and Clee Hill. As we had seen on the Thaxted coach tour, these guys were good dancers, lively characters and in possession of a good song or two. Our instructional day was easy from the point of view of teaching people who wanted to learn. And our reward was that we were all going along to the pub that evening, no doubt to keep the Border conversation going.

Smudge and I were staying with an unruly nonconformist called Mike, who took us to the pub after a meal at his place. It was pints for everyone and Smudge and I bought a round apiece. Then it was Mike's round.

"Do you want Woods?" he asked Smudge.

"Oh, great!" Yes please," said Smudge. Woods bitter was one of his favourite brews. But that's not what Mike meant – he was referring to Woods 100-proof Navy Rum, and he had learned from us that one or two of us were partial to a drop of this real rum.

"Oh," said Smudge, the picture of disappointment on being handed a little glass, "Oi don' like rum . . ."

"You try a spot o' this, boy," suggested Mike in a perfect Norfolk dialect. Odd, in the middle of Essex.

Smudge took a sip.

"Cor! That's bloody luvly, that is! Huh! Huh! Huh!"

With this sudden change of loyalty from bitter to spirits, our man was on a roll, getting through another six little glasses during the course of the evening. After the first one, he fell asleep on the bar billiards table, but kept waking up to order another. In one of his waking moments he was set up by the Belchamp lads to do some serious chatting up.

"Go on," they urged him, "she's divorced – looking for a man. And you are the man of her dreams!" Smudge knew that, of course. He was the man of all women's dreams.

"She *is* a vision of nubile callipygian pulchritude, Smudge," I pointed out.

"Eh? What're you on about?"

"She is a sexy beauty blessed with perfectly shaped buttocks," I translated. He still looked baffled.

"She's got a lovely arse," said the Belchamp spokesman, by way of further simplification.

"Oh . . . *right*. Yeah, she has an' all. Huh! Huh! Huh!"

"And she's dyin' for you to come over and make her dreams come true," concluded the Belchamp man.

"Oh, all roight then . . ."

Like a progammed missile, Smudge was instantly at her side. Within seconds of his, "Ullo, wot's yore name then?" his hands were on the move whilst his mouth was passing favourable comments about various parts of her anatomy. His conquest failed when, standing behind her, he fell asleep over her shoulder with one hand up the back of her jumper.

As the evening progressed, we played some tunes and sang some songs. We gave them our favourites and they gave us theirs, although there seemed to be an air of rivalry about it all. Willy was convinced they were trying to upstage us – not difficult after our long drive over that morning and then spending the day teaching them to dance. We just wanted to relax. However, if they were trying to upstage us, they would discover that Willy was someone who always had an extra trick or two up his sleeve. When Belchamp were singing *I'm Climbing Up The Sunshine Mountain*, which of course they had borrowed from us, Willy went for the winning goal. As they got to the line, 'faces all aglow . . .', he set fire to his beard with his Zippo.

While this had been going on, Smudge had woken up again and moved to a new challenge, having finally worked out that he'd blown it with the divorcee. At first, none of us noticed that he had moved, but what we did see was a blonde girl at the back of the room. She seemed to have at least two pairs of hands. One pair was occupied with a drink and a cigarette, whilst she caressed herself sensuously with a second pair. And then we finally noticed Smudge. Oddly though, he seemed to be asleep again, draped over her shoulders like a large backpack with legs.

Come Sunday morning, with Smudge still drowsy and suffering from the excesses of the previous evening, we were taken to a beautiful thatched pub called The Half Moon, in Belchamp St Paul itself. Overlooking the lush village green, it was a wonderful venue for a lunchtime session. The Belchamp crew commented favourably on the size and competence of our band, and a conversation began about our recently trialled role as a ceilidh band. Inevitably, by the time we left that day, we had been booked to play at a ceilidh for them in July 1991.

Before the date had come round, our paths crossed again when they arrived at the Upton Folk Festival in the spring of 1991. Eagerly they demonstrated for us all they had learnt during our instructional. They were very positive about themselves and told us that they probably had enough material to go out as a Border side. Little comment was passed by us, and we thought no more about it. After all, many Cotswold sides at that time had been bitten by the Border bug and would go out as a Border side just for a change. As far as we were concerned, it all helped to promote our local dances.

Shortly after the Upton weekend, a rumour turned up at the Horse and Jockey one practice night that Belchamp's Border kit was just like ours.

"Don't be daft," said Mick. "Nobody would be stupid enough to copy our kit!"

"You better believe it," said Willy, looking deadly serious, "I was talking to them at Upton."

"They're woindin' you up," suggested Smudge.

"I don't think so," Willy concluded emphatically, turning his attention to his pint.

Unconsciously evading any further exploration of these uncomfortable thoughts, the subject was changed. Over the next few months this conversation slipped from our memories and was gone by the time we went to play for their ceilidh. The plan was to meet for the usual Friday evening pub session, enjoy a joint Border tour on the Saturday and then play at the ceilidh in the evening.

Staying with their squire, I wasn't thinking about what kit these guys would be wearing, even when he and I were both blacked up and ready to go. He was of course somewhat low-key, being prepared to go out without hat, bells and other accessories, whereas I was top-to-toe Silurian, right down to my triangle hanging from my belt and my tankard hanging from my triangle.

The wake-up call happened as we entered the pub at the first spot. It came as a real shock.

Everywhere I looked there were black faces, bowler hats with Silurian sashes and black tailcoats. For a few seconds I was bewildered. "Who the hell are *all these people*?" I asked myself. Then of course I realised they were mostly Belchamp men. John Willy's rumour had turned into reality.

Once outside, it was easier to tell us apart, because they were wearing knee breeches and coloured socks but, from the waist up, and especially from behind, they were pure unadulterated Silurian. It felt very awkward, akin to the experience a woman might have of turning up at a party and finding someone else wearing the same dress, but a bit more sinister. This was more like knowing that your stalker has been following you on shopping trips.

"Wha' did they wanna go and do that for?" Smudge asked in hushed but plaintive tones, as we gathered in a little knot before moving off for the day's dancing.

"Bunch of bloody tossers!" said Burco, also under his breath.

"Like seeing yourself in a bad dream," suggested Keith.

"What? You mean the technicolour socks?" I added.

"Well," Willy said, "I don't much fancy a day's dancing with 'em, so we'd better show 'em who's in charge at the ceilidh tonight."

For us, the day went downhill from there. The dancing was flat; the pub session mediocre. We didn't know whether to laugh it off or be indignant, but either way we were amazed that anyone should have the temerity to copy a kit so distinctive and exclusive. It is said that imitation is the sincerest form of flattery, but this didn't feel like flattery. This felt more like some new form of plagiarism: our kit being worn by another side – even down to the tailcoats!

There would come a time when the vicar of Thaxted would see this attempt to copy us and be moved to evaluate the two sides, describing Silurian as 'anarchic but genteel' and Belchamp 'vulgar by comparison'. We would be comforted by his positive appraisal but, on that day in 1991, we were stunned by the impudence of this Cotswold chimera. As the day wore on, it became increasingly obvious that this was a clone side we were looking at. Little Silurian details kept coming to our attention – the round hippie sunglasses, the pheasant feathers, the bell pattern under the knees.

We changed back into our ordinary clothes for the ceilidh on the Saturday night. Though nothing more was said following Willy's comment earlier in the day, we intuitively knew what we had to do to prove that Silurian was peerless, even as a band of musicians, and we undoubtedly hit the spot. The music flowed. As for me, my spirits were lifted high when, at the end of the evening, Willy said, "Thanks, Rob – that drumming was bloody great!"

On Sunday morning, the uneasiness was palpable. We didn't really want to spend any more time with these clones, and we left as soon as it was polite to do so. Inevitably we talked about it most of the way home.

"It's bad enough them wearing our kit," muttered Burco, "but they're trying to copy our attitude too! That really pisses me off – nobody copies my bloody attitude!"

"That's not the biggest problem," Keith pointed out. "They're not as good as us. So when they go out dressed like us and people see them, they'll be thinking Silurian's gone down the pan!"

"Have you seen their band line-up?" I said. "Even that looks like us. I'm surprised they haven't got a melodeon player in a Guard's uniform!"

"Give 'em time . . ." said Willy.

Vas was particularly upset, and felt somewhat betrayed, having spent all that time the previous November teaching them the dances. Now here they were showing their gratitude by cloning us instead of coming up with their own original Border kit. The flattery card that they might have waved at us was simply not going to work. It was just bad form to copy another side's kit. Unoriginal and impertinent.

"I can see what's going to happen," said Vas. "At future ring meetings, eventually all sides will look like us!"

"Cotswold morris will die out," said Keith helpfully. Or was that 'hopefully'?

"It'll become as rare as Border is now," I ventured. "Photographers and reporters will be scouring the country looking for a Cotswold side. And morris dancers in a couple of generations will rediscover Cotswold – and they'll be saying 'Wow! *That* looks interesting – let's do that!'"

Human beings have many failings, amongst which are envy, covetousness and theft, all of which were on display that weekend.

But, if the Belchamp boys thought they could simply purloin the Silurian enigma, they were adding another failing to that list: credulity. It is impossible to duplicate something unique. Silurian represented a matchless confluence of disparate yet compatible anarchic personalities held together by an invisible force that, through some kind of alchemy, resulted in an entity that was greater than the sum of its parts. In 1991, this band of brothers was at its peak. To observe this from outside and believe that it is possible to recreate something almost mystical merely by dressing the same way is naïve. And to believe that copying someone else's look, and then acting up in a vaguely antisocial way, is going to produce an exchange of energies with onlookers, is to misunderstand the nature of energy.

In the great scheme of things, there is always someone willing to steal someone else's idea, always freeloaders who prefer to profit by another's efforts, and there is nothing to be done about it except let it go. And that was what we did.

As our journey home continued that Sunday, we swiftly concluded that it mattered not what other sides may or may not do. What counted was what we did.

"I'll tell you what, though," said Willy, in reflective mood and looking at Smudge.

"Wot?" said Smudge guardedly, looking for the catch as ever.

"Nobody's ever going to be like us," continued Willy.

"No," said Smudge, adding, just to be on the safe side, "Why's that, then?"

"Cos, for a start off, Smudge, nobody else has got one of you!"

"And nobody's got one of you either, Willy," I said.

THE END . . . (of an era)

And Finally . . .

• • • • •

In a box at the back of the room where I write, I found a small sheaf of notes under the heading of 'Book Three'. The original finished draft of the Triangle Player had been split into two for publication and, excited by that prospect, I had evidently set to work on the next instalment. The second part of the Triangle Player was never published, however, and I progressed no further with a third volume other than those few pages of notes.

Looking at them now, and with a little help from the old boys of Silurian, I could just about put together a sequel, and indeed might do that one day. But the truth is that it is not needed. The history of Silurian can be compared to the life of anything that finds itself in the public domain, in that its rise in popularity can be plotted on a bell curve graph. Between the years of 1985 and 1991, this mercurial bunch of anarchic wild men were at the top of their own curve. To continue the story beyond this point would be to examine the inevitable descent from that peak. That could be seen as unfair to those who proudly carried the Silurian banner in the ensuing years.

It is no slight on these original exponents of Welsh Border morris that they were unable to stay at the top of their game indefinitely. Such a feat has never been achieved. Though this treatise is not the whole story of Silurian, I am satisfied that I have documented in sufficient detail the best years of this band of comrades. What they achieved in those few years was unique, astonishing and unprecedented in the history of the 20th Century morris revival. I hope my writing goes some way towards explaining the galvanic effect we had on the morris world, which precipitated a huge spike in interest in Border morris clearly visible today. Ultimately, there is a limit to how far I can go in relating anecdotal incidents about morris dancing and the consumption of beer. What is more pertinent, more rewarding and more valuable is to reflect on the legacy of Silurian and the elemental energies they exposed, albeit briefly and almost unwittingly.

After an absence of nearly twenty years, I have returned to a substantially altered morris world. I have witnessed none of the incremental changes over that period, so the difference is starkly visible to me. At the point where my story ends, Border morris was still seen as part of the lunatic fringe, performed by only a handful of sides, with Silurian popularly seen as towering above the rest. Today, there are Border sides everywhere and Silurian is simply one amongst many, no longer as fleet of foot, iconoclastic or mercurial, and virtually isolated in being an all-male side.

This predominance of Border sides came to my attention on a visit to Chepstow in 2016, on the recommendation of Kim Barrett, co-owner of the wonderful other-worldly Green Man and Gatekeeper shop at Taurus Crafts near Lydney in Gloucestershire. One day, I had been chatting to Kim about the more mystical aspects of morris, and she said, “You must go to the Chepstow Wassail – you won’t be disappointed.” She was right. I was impressed by the number of Border sides filling the town, and I even picked up more than a hint of the mystical undercurrent that must have been the driving force of morris millennia ago.

The upsurge in Border morris is exhilarating, and what I have witnessed since the Chepstow Wassail is very encouraging. What I don’t see though is another dramatic step change in the offing – but there will be one, I am sure of that. It seems the spread and ubiquity of Border sides is now the new norm, following the tipping point and subsequent paradigm shift of Silurian’s entrance into the world of morris nearly half a century ago. Vas Deshmukh’s jokey prediction in 1991 that, “Eventually, all sides will look like us,” has partially come true. There is now a new ‘level playing field’ on which these latter-day Border sides all perform. Amongst them, we have the good, the bad and the mediocre. Some are brilliant, some are not as good as they think they are and some are better than they think they are. From my observational point of view, there are quite a few that really are 'out there' and have the potential to rise head and shoulders above the rest, so there is plenty of scope for that to happen and very soon. Silurian, in its peak years, was a one-off, an accident, a happy bit of synchronicity that brought together the right people at the right time to rescue the ancient remnants of the dance before they slipped into obscurity. Border morris is now alive and considerably more vibrant than it was when Dave Jones first had the dream. His dream became reality, and the reality has blossomed into a huge flowering tree growing vigorously in fertile ground. On some branches, I can see lush fruit about to form, and I await the day when we can all enjoy the nourishment this fruit will bring.

Nearly four decades have passed since Silurian first ventured forth as a dedicated Border side, displacing the idea of a static dance display and replacing it with what we saw as lively street theatre, but which quickly became a key to a hidden portal. Audiences woke up as they were 'invited' to participate in the performance. Much has changed since then, however. Most significantly, life for everyone has become less spontaneous, more ordered and burdened with unsustainable schedules. When Silurian were donning their new kit and taking Bromyard by storm, home computers and personal phones were little more than exotic new ideas on the frontiers of the electronics industry. Subsequently hailed as the latest devices to 'make life easier', they of course did no such thing. They simply allowed us to cram even more into our very busy lives. Now they are commonplace, and there is an increasing temptation for people in the audience to record events on their phones, distracted by the aim of updating their social media pages rather than being captivated directly with what is in front of them. This has a negative effect on the connection between audience and performers, because to look at life through a lens is to run the risk of detachment.

Technology is a useful tool, but over-reliance can exacerbate human disconnection from the universal force so many of us are trying to be part of, a disruption which really kicked in with the emergence of the Industrial Revolution and has accelerated exponentially since then. Energy is the portal to this force, but it is elusive, and still threatened by the male dominance that disturbs the essence of yin-yang, without which it is impossible to be adequately receptive. Yin-yang illustrates the vital holistic balance of female/male energy in which two seemingly opposite forces are in fact interconnected, complementary and interdependent. For the most part, this is now lost to us. The advent of mixed morris sides is a move towards regaining the balance, but we are not there yet. In merging female and male energies in this way, there is a danger of jeopardising both, so we must take care.

We are on the right path though. I have seen one morris side that is addressing this issue by putting male and female energy on an equal but separate footing, and what I see there is impressive. Life in the 21st Century is in a turbulent state of flux, and morris dancing is caught up in that. I am sure that what I perceive today, in morris as well as in other aspects of life, is part of a transition leading to greater awareness of how we might achieve the balance we seek. And I sense that the goddess, suppressed and somnolent for so long, is awakening at last.

Many of the features we see in contemporary morris dancing are vestiges of rituals and ceremonies that predate monotheistic religions, suggesting that morris dancing has roots that go back at least three millennia. It is my belief that the roots reach right down to our hunter-gatherer days, but it would be difficult to explore this idea within the context of this personal story. Some aspects of life in our earliest agrarian communities have been covered, and it is worth highlighting the salient points. The basic dance movements of circle, figure-of-eight and crossovers have a part to play in calling up and maintaining energies. Long staves, bells and black faces are symbolic relics of those parts of the ancient dance relating to confronting negative 'spirits', protecting and sanctifying 'place' and celebrating the turning of the year through birth, fecundity, death and rebirth.

Staves have replaced swords, which had a far-reaching history in the dances of fertility rites. However, as E K Chambers points out, in his treatise, *The Mediaeval Stage*, swords were not associated with the cult of war, but with protection. They were concerned with the symbolism of ritual, sacrifice and other seasonal agrarian concerns, wrapped up with the god Mars in his more primitive role as a fertility spirit. Bells were a prerequisite in ancient times in warding off evil spirits as well as penetrating the thin veil that exists between this world and the other. As Tracy Boyd points out, sounding the bells was seen as specific to a clearing of the ways, a crossing of the boundary between the profane and the sacred, in the course of a transcendental progress to a higher plane. For me, it seems morris without bells is like chips without salt. And then there is the black face, a subject of some contention today. The black face in particular is highly significant in association with disguise and fertility, and there are clear indications that this has almost certainly been an essential part of the ritual fire festivals since the beginning.

Morris in the past has often had to tangle with authority of one kind or another – the Church, the Crown, the magistrates and the literate classes in general. And now it is being challenged once again. Through a combination of misinformation, assumption, rumour and indeed prejudice, the advocates of political correctness accuse black-faced morris dancers of racism. I cannot leave this book without saying something about that. Some people believe that racism is a morris dancer with a black face. Some people believe the world was created in six days 6000 years ago. And some people believe that eating saturated fat will fur up their arteries and kill them. None of the above is true. We live in a world of fantasy and fiction, disinformation and deviousness. A good motto to live by today would be: trust no one, not even yourself;

question everything. And, to the PC lobby out there I say, "Before you pass judgement, stop and *think*!" Under the law of this land, where one is innocent until proven guilty, it is incumbent on those in the seat of judgement to examine all evidence from both sides before delivering a considered verdict.

Racism is not morris dancers blacking their faces. Racism is Maggie Thatcher calling Nelson Mandela 'that grubby little terrorist'. Racism is an English colonial policeman in 1956, giving an indigenous Kenyan freedom fighter 50 yards start before shooting him in the back. Racism is a mainstream newspaper dropping the word 'refugee' and rebranding the victims of war and violence as 'migrants' seeking to undermine our 'civilised society'. To a great extent, racism is the spawn of colonialism and imperialist hauteur, which in itself goes right back to our tribal past. At the heart of human behaviour is the need to establish and protect territory, as with all living things on this planet. Indeed the roots of morris go back to this basic principle, but that does not make it racist. Territory and a community's sense of place are innate. I cannot say, for instance, that the robins and sparrows in my garden, so vocal in the spring in declaring their own territories, are in any way being racist. No, the problem of racism is a human one, because of the complexities and erroneous thinking with which this species has surrounded itself, including certain fictions that have generated followers and adherents on a global scale.

In the last 10,000 years, since we first began to dabble with the idea of cultivating the land to produce food, human society has become increasingly convoluted, fragmenting into myriad cultures, protected by nationalism and unnatural religions. Human society has become toxic in its pursuit of these elaborate fabrications. We began by recognising that differences exist between 'tribes'. We then graduated to being wary of and then mistrusting neighbouring tribes, to attacking and conquering those tribes and finally to promoting hate for anything 'other'. Our fundamental instinct to establish and protect individual communities has descended into the rabid paranoia of racism. The fear and loathing of 'other' can be seen, not just in 'white' against 'black' (which is another fiction, and the product of our obsession with binary thinking). It can be seen, for example, with Hutus against Tutsis, Kurds against Iraqis and, less obviously, English against Scots or the Arsenal 'tribe' against the Spurs 'tribe'.

Trying to contain all this in the blackened face of a morris dancer is absurd. Morris dancers are nothing more than easy targets, because the real problems of racism are now far too complex to unravel. They are laminated between tightly bonded layers of religion, corrupt commercialism, self-serving government leaders, human arrogance and the superglue of our socio-economic system. This in itself is another 'fiction', based on authoritative social hierarchy, top-down control, consumerist greed and a winner-takes-all ideology. There is no hope here for anyone who is not on the top floor of this teetering, unstable edifice. With all that we have to worry about, morris dancers are the least of our concerns. In fact, because their raison d'être is music, dance, song, laughter, fun and benign spirituality, they are part of the solution. I have never met a morris dancer who is not friendly, outgoing, welcoming and inclusive. To oppose this view is to breed hate and fear where none exists.

Whilst human society seems determined in so many ways to descend into anxiety, self-loathing and destruction, morris dancers are amongst the lantern bearers, lighting up our darkness and showing us the path ahead. They have always been part of the festival spirit and carnival atmosphere of ancient high days and holidays, full of exuberance, pleasure and the joy of living. In an age when spontaneity has been suppressed, and living for the moment is something we now need a therapist to explain to us, those free-fall, fun-loving morris dancers can give us a few clues about what is really important. Along with painters, poets, sculptors, craftspeople and artists of all kinds, they show us the side of human character that will help us to return to being the empathetic, cooperative, altruistic and *connected* species we truly are.

Morris today also appears to be reaching back to something more elemental, helping us to visualise a meaningful spirituality. The mystique that Silurian awakened is coming back, but of course it faces challenges. The 'tribal' context of morris dancers as warriors and protectors is gone, male and female energies have become mixed, and the new spirituality is fighting for breath in a tech-reliant world. But all the signs are encouraging. I feel that morris will come back into its own because it carries the last sparks of ancient energy with it, and the planet needs that energy right now. Morris is a survivor. It speaks to us from our distant past, but it is not that far away that it cannot be heard. Silurian proved that forty years ago.

By looking at morris in a fresh way, Silurian woke up the slumbering beast. It breathed life into the dancers, and it worked, because we delivered what we believed in – no compromise. We gave up our individuality whilst retaining our characters, and we involved the audience whether they liked it or not. Street theatre was what we were displaying – doing flash mob before it was a 'thing'. My elder son, who is a musician, says he likes music with groove, funk and attitude, and he liked Silurian because we presented that combination, even in a folk context. Above all, wearing a costume that today would be described as low-key, we managed to look ordinary but a bit edgy and unsettling.

The future of morris cannot be predicted but, if it is to flourish, there is a need to free-fall, to let go of the interminable academic discussions about the etymological possibilities of the name and the historical references to morris dancers, the earliest of which is less than 600 years ago, hardly long enough to establish anything definite. Examining individual pieces of a jigsaw puzzle has limited use in trying to visualise the whole picture. In looking back to the origins of morris, we have to use our imagination as well as all known references and other archaeological clues. We cannot know how people *felt* centuries or millennia ago. But, if we just use our vision, intuition and instinct as well as the physical clues from the past, we might come to understand that actually those ancient ancestors were much like us. All that they felt is well within the grasp of our own comprehension, and could be released with the simple turn of a key in a metaphorical lock.

Today we live in a strange, dysfunctional world, in which we are rapidly losing connection with one another, let alone the spirits and energy forces that ancient man might have drawn on to give the harvest a helping hand. Since at least the time of Descartes, we have attempted to understand the universe through reductionism, but this is not possible in isolation. We must think holistically. It is conceited to deride our ancestors for their 'primitive' thinking. They may not have been quite right in their understanding, but they were not completely wrong either, and it is clear that they did understand certain fundamentally important things that we have long since lost.

All that makes us human is still with us. Despite our so-called 'progress', our basic nature as creatures of this earth is just below the surface, and there is a vital need to reclaim it now. The old has never quite given way to the new. Taking our cues from certain aspects of ancient thinking, we must be more inspired as well as remaining circumspect. We must not cloud our thinking with relatively modern narratives, such as troublesome morris dancers in local alehouses, or unemployed itinerant labourers cadging money (particularly as there was a time when festive morris had been used by the Church to collect money on its behalf). Morris is older and more dignified than that, and was most certainly not even called 'morris' two thousand years or more ago. We cannot know what it was like, but we can be certain that the seasons and the turning of the year would have been vitally important to those old agrarian communities, as indeed they are now, if only we knew it.

So, I say to any black-faced morris dancers that may be reading this, "Be proud of this legacy, this treasured heritage, this ancient and sacred celebratory dance. Make it live again. Don't be led astray by misinformation or bias. Tell people you are celebrating the earth cycle, the changing seasons and that eternal symbol of fertility and new life, Mother Earth, through which we will return to our true place within the connectedness of the universe."

The future is bright – the future has morris.

Appendix 1
The Battle of Worcester Bridge

• • • • •

A song for the Faithful City

Silurian and Faithful City had a history of banter with an edge to it. It takes very little to tip the balance and create a cutting edge, but this is what happened at Lassington Oak and was further exacerbated during Faithful City's 21st Birthday weekend.

We resolved to commemorate this fall from strained mutual tolerance to something approaching enmity by writing a song. For the benefit of the uninitiated, I should point out that the song is in fact dedicated to the Criss Cross Morrismen, a side invented by Cadbury's to promote their new corn savoury criss-cross bars. Before this happened, Silurian already had a healthy disdain for all things Cotswold, but it was felt that selling morris to a major corporation for thirty pieces of silver was worthy of severe derision.

The Criss Cross Morrismen bore an uncanny resemblance to Faithful City, but that may just have been an unfortunate coincidence.

Historical note: the criss-cross bar never went into full production, thus the bar and its morris side thankfully disappeared forever from the face of the Earth.

For all you dedicated archivists out there, the words are set to the tune of that well-known song, popular in folk clubs at that time, *The Battle of Sowerby Bridge*.

The Battle of Worcester Bridge

Oh, the Battle of Worcester Bridge were fought
On the forty-fourth of March.
The Criss-Cross Morrismen were there,
Their hankies stiff as starch.
We marched as far as Powick Bridge
When the enemy came in sight,
And they called our bagman nasty names
And challenged us to fight.

Chorus:
We were amongst them, we were amongst them.
Oh we slished and we slashed,
And we slaughtered and we slew,
'Til the air for miles around were blue.
For an hour and a quarter,
We held the foe at bay.
There were only two were left that day,
And we were amongst them.

At break of day down Tudor Way,
We went to fight the foe.
Our good scout Andy Griffin
Came and told a tale of woe.
He said they're doing Upton Stick,
So we did Bromsb'row Heath,
And when they did the three-tops hey,
We smashed them in the teeth.

Chorus:
We were amongst them, etc.

The enemy then retreated
To the Barneshall laundrette,
Cos they'd all shat their breeches
From the criss-cross bars they'd ate.
They hung young Wotsit out to dry
And left him there all night,
So we stuffed his arse with criss-cross bars
And challenged them to fight.

Chorus:
We were amongst them, etc

The enemy danced around the town
Til they bored us all to tears,
So we retired into the pub
To buy a few more beers.
Then the Criss-Cross boys came to the pub,
A round of drinks to buy.
"I'm sorry lads," the landlord cried,
"Silurian's drunk us dry!"

Appendix 2

Having the *craic* at Killorglin Puck Fair

Shortly before I left Silurian, we were invited to the Puck Fair in Killorglin in 1997, by which time I had added an oboe to the list of accessories that accompanied me on morris outings. So here is a little snippet I would like to share with you regarding this instrument and, just so that you know you are getting your money's worth, another brief snapshot of what it is like to be in Ireland at festival time.

Though I still believed that my route to musical fame was through my triangle, I had become fascinated by the oboe as a folk instrument and had used it as my entry visa to that lawless and unpredictable gaggle of enthusiastic amateurs known as the Silurian ceilidh band. I had learned by ear a small selection of the more popular folk dance tunes and could just about get away with being in the band. Obviously in Killorglin, or in any other Irish town come to that, there was no way I was going to put my unprotected musical head above the parapet in a land where music is the lifeblood of the people. So, when I was in kit but not ensconced in the comfort zone of the Silurian band, I simply carried the oboe around in an authoritative kind of way, hoping that no one would call out, "Give us a tune then!"

At one point, watching some antics in the main square, I was leaning against a wall, a Guinness in one hand and cradling the oboe in the other, when my heart gave a frightened jump on being approached by someone whose accent gave him away as being local. It was too late to get away, so I tried to look nonchalant behind my round hippie shades and black face. Was he going to ask for a tune!?

"I was wondering," he said, "whether ye might settle an argument I'm having with me mate . . . is dat an *obee* you've got there?"

"It certainly is," I assured him, my sense of relief at not being asked to play making me sound quite cheery. "It's actually an Obi Wan Kanobi."

"I thort so," he replied. "An' him thinkin' it was a clarionet."

Much pleased with himself, he wandered back to his mate, and I heard him say, "Didn't I tell ya? It's an obee one-canna-be – or somethin' like that."

What a marvellous place, I thought. Music, Guinness and the highest order of banter. What more does one need to gladden the soul?

The other story concerns something far more mundane – a hunt for cigarette papers. On the last day of the festival, I was with Micha Jarvis, one of the latter-day stalwarts of Silurian, and cigarette papers were priority. In a town full of shops enjoying the benefits of what one might call multiple retailing (O'Connell's Hardware and Unisex Hairdresser – that sort of thing), Jarvis was spoilt for choice but, playing safe, picked one that had the word 'tobacconist' amongst the other options over the door.

"Afternoon!" said Jarvis, entering the shop.

"How's it goin'?" replied the genial shopkeeper.

"It's goin' well," said Jarvis, "but it will go much better if I could find some cigarette papers. Do you sell cigarette papers?"

"Ah well, yes – we do sell cigarette papers."

"Oh good," said Jarvis, visibly relieved.

"And what sort would you be after?" asked the shopkeeper.

"What sort have you got?" replied Jarvis.

"Ah well, we have da Rizlas. We have the red, the green, the blue and we have the kingsize red, and the lickeriss . . . . . . *normally.*"

"Normally?" echoed Jarvis.

"Ah yes, we have all those normally. But not today. Today we're all sold out. 'Tis always the same when da fair's in town."

This book would not have come to life without the support and commitment of those whose pledges made this Crowdfunder project successful. I thank you all.

Adrian Pitt • Alan Perrow • Alana Michael • Alan Smith • Andy Wooles
Andrew White • Andrea Stewart • Angie Latham • Anna Swaithes.
Anne Tarrant • Annie Balen • Annie Jones • Ant Veal • Bernard Smart
Beth Haverly • Bev Langton • Brett Davenport • Brian and Ella Dean
Bruce Jarvest • Caroline Yeates • Chloe Garner • Chris Lamb
Chris Morgan • Chris Mulvey • Christina Pritchard • Dave Fisher
Dawn Smith • Derek Ambler • Dion Cochrane • Ed Elliott
Elaine Huntingdon • Elen Sentier • Eva Harvie • Fiona Provan
Frederick John Williams • George Causley • George Elliott
Georgia Askew • Gerard Edwards • Gill Swaithes • Grace Orton
Graham Baldwin • Gren Penn • Gurdyal Simm • Heather Weaver • Ian Carter
Ian Wild • Jackie Denman • Jacky Smith • James Massey • Jane Watts
Janet Matthews • Jayne West • Jean McDonald • Jess Allen • John Exton
John Smith • John Tose • Jon and Emma Proctor • Josiah Lenton
Judith Beamand • Judith Williams • Kat Terry • Kate Wood
Keith and Jen Close • Laine Lainy Mills • Laney Elliott
Les and Elizabeth Scott • Lisa McDermott • Mandy Pullen • Marcia Martinez
Martyn Goodwin • Martyn Kington • Matt Simons • Mel Wilson • Micha Jarvis
Michael Ridley • Mick McTiernan • Mick Quinn • Miranda Bedwin
Nada Meredith • Nigel Wilkie • Pamela Thom-Rowe • Paul Howland
Peter de Courcy • Peter Johnson • Peter Ramsbottom • Richard Gott
Robert Dean • Sally Dean • Sam Davey • Sandra Clare • Sarah Crofts
Simon Jam Wall • Simon Pipe • Steve Podger • Sue Rogers. • Tammy Macenka
Tim Dexter • Tom Oliver • Tony Price • Tony Roberts • Tracy Boyd
Tracy Wood • Vanessa Everett • Veronica Maynard.

Acknowledgements

• • • • •

Aside from the 105 supporters whose crowdfunder pledges enabled this book to be published, and whose names appear in a separate list, there are others whose support, encouragement and technical skills have helped to create the book you hold in your hands today.

Firstly, the people who lit my fuse and gently coaxed me into writing this story: Angie Latham, Keith Close, Kim Barrett and my partner Sally Dean. A special kind of thank-you goes to my two sons, George and Ed, who confessed to being huge childhood fans of Silurian, and painted a picture for me of how they perceived the heroes of this story to be mesmerising, scary, totally 'other' and clearly from another planet. Also, big thanks to Phil Rickman for his time, his observations and his willingness to share with me some very valuable source material on the roots of the Morris. With reference to source material, my thanks and admiration go to Tracy Boyd for her truly impressive and ongoing resource www.sacredthreads.net in particular the section on Morris.

As a typical angst-ridden author, I am humbly grateful to Sally for her editing skills, her patience and calmness in coping with my turbulent mood changes whilst this was a work in progress. Further thanks also go to Angie Latham and her husband Dougie for their technical skills in creating the video and other artwork for the Crowdfunder project and Facebook page, whilst being willing to guide me, a Facebook virgin, through the mysteries of social media.

For the culmination of this project as a published book, I thank the team at Orphans Publishing, particularly Emma Holtz for her valuable spectrum of skills, as well as Helen Bowden, Duncan

Betts, Chris Knight, Peter Swain, Allan Hall and Leon Bateman. And, for their contributions to the project pledge rewards, I thank Andy Griffin for his cartoons, Dave Smith for his photograph and Dennis Gould for his letterpress work.

Further reading

• • • • •

This book is clearly not an academic treatise. It is just a simple story about some wild morris dancers from the badlands of the Welsh Border. There is much more that could be said about the Morris, its history and its place in the great scheme of all things, but not here. For those of you who are interested in exploring these ideas further, here is a short list of other sources of information that I would recommend.

Boyd, Tracy : "The Daunce of Nine-Men's-Morris and the Boundaries Between Worlds" at www.sacredthreads.net/morris.

Cawte, E C : *Ritual Animal Disguise*, Cambridge, D S Brewer Ltd (1978)

Cawte, E C : *The Morris Dance in Herefordshire, Shropshire and Worcestershire*, Journal of the EFDSS. IX.4 (1963)

Chambers, E K : *The Mediaeval Stage*, Dover Publications (1966)

Heselton, Philip : *The Elements of Earth Mysteries*, Element Books (1991)

Jones, Dave : *The Roots Of Welsh Border Morris*, Annie Jones (1995)

Jones, Evan John : *Sacred Mask, Sacred Dance*, Llewellyn Publications (1997)

Karpeles, Maud : *Dances Of England And Wales*, Max Parrish (1950)

Leather, Ella Mary : *The Folklore Of Herefordshire*, Lapridge Publications (1991) reprint of the original 1912 edition

Trubshaw, Bob : *Explore Folklore*, Heart of Albion Press (2002)

Author Profile

• • • • •

Since being commended at primary school on his 'composition' entitled My Holiday, Rob Elliott has written millions of words, mostly in the form of diaries, letters and articles. His first tentative venture into the world of books was through *Don't Blame Me, I'm Only The Triangle Player* in 1991. In 2008 and 2009 respectively, he had two books published on the industrialisation of food (*The Food Maze*) and the spiritual antidote to this dystopia (*How To Eat*). This is his fourth book. Rob lives in Herefordshire just a few miles from the Welsh Border. He can be contacted through Facebook.

Praise for *Don't Blame Me, I'm Only The Triangle Player*

The incoherent ramblings of an inebriated rustic
TIME OFF

Reading it is as easy as falling off the bog
METROPOLITAN

Funnier than shooting wasps with a .22
EVENING VANGUARD

Threadbare plot and see-through characters
FINANCIAL SCAMS

The biggest fiasco since the Indian Mutiny
NEW DELHI RHYMES

Split my sides laughing, but only because the book fell in the fire
DAILY WAIL

I've seen more appealing things crawling out of the sewer
GUTTER PRESS